Communicative skills { *Listening Speaking Reading Writing* }

FIFTH EDITION

Sheltered Content Instruction

Teaching English Learners with Diverse Abilities

Jana Echevarría
California State University, Long Beach

Anne Graves
San Diego State University

PEARSON

Boston • Columbus • Indianapolis • New York • San Francisco • Upper Saddle River
Amsterdam • Cape Town • Dubai • London • Madrid • Milan • Munich • Paris • Montréal • Toronto
Delhi • Mexico City • São Paulo • Sydney • Hong Kong • Seoul • Singapore • Taipei • Tokyo

Vice President, Editor in Chief: Jeffery W. Johnston
Senior Acquisitions Editor: Julie Peters
Editorial Assistant: Andrea Hall
Director of Marketing: Margaret Waples
Executive Marketing Manager: Krista Clark
Program Manager: Laura Messerly
Project Manager: Annette Joseph
Project Coordination: Electronic Publishing Services Inc., NYC
Photo Researcher: Electronic Publishing Services Inc., NYC
Operations Specialist: Linda Sager
Cover Design: Jennifer Hart
Cover Image: Blend Images/SuperStock

Credits: p. 73 (bulleted list): © Copyright 2010. National Governors Association Center for Best Practices and Council of Chief State School Officers. All rights reserved; **p. 77 (class example):** Teacher communication in regular and sheltered science classes. California State University, Long Beach; **p. 85 (class example):** Echevarria, J. (Producer & Writer), & Silver, J. (Producer & Director) (1995). [Videotape]. Instructional conversations: Understanding through discussion. Santa Cruz, CA: National Center for Research on Cultural Diversity and Second Language Learning.

V011
10 9 8 7 6 5 4 3

ISBN 10: 0-13-375426-X
ISBN 13: 978-0-13-375426-1

For my family, whose love and support mean the world to me.
JE

For John Forren and our daughter, Grace.
AG

ABOUT THE AUTHORS

Jana Echevarría

Jana Echevarría, PhD., is professor emerita of Special Education at California State University, Long Beach, where she received the honor of being selected as Outstanding Professor. She has taught in elementary, middle, and high schools in special education, English as a Second Language, and bilingual programs. She has lived in Taiwan, Spain, and Mexico and is an internationally known expert on second language learners. Her research and publications focus on effective instruction for English learners, including those with learning disabilities. She has presented her research across the U.S. and internationally including Oxford University (England), Wits University (South Africa), Harvard University (U.S.), South East Europe University (Macedonia), and University of Barcelona (Spain). Publications include the popular SIOP book series and over 50 books, book chapters, and journal articles.

Anne Graves

Anne W. Graves, PhD., is a professor at San Diego State University (SDSU) teaching and conducting research on instruction in reading and writing for learners with disabilities from diverse backgrounds since 1990. Beginning in 1975, Graves taught in special education settings in the public schools for 6 years. After receiving her PhD. at the University of Wisconsin–Madison in 1984, she was a professor at University of South Carolina–Coastal Campus and Sacramento State University before joining SDSU. Her research on efficient and effective instructional approaches and interventions has resulted in numerous publications and presentations at local, state, and international conferences. Graves is part of a research team at San Diego State that conducts studies of intensive small group instruction for struggling readers in culturally and linguistically diverse settings. Currently, she is principal investigator on a grant that supports cultural and linguistic emphasis in teacher preparation for candidates seeking credentials in both special education and bilingual elementary or secondary education known as ADELANTE funded by Office of English Language Acquisition in the U.S. Department of Education.

CONTENTS

Preface   xi

chapter *1* **Teaching English Learners with Diverse Abilities   1**

Student Profiles   2
Native-Language Knowledge   5
    Assessment   6
    Instruction   6
English-Language Knowledge   10
    Assessment   14
    Instruction   16
Academic Background and School Experience   19
    Assessment   21
    Instruction   21
Learning and Behavior Challenges and Giftedness   22
Search for Interventions: A Three-Tiered Model   23
    Tier 1   24
    Tier 2   25
    Tier 3   26
    Instruction   26
Student Profiles Revisited   28
Summary   29
Activities   30

chapter *2* **Theoretical and Historical Foundations   31**

History of Education of Students Learning English in School   32
    Immigration   32
    Rights of English Learners   32
    Students with Disabilities   33
    Programs for English Learners   33
Theories of Second-Language Acquisition   35
    The Contributions of Cummins   36
Factors That Affect Second-Language   38
    Language Learner Factors   38
    Socio-Contexual Factors   41

Teaching English Learners: Theory to Practice   43
  Humanistic Learning Theory   43
  Developmental Learning Theory   44
  Social Interactionist Learning Theory   45
  Cognitive Learning Theory   45
  Behavioral Learning Theory   46
Summary   47
Activities   48

chapter 3 **Sheltered Instruction in the Content Areas   49**

Definition of Sheltered Instruction   50
The SIOP® Model   51
  A Well-Planned Lesson   56
Sheltered Instruction and Effective Instruction: A Comparative
  Case Study   61
  Discussion of the Case Study   67
Specific Considerations for Students with Learning
  Disabilities   69
Summary   70
Activities   71

chapter 4 **Understanding, Adjusting, and Teaching the Language of the Classroom   72**

Understanding the Language of the Classroom:
  All Teachers Are Language Teachers   73
Teaching Language through Objectives   74
Developing Oral Language Proficiency   76
Adjusting Language with Sheltered Instruction   76
Using Instructional Conversations for Language
  and Concept Development   80
Summary   86
Activities   86

chapter 5 **Promoting Affective and Cultural Connections   87**

Providing Reading and Writing Activities
  That Promote Success   89
Providing Ample Practice and Careful Corrections   91

Focusing on Relevant Background Knowledge
and Cultural Connections   92

Actively Involving Learners   93

Using Alternate Grouping Strategies   94

Providing Native-Language Support   95

Focusing on Content and Activities That Are Meaningful to
Students Both Emotionally and Culturally   97

Creating Roles in the Classroom for Family and
Community Members   97
Family Literacy Nights   98

Holding High Expectations for All Learners   99

Being Responsive to Cultural and Personal Diversity   100

Summary   101

Activities   102

chapter 6   Learning Strategies   103

Types of Learning Strategies   104

Examples of Specific Strategies in the Content Areas   107
Teaching Reading Strategies in Content-Area Classes   108
Teaching Writing Strategies in Content-Area Classes   110

Guidelines for Selecting a Learning Strategy   113
Determine Levels of Knowledge and Language
Proficiency   114
Determine Which Strategies Will Be Most Useful   114
Decide Order of Instruction   115
Use Simple Wording and the Fewest Number of Steps   115

Teaching Learning Strategies   116
Determine Preskills and Preteach Them   116
Include an Opening, a Body, and a Closing   117
Plan a Series of Lessons   118

Presentation Methods Used to Teach Learning Strategies   119
Active Student Involvement   119
Appropriate Pacing   120
Monitor and Correct Errors   120
Controlled, Grade-Appropriate Practice and Independent
Practice   121

Summary   122

Activities   122

chapter 7   Differentiated Instruction   123

Demonstrating Sensitivity to Cultural and Linguistic
Diversity   124

Providing Adequate Background Knowledge   126

Building Academic Proficiency   127
  Content Knowledge   127
  Academic Proficiency Skills   128
Providing Language Development Opportunities   129
  Language Proficiency   129
  Academic Language   130
  Discipline-Specific Vocabulary Development   131
Modifying Lesson Plans and Text   132
  Modifying Assignments   138
  Preparing for Advanced Academic Engagement   141
Summary   144
Activities   144

chapter 8 **Becoming a Reflective Practitioner   145**

The Importance of Reflective Practice   145
Professional Development   146
  Inservice Sessions   147
  Action Research   147
  Professional Learning Communities (PLC)   148
The Value of Video Reflection and Analysis   150
Self-Evaluation and Goal Setting   151
Revisit Student Vignettes and Reflect on Practice   153
Summary   156
Activities   157

Glossary   158
References   161
Index   169

PREFACE

In this fifth edition of *Sheltered Content Instruction*, we set out to prepare teachers to deliver content area instruction to English learners using a sheltered instruction approach. English learners are the fastest growing segment of the U.S. school population, and they vary from one another greatly in their educational needs. Some students come with grade-level academic preparation, some are gifted, and others are underprepared for the high academic standards of school. This edition reflects the recent research, best practices, and policies that impact the education of English learners. With standards that are intended to prepare students to be college and career ready, it is reasonable to assume that many students will be challenged to meet these high standards and teachers may question some students' abilities to do so.

We have designed this book to assist teachers in thinking about their own practice and the issues they should consider when teaching English learners, especially when they struggle academically. There is a need across the nation to include courses that focus specifically on these learners in teacher preparation programs. Many textbooks used in teacher preparation—general education and special education—are inadequate for preparing teachers to work effectively with diverse students.

New to This Edition

This book is now available as a Pearson eText with video illustrations of key content. The "play" button icon and written introductions to video clips guide students and instructors in viewing these videos. See examples on pages 3 and 5.

Since the publication of the previous edition of this text, the number of English learners has increased substantially, with tremendous growth in this population in states that have not previously had large numbers of culturally diverse learners in their schools. Some of the changes to this edition are listed below.

Chapter 1 includes:

- A discussion of the importance of a separate block of time for English language development, including optimal learning contexts for promoting language acquisition.
- Connections to Common Core Standards and Career and College Readiness Standards.
- Connections to state standards for teaching English learners.
- Examples of the kind of academic language used in content-area classes.
- Various models of the levels of language proficiency, including current language related to "levels" of proficiency.
- A discussion of learning and behavior challenges and giftedness.
- A description of tiered instruction.

Chapter 2 includes:

- A revised and updated discussion of the history of education for English learners, including the history of services for students with disabilities.
- A revised section, "Factors That Affect Second-Language Acquisition." Additional factors based on recent research have been added and the section was reorganized around factors inherent in learners and those that are influenced by context.
- Updated information from the *Nation's Report Card*.
- Updated research throughout.
- Revised end-of-chapter activities and a new feature, "Your Turn," in which readers apply the chapter content to their practice.

Chapter 3 includes:

- A revised SIOP Language Arts lesson plan that shows how the features of the SIOP® Model work together in lesson planning and delivery to meet the Common Core State Standards.
  - A reorganized and revised section on the SIOP® Model.
  - An updated section called "SIOP Techniques for Making Lessons Comprehensible."
- A discussion of the way the SIOP® Model of sheltered instruction prepares students to be college and career ready.
- Updated research throughout.
- Revised end-of-chapter activities and a new feature, "Your Turn," in which readers apply the chapter content to their practice.

Chapter 4 includes:

- A new section on the importance of understanding the language of the classroom and how it differs from everyday language proficiency.
- A new section on writing effective language objectives and their importance in the role of language teaching within content classes.
- Alignment of sections on adjusting language with sheltered instruction and using instructional conversations with the way they help English learners be college and career ready.
- Updated research throughout.
- Revised end-of-chapter activities and a new feature, "Your Turn," in which readers apply the chapter content to their practice.

Chapter 5 includes:

- Revised connections of affective and cultural issues to the education of English learners.
- A focus on the importance of appropriate assignments and realistic expectations for English learners.
- Many examples of projects or lessons that support cultural and linguistic diversity.

Chapter 6 includes:

- A revised focus of strategy instruction to improve outcomes for English learners.
- Connections to college and career readiness goals.
- Connections to standards for the teachers of English learners.
- Explanations of the use of strategy instruction in the context of Response to Intervention.
- Applications of strategy instruction in content areas for students in middle and high school.

Chapter 7 includes:

- A new orientation based on instruction that supports all students.
- An emphasis on differentiating instruction to enhance language development.
- New descriptions of vocabulary development with a focus on teaching "academic language."
- Differentiating instruction with an emphasis on Common Core Standards or college and career readiness.
- Modifications and adaptation with emphasis on standards for teaching English learners.

Chapter 8 includes:

- A reframing of the chapter to focus on being a reflective practitioner.
- A new section on reflective practice.
- A new section on professional development that highlights inservice sessions and action research.
- A revised section on Professional Learning Communities to enhance teaching for English learners.
- Updated research throughout.
- Revised end-of-chapter activities and a new feature, "Your Turn," in which readers apply the chapter content to their practice.

The addition of a Glossary of Terms will assist readers with navigating the content of the text.

Overview of the Book

Some of the terms used in this book may differ from those used in your area; terminology varies from region to region and has different meanings for different people. In this book, the term *sheltered instruction* indicates the teaching of content area knowledge and skills in a more understandable way while also developing students' English language proficiency. Some similar terms are *content ESL, structured English immersion (SEI),* and *specially designed academic instruction in English (SDAIE).* In many districts there are no classes designated as "sheltered"; however, any time content material is taught to English learners, a sheltered instruction approach should be used to make the material comprehensible.

One of the goals of this book is to define what a sheltered lesson is and to describe how it can be used on a daily basis in the classroom. Little has been written about the challenges caused by the varying levels of educational background and abilities of English learners. Teachers frequently report that they struggle to accommodate the diversity of skills and abilities of the students in their classes. These diverse skills and abilities are even more difficult to understand for those teachers who lack training and knowledge about second-language acquisition and related issues.

English learners will experience predictable and understandable challenges as they learn in a new language. Other students may have needs that require specialized attention, such as those who are undereducated and those who have learning difficulties. Sheltered instruction is appropriate for English learners, regardless of whether they are (1) in small groups or large groups, (2) in primarily bilingual or English language placements, or (3) identified for special education services.

In writing this book for teachers and for students studying to become teachers, we have reviewed theory, research, and practice in the areas of second-language acquisition, general education, multicultural education, and special education, including updates from our own ongoing research. This new edition provides the most current information available about students who are learning standards-based content in English.

Organizational Overview

This book begins by laying a foundation in issues surrounding the education of students learning English. Chapter 1 describes the target population for the book, provides student profiles, and discusses the areas of assessment and instruction for this population. These areas include native-language knowledge, English-language knowledge, academic background, and behavior and learning patterns. Common Core State Standards (and college and career readiness standards) are added to this edition. Considerations of language proficiency and Standards for Teachers of English Learners are added with examples of how to use language levels to determine the type of instruction. This chapter also describes procedures for informal assessment and instructional planning. Programmatic decisions can have a significant impact on instruction, so we have elaborated the section on program options.

Chapter 2 provides an overview of the historical background and theories that explain and support procedures for the instruction of English learners in school, including those with disabilities. It includes information on the history of second-language learners in the schools, an overview of theories of second-language acquisition, and learning theories. It also includes a discussion of the factors that affect second-language acquisition and the influences on an individual's rate and level of learning a new language.

Chapters 3 through 8 provide specific information on differentiated instruction for all students, with special emphasis on English learners. Each of these chapters includes specific examples of teaching situations as well as activities for discussion. Chapter 3 introduces sheltered instruction and gives specifics for its effective implementation in the content areas, including a discussion of the research-validated SIOP® Model. Chapter 4 focuses on the language of the classroom and what teachers and students alike need to recognize about its importance. Chapter 5 emphasizes the importance of culturally and affectively responsive teaching, including information and strategies regarding the appropriate school environment for students, teachers, and parents. Chapter 6 includes research on learning strategies, descriptions of those strategies, and specific examples of strategies that are likely to improve school performance. Chapter 7 describes differentiated instruction, particularly in the context of language proficiency levels and curriculum adaptations with specific examples of accommodations, adaptations, and modifications for all students, with special emphasis on those who are learning English. Chapter 8 encourages teachers to be reflective practitioners. It includes an overview of the material presented in the book and a framework for readers' self-reflection.

Most professionals agree that teaching content material to students who are learning English is one of the greatest challenges teachers face today. One of the reasons is the range of skills and abilities that these students bring to learning tasks. This practical guide for teachers recommends a variety of methods and techniques for making grade-level instruction meaningful for English learners.

Acknowledgments

First and foremost, we'd like to express our appreciation to Aurora Martinez, for her support and direction. The editorial team, led by Kathryn Boice, kept us on track through the process. We further acknowledge the contributions of our copy editor, Kathy Smith. Thanks.

A book such as this is developed over time, as a result of many discussions, observations, teaching experiences, and interviews. In particular, we owe a debt of gratitude to the many teachers and school personnel, too numerous to mention individually, whose cooperation and generosity contributed to this book being grounded in classroom experiences and practices.

The districts represented include Lennox Unified School District, as well as Long Beach Unified, including the teachers and staff at Hill Middle School, Los Angeles Unified School District, Los Alamitos Unified School District, Santa Barbara Unified School District, and San Diego City Unified School District, including the teachers and staff at Mann Middle School.

We thank the following reviewers of the earlier editions for their comments and suggestions: Eileen Ariza, Florida Atlantic University; Mary Carol Combs, University of Arizona; Joseph DiLella, Eastern New Mexico University; Jay Richard Fuhriman, Boise State University; Theresa Garfield, Alamo Community College District; Else Hamayan, Illinois Resource Center; Socorro Herrera, Kansas State University; Robin LaBarbera, Biola University; Mary E. McGroarty, Northern Arizona University; Carla Meskill, University of Albany, State University of New York; Teresa Pica, University of Pennsylvania; and Kyounghee Seo, St. Cloud State University. We also thank the reviewers of this edition: Todd Bunnell, Mississippi University for Women; Elizabeth England, Shenandoah University; Yolanda Ramirez, University of Texas of the Permian Basin; Ellen Skilton-Sylvester, Arcadia University.

Sheltered Content Instruction

CHAPTER I

Teaching English Learners with Diverse Abilities

LEARNING OBJECTIVES:

- Contrast native-language knowledge with second-language knowledge.
  - Consider how each should be assessed and what the important considerations for instruction are.
- Identify the stages of second-language proficiency.
- Describe the importance of academic language, and explain why it is critically important for school success.
- Discuss the types of learning and behavior challenges that a struggling English learner could have, and explain why they might occur.
  - List types of assessment and instructional support than support learning and behavior changes.

[handwritten note: diff from conversational]

[handwritten note: N.C.E.L.A.]

nglish learners constitute the fastest growing part of our school population. The number of English learners in the United States schools has tripled since 1998 (National Clearinghouse for English Language Acquisition, 2013). English learners continue to be most concentrated in California, Florida, Illinois, New York, and Texas, but many other states such as Nebraska,

[handwritten note: in some states, its a huge % of population]

Monkey Business/Fotolia

1

Oregon, Nevada, North Carolina, and the District of Columbia have experienced an influx of families who speak languages other than English. While some of these students from diverse linguistic backgrounds are similar to one another in that they must learn a second language, each one is unique, with his or her own level of English proficiency, language and academic abilities, and educational background. In this chapter, we offer a systematic way to assess English learners' needs and provide appropriate education so that they can experience success in school and beyond.

Some students learning English do well in school, while others experience special challenges (Banks & McGee, 2001; Garcia, 2000; Genesee, Lindholm-Leary, Saunders, & Christian, 2006; Graves, Gersten, & Haager, 2004; Saunders & Goldenberg, 2010). English learners are learning in and through a new language, and find themselves in a cultural environment that may be significantly different from their own. The influence of English-speaking teachers on their culturally diverse students has been well documented, and unfortunately this mismatch of language and culture may contribute to some students' poor performance in school (Agirdag, 2009; Artiles, Rueda, Salazar, & Higareda, 2002; Gay, 2000; Harry & Klingner, 2005; Harry, Torguson, Katkavich, & Guerrero, 1993; Villegas & Lucas, 2007). Further, some schools have effective parent programs that are inclusive of all families while at other schools only mainstream families are represented. As we better understand these important relationships, educators are giving greater attention to the impact that ethnicity, language, culture, and background have on students' learning (Au & Blake, 2003; August & Shanahan, 2006; MacSwan, 2000).

Clearly, we as educators need to consider each student's unique abilities in order to provide an appropriate education to English learners. Are the students' parents professionals or migrant workers? Did the students learn English while living in a refugee camp or through a private tutor? Is the student a recent immigrant or U.S. born? Do the parents support primary-language instruction or not? Have the students been educated at grade level, or do they have significant gaps in their education? The answers to these questions may impact programming decisions.

Student Profiles

While the diverse backgrounds of individuals do not fit neatly into categories, four general profiles emerge among English learners:

1. Balanced bilingual
2. Monolingual/literate in native language
3. Monolingual/preliterate in native language
4. Limited bilingual

Nico is a tenth-grader who was born in Guatemala. He moved to Southern California in the second grade. Before coming to this country, he was a good student and learned to read and write in Spanish. When he began school in the United States, he was placed in a bilingual classroom where he received some native-language support before transitioning into English instruction. Now in high school, he is performing at or above grade level in mainstream classes. Because Nico can speak, read, and write well in both languages, his teacher is considering him for the gifted program at his school.

Your Turn

If a student who is an English learner is struggling on tests and in class assignment, what are several steps that teachers need to take to support this student?

Nico and other students like him are not the subject of this book because they have achieved a balanced-bilingual status. Indeed, duplicating his experience is the goal of this book: helping individuals to become academically successful in English while maintaining their first languages. We have written this book to assist teachers in providing a high-quality education to all students—including those from diverse backgrounds who are not yet proficient in English, as well as students who have learning challenges.

Students who have not yet achieved balanced-bilingual status are of concern to us; they are monolingual literate or preliterate in their native language or limited bilingual status students. These students require special attention, knowledge, and strategies including assessment and review to enhance their opportunities to learn and help them succeed in school.

 Watch the following video clip and list the ways a teacher can adjust assessment, review, and teaching strategies to support English learners.

Rahul is a recent immigrant who attends middle school. He has grade-level academic ability in his native language but speaks very little English. Because he has lived all his 13 years outside the United States, certain kinds of cultural knowledge present difficulties for him. Rahul is quite shy and does not seek help readily. He has excellent social and academic language skills in his native language and has studied English for a few years, but his proficiency is quite limited. His history of learning and behavior at school, at home, and in the community is positive. He is described as a good citizen and a student who demonstrates appropriate behavior in most settings.

When *Agnessa* was 6 years old, an American family adopted her from an orphanage in Russia. She has an older brother who is the biological child of her parents. Now in third grade, Agnessa has very limited literacy skills. Even her spoken English is quite limited when she interacts with students and the teacher in class. Her family is concerned that Agnessa doesn't seem to be making sufficient academic progress, and she has had a number of behavior problems in school. She has been caught stealing twice this year, and she is often uncooperative in class.

Born in an urban U.S. city, *Luisa* is a friendly 15-year-old who sits quietly in class as if she understands everything. When written assignments are given, she writes them down and begins to work. Her handwriting, however, is illegible, and her spelling is extremely poor. Spanish is her first language, although her family speaks a mix of English and Spanish at home. She writes in English in a knowledge-telling mode without recognizable structure in her sentences or paragraphs. Luisa can converse quite well in both languages, but for some reason has not made academic progress in either language. Although she is popular at school, she is at risk of dropping out because of consistent underachievement.

The purpose of this book is to provide information for teaching English learners with diverse abilities, such as Rahul, Agnessa, and Luisa. Learning a new language while learning in and through that language is a complex endeavor affected by a variety of factors, some of which are shown in Figure 1.1. Effective programs for English learners take a systematic approach in evaluating the needs of these students and then providing the kind of instruction that meets their needs. For all students in our schools to achieve their potential both as learners and as productive members of our society, high-quality programs are essential.

Because of the tremendous influx of English learners into our schools, the need for programs—as well as procedures for placing students in programs—has often outpaced program development. As a result of this uneven growth, terminology varies from state to state and region to region, and the terms used in this book may differ from those used in each school.

High-quality programs include evaluation of English learners in a variety of areas to determine their needs, including native-language knowledge, English-language knowledge, school experience and academic background, and learning and behavior patterns (see Figure 1.2). Once an appropriate assessment has been done, instructional

FIGURE 1.1 Visual Display of Language-Learner Dimensions

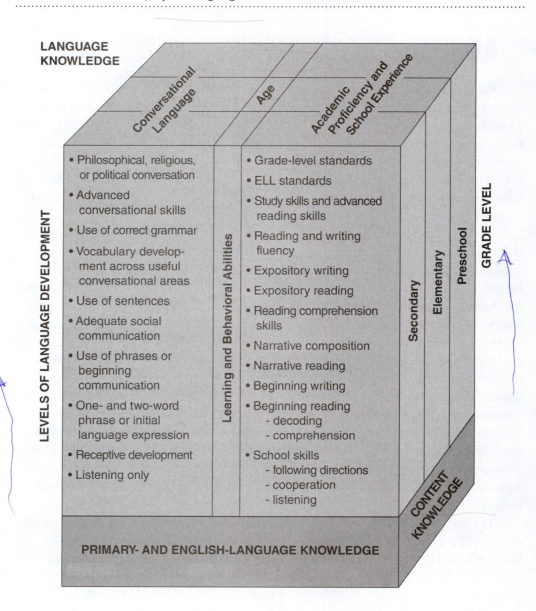

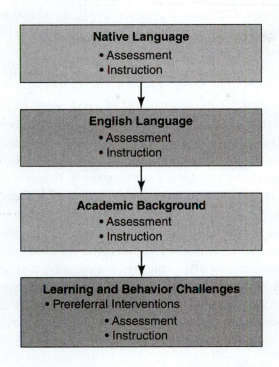

plans can be developed to support learners in attaining grade-level standards. Let's take a look at each aspect of the assessment process.

Native-Language Knowledge

As mentioned, students enter school with varying levels of native-language development. These levels range from low-proficiency to above-grade-level skills in oral language, reading, and writing. We know that students who speak their native languages fluently and have developed age-appropriate literacy skills have increased opportunities for developing language and literacy skills in English (August & Shanahan, 2006; Baca & Cervantes, 2004; Cummins, 1989; Saunders & Goldenberg, 2010). Further, those who have developed a rich repertoire of knowledge and concept comprehension in their native languages have better opportunities for learning English because their knowledge can be transferred to English (Barratt-Pugh & Rohl, 2001; Cazden, 1992; Krashen, 1982). For example, an individual who understands that the earth rotates around the sun would know that concept regardless of the language the teacher speaks when talking about it.

 Watch this video clip of a dual language classroom and note some of the concepts that students may learn in Spanish that may warrant native language assessment.

Your Turn

What are the benefits of Native language development in students in school in the United States? Reflect on the strengths and challenges of Native language instruction.

Those students who have not had solid literacy models in their native languages have more difficulty developing literacy in another language (in this case, English) (Franklin & Thompson, 1994; Howard, Christian, & Genesee, 2003). An assessment to determine the student's level of native-language proficiency will provide valuable information for making placement and instruction decisions.

Assessment

In Agnessa's case, a home language survey would be given when she enrolled in school to determine her native language, as required by federal law. The result would indicate that her native language is Russian. Next, a competent speaker of Russian would assess Agnessa's native-language knowledge (Cloud, Genesee & Hamayan, 2009). If native-language professionals are unavailable, personnel from other districts or geographic areas may be hired. Finally, if trained personnel are completely unavailable, community members may be used to ascertain the student's abilities. When using this option, it should be indicated on the record that the student could not be adequately assessed and that valid, reliable judgments about the language and cognitive abilities of the student could not be made (Baca & Almanza, 1996). This is especially important when the student is being considered for special services, such as special education. Another good resource for school personnel is the student's family since they are able to provide input and insights into the student's range of skills, including daily living skills (Chang, 1992; Gonzalez et al., 1993).

An assessment of Agnessa's native-language skills includes measuring oral-language proficiency and reading and writing skills (Hoover & Patton, 2005; Schiff-Myers, Djukic, Lawler-McGovern, & Perez, 1994). Once Agnessa's native-language skills have been assessed, results can be compared to grade-level competencies as much as possible (Hoover & Patton, 2004; Perez, 1993; Saville-Troike, 1984). If as a third-grader Agnessa can write a comprehensible 50-word story that is organized and uses a variety of interesting vocabulary words, then the native-language evaluator will list those skills and determine her approximate academic grade level. Agnessa has approximately first-grade level writing and has good comprehension when a story is read to her, but because she is below grade level in literacy in both languages, Agnessa will need more intensive literacy interventions.

 Watch this video of an individualized math assessment that also allows for the assessment of language including academic language in math. What does the teacher learn by asking this student questions about fractions?

Instruction

There are a variety of program models for teaching English learners, summarized in Table 1.1. They include sheltered instruction, transitional bilingual education, developmental bilingual education, two-way immersion, English language development, and newcomer programs. While *Lau v. Nichols,* the landmark case that affirmed the rights of English learners to receive an education equal to that of their English-speaking peers, gave preference to bilingual education for meeting the needs of these students, the law was written broadly enough that its interpretation has led to a number of different programs being implemented for English learners (Aguila, 2010; Gandara, Moran, & Garcia, 2004).

Sheltered Instruction	Promotes use of techniques and strategies for making grade-level content comprehensible for English learners while promoting their English-language development. Although native language may be used for clarification, English is the medium of instruction.
Transitional Bilingual Education	Teaching in students' native language provides support as they transition into English instruction, usually within 2–3 years. Sheltered instruction is used during instruction in English to scaffold students' understanding.
Developmental Bilingual Education	With the goal of bilingualism and biliteracy, students are taught in two languages for multiple years. Sheltered instruction techniques and strategies assist students' comprehension in English.
Two-Way Immersion	English learners and English-speaking students are taught together in two languages. Students communicate in authentic, meaningful ways that promote dual-language development for both groups. Sheltered instruction techniques are utilized when teaching content through the second language.
English Language Development	Also commonly referred to as English as a Second Language (ESL) instruction; a separate block of time each day is set aside to focus on specific skills leading to English proficiency.
Newcomer Programs	The goals of newcomer programs are to acculturate immigrant students with limited English proficiency to U.S. schools, to assist students in acquiring beginning English language skills, and to develop core academic skills and knowledge.

Choice of program alternatives is influenced by a host of factors, such as the number of students from the language group; the philosophy of the school, district, or state; parent preference; and the availability of necessary resources such as bilingual personnel, trained staff, and leadership (see Dolson & Burnham-Massey, 2010, and Genesee, 1999, for a complete discussion of program alternatives).

Sheltered Instruction. The primary goal of sheltered instruction (SI) is to make grade-level academic subject matter comprehensible to English learners, while at the same time developing their English proficiency. Sheltered teachers are certified in content areas (e.g., multiple subjects for the elementary level, and science, mathematics, history, or literature at the secondary level) and have had training in ways to effectively teach English learners, including knowledge of second-language acquisition, cultural considerations, and research-based instructional practices for teaching English learners. Such training may take place through preservice or inservice courses.

This type of instructional approach serves as a support until the student is ready for mainstream classes. Sheltered instruction is both an instructional approach and a program option. Some schools offer in their instructional program sections of content classes that are designated as "sheltered" (e.g., sheltered science, sheltered math, sheltered social studies). These classes provide support for English learners until they have developed sufficient English proficiency to be successful in mainstream classes. In other situations, such as in schools that have high numbers of English learners, sheltered instruction is often the instructional approach used by teachers in mainstream classes with all students. In these typically urban settings, most students benefit from an emphasis on language development and providing access to the content, so sheltered teaching is appropriate. Sheltered strategies and techniques are also appropriate in programs such as two-way immersion so that instruction being delivered in students' second language is made comprehensible.

Sheltered teachers design lessons that use English in a variety of ways, including reading, discussing, and writing about standards-based ideas, processes, and information. This approach integrates natural second-language-acquisition features with principles of effective instruction. Since the emphasis is on meaning, not form, students learning English are able to interact with peers and teachers at their own levels of English-language proficiency. Students practice using English while participating in discussions centered around content area material, thus increasing language acquisition while developing academic concepts. (Chapter 3 discusses specific features of high-quality sheltered instruction.)

Transitional Bilingual Education. Also known as *early-exit bilingual education,* transitional bilingual education (TBE) is the most common form of bilingual education. The focus of TBE is to provide native-language support by teaching literacy and academic content areas using the student's first language while developing oral proficiency in English. Some nonacademic subjects may be taught in English using sheltered instruction techniques. As students gain proficiency in English, more academic subjects are taught in English, usually beginning with math, then reading and writing, science, and finally social studies. The purpose of TBE is to support English learners in their native languages as they move or transition toward academic instruction taught entirely in English, usually in grade 3.

Developmental Bilingual Education. Developmental bilingual education (DBE) is also referred to as *late-exit bilingual education* and is an enrichment program that focuses on producing bilingual, biliterate students. This is done by teaching English learners in both English and native language, emphasizing the cognitive, linguistic, and academic benefits of learning in two languages. When instruction is in English, sheltered instruction is used to make the content comprehensible for English learners. Rather than viewing the native language as simply a bridge to English proficiency, DBE programs capitalize on the students' linguistic resources and aim to provide the benefits that result from full development of the students' native language (Cummins, 1996; Lindholm-Leary & Genesee, 2010). Students receive bilingual instruction throughout elementary school and through middle and high school when possible.

The most effective model of TBE or DBE is one in which teachers fluent in the students' native language provide instructional support as needed, with beginning speakers requiring more native-language instruction than those with greater English proficiency. Bilingual instructional aides (IAs) are a valuable resource when a certified bilingual teacher is unavailable. In this model, the teacher maintains responsibility for instruction, but works together with the IA. The teacher plans lessons, monitors instruction, and develops assessment of student progress; the IA works with a group of students, carrying out lessons in the native language. The IA also documents students' progress and communicates with the teacher. Since IAs are closely involved with the students' education, they assist in developing good working relationships with families. In exemplary bilingual programs, parents, educators, and the community value cross-cultural experiences and are actively involved together in school activities and programs as well as the school's decision-making process.

Two-Way Immersion. Two-way immersion (TWI), also known as *two-way bilingual education* and *dual-language immersion,* is unique in that each TWI class is structured so that it is usually composed of 50 percent native-English speakers and 50 percent speakers of another language. Academic instruction takes place in both languages so that all students have the opportunity to be both native-language models and second-language learners. The non-English language is used at least 50 percent of the day.

TWI draws on sociocultural theory that asserts that learning occurs through social interaction (Vygotsky, 1978). Students from different language backgrounds communicate in authentic, meaningful ways that promote language development for both groups. The most successful TWI programs recognize the importance of family and community involvement, making sure that the cultures of both groups are valued equally and all parents are involved in decision making (Howard et al., 2007; Lindholm-Leary & Genesee, 2010).

English Language Development. Recent research indicates that exposure to English and interaction with peers and teachers might help promote fluency and communicative competence, but they are not sufficient for native-like English proficiency (Saunders & Goldenberg, 2010). There needs to be an intentional effort to make academic language—the cognitively complex language of formal education—understandable for English learners. The importance of developing academic English has become more apparent in recent years, and a separate block of classroom time devoted to English language development (ELD) has become the norm in regions where there are high numbers of English learners.

Each of the various program models discussed in this section calls for a specific time when attention is given to learning the English language. Teachers trained in second-language acquisition theory and methods provide instruction that focuses on developing oral language, reading, and writing in English so that English learners can participate more fully in classroom instruction. English as a second language (ESL) instruction and English language development (ELD) are both most often taught by a specialist and are typically provided either on a pull-out basis or as a scheduled time for one or more periods during the day. ESL and ELD standards can provide a framework for this type of high-level language development (McKay, 2000).

Currently, there is an increased awareness of the importance of integrating academic content areas with language instruction. Rather than being introduced in a series of isolated units, language instruction is most effective if it simultaneously provides access to subject matter texts, discussions, and class activities (Echevarria, et al., 2013; Short, 1991). College and career readiness standards, including Next Generation Science Standards and Common Core Standards, are likely to benefit English learners because of their emphasis on text complexity and language, building knowledge from informational text, and an expectation that students will produce and use evidence in text to justify their views (Santos, Darling-Hammond, & Cheuk, 2012). The newly adopted standards' focus on meaningful activities, problem-based learning, and the enhancement of critical thinking creates higher expectations for all learners. There are currently many recommendations that the learning of English occur more in the context of content area learning such as science (Lee, Quinn, & Valdéz, 2013).

Many have put considerable effort into developing systems designed to adapt new standards for English learners in the context of varying levels of English proficiency and specific content areas such as Language Arts and Mathematics, with standards in science and social studies either very new or soon to be published (Lee & Buxton, 2012). Content area and English as a Second Language teachers will make systematic decisions vis-à-vis content area and English language development (or proficiency) standards. They must first assess students to determine current content area skills and level of academic achievement. All of this is happening at once and great consideration must be given to each part as

FIGURE I.3 Important Considerations in the Development of Standards for English Learners

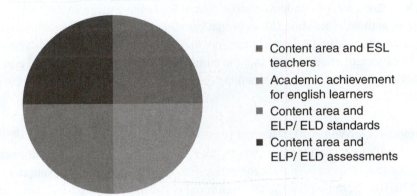

- Content area and ESL teachers
- Academic achievement for english learners
- Content area and ELP/ ELD standards
- Content area and ELP/ ELD assessments

depicted in the pie chart in Figure 1.3. Differentiated instruction for English learners may be needed, including additional time, appropriate instructional support, and aligned assessments to facilitate the acquisition of both English-language and content area knowledge (see Chapters 6 and 7 for more information on this). All of these considerations are important when considering educational profiles of students who are learning English.

Newcomer Programs. Newcomer programs are designed typically for middle and high school immigrant students who have limited English proficiency, although there may be such programs at the elementary level as well. The goals of newcomer programs are to acculturate students to life in the United States, to assist students in acquiring beginning English language skills, and to develop core academic skills and knowledge. Many new-comers have limited literacy skills in their native languages, often due to limited formal schooling. There is wide variation in how newcomer programs are implemented (Short & Boyson, 2004). Some programs are located within a school so that when students exit the program they remain at the same school while others are at designated school sites or at district intake centers. Most programs include families in the school by offering adult ESL classes, arranging family events, and assisting families in accessing community health and social resources.

In summary, for students learning in bilingual settings, the steps for instruction are

1. Assess native-language proficiency.
2. Design and implement an instructional plan that includes ESL/ELD, native-language support, and sheltered instruction, as appropriate.
3. Conduct ongoing, informal assessment to determine the student's progress in language, academic, and content acquisition (Cloud, 1994; Genesee et al., 2006; Ortiz & Graves, 2001).

English-Language Knowledge

English proficiency is one of the greatest predictors of school success. When insufficient time and attention are devoted to the systematic development of English, the consequences are grave. Inadequately developed English skills are associated with lower GPAs, repeated grades, lower performance on standardized tests of academic content knowledge, and low graduation rates (Abedi & Lord, 2001; August & Shanahan, 2006; Ruiz-de-Velasco & Fix, 2000).

insufficient English → dire consequences

As important as English proficiency is, we need to be cautious about attempting to "force" accelerated proficiency on students. Second-language development is a process, much like learning one's first language. We would not expect a 3-year-old to have completely developed language any more than we should expect a student with three years of exposure to English to be fluent and performing at grade level in English. Accountability measures may pressure school administrators and teachers to have unrealistic expectations of students, who themselves may be feeling pressure to learn English.

Given the important agenda of preparing teachers for classrooms and educational settings with large numbers of English learners, many states have moved toward the establishment of standards for addressing the knowledge, skills, and abilities that teachers need. For example, the California Department of Education has developed a new set of requirements for Teachers of English Learners (CTEL) (http://www.ctel.nesinc.com):

DOMAIN 1: Language and Language Development

A) Language structure and use
B) First and second language development and their relationship to academic achievement

DOMAIN 2: Assessment and Instruction

A) Assessment of English learners
B) Foundations of English/literacy development and content instruction
C) Approaches and methods for ELD and content instruction

DOMAIN 3: Culture and Inclusion

A) Culture and cultural diversity and their relationship to academic achievement
B) Culturally inclusive instruction

In the first CTEL domain, language knowledge and language development are critically important for teachers of English learners. Teachers need to have a good command of the structure and use of the language in order to instruct students effectively. In English, the structure of the language includes knowledge of phonology (sounds), morphology (basic units of meaning), syntax (grammar), pragmatics (function), and semantics (meaning) across content areas (see Figure 1.4). Students must understand

FIGURE 1.4 Domains of Language

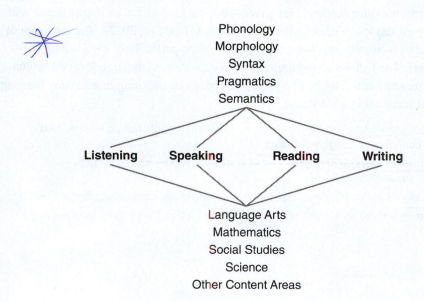

Phonology
Morphology
Syntax
Pragmatics
Semantics

Listening   Speaking   Reading   Writing

Language Arts
Mathematics
Social Studies
Science
Other Content Areas

English grammatical and syntactic patterns and rules when they read, write, speak, and listen to English. More on first- and second-language development and a comparison of the two can be found in Chapters 2, 3, and 4.

A major foundational skill for teaching language and literacy development, which was made popular by Jim Cummins (1981, 1989, 1994, 2003), is the ability to make a distinction between everyday conversational ability and the academic proficiency required for scholastic success.. Teachers need to carefully consider the difference between the conversational proficiency needed in everyday situations, which is termed *basic interpersonal communicative skills* (BICS), and the more cognitively demanding language necessary for school success, which is called *cognitive/academic language proficiency* (CALP). Although the terms BICS and CALP are still widely used, Cummins (2003) has more recently used the terms *conversational language* and *academic language.* Once the differences are understood, assessments need to be made in each area and techniques for assisting students in transferring conversational language into literacy development need to be explored (see this chapter for more on assessment and Chapters 3, 4, 5, 6, and 7 for adaptations and differentiation of instruction).

Further exploration of the foundations of language development provides an organizational framework for assessment and instruction, CTEL Domain 2. Assessment of conversational proficiency is relatively easy to accomplish, yet it is essential. Although a person can learn and understand basic words and phrases in a matter of hours, with fluency usually attained in one to three years, it is critical that this conversational knowledge be transferred into reading narrative genre. In Cummins's conceptualization of bilingual proficiency, conversational proficiency is just "the tip of the iceberg"; below the surface lies the more critical language proficiency required for academic tasks.

The language of school, academic language, is more complex and more cognitively demanding than everyday language. It is the kind of language needed for comprehension of text, as well as for analysis and synthesis of material. If a student speaks little or no English, then the acquisition of new concepts will be expedited when they are presented in the language the student understands—his or her native language.

Content area instruction, which relies on academic language proficiency, demands more from the student than simple understanding of spoken English (Graves, August, & Mancilla-Martinez, 2012). Conversational skills are not sufficient in content areas, because each subject area uses a language of its own. For instance, the language of mathematics is different from the languages of literature or science. Each academic content area has its own standards and associated vocabulary terms. These standards and vocabulary terms are pure academic language—not the kind of words that students will encounter in everyday experiences (Short, Fidelman & Louguit, 2012). The language of each content area is usually decontextualized and can be particularly challenging for English learners. The following vocabulary terms demonstrate the high level of language each content area requires. Notice that words can have one meaning in everyday language and a different meaning in a subject area:

English-Language Arts: homographs, characteristics of nonfiction, citations, text features, conjunctions, logical fallacies

Mathematics: divisibility, histogram, front-end estimation, unit conversion, variability, expanded notation

Social Studies: conflict, colonization, interpret, relief map, longitude, plateau

Science: magnetism, attraction, consumers, investigation, prediction, igneous rock, bar graph

grasp
faster
concepts in
native language

demands of
fluency
vary subject
to subject

(For further discussion of the language demands of each content area, see the book series *The SIOP® Model for Teaching English-Language Arts to English Learners, The SIOP® Model for Teaching Mathematics to English Learners, The SIOP® Model for Teaching History-Social Studies to English Learners,* and *The SIOP® Model for Teaching Science to English Learners.*)

With each succeeding grade level, the ability to learn content material becomes increasingly dependent on interaction with and mastery of the language that is connected to the specific content material. The ability to demonstrate knowledge also requires increasingly sophisticated oral and written forms of language. McKeon (1994) suggests that "careful planning of instruction is needed to help students develop the decontextualized language skills they will need to master the cognitively demanding content in higher grades" (p. 25).

Cummins's conceptualization of language proficiency is not without its critics (Edelsky, 1991; Rivera, 1984; Romaine, 1989; Troike, 1984). Baker (1993) characterizes the limitations of the BICS/CALP distinction as an oversimplification of the reality of how complex and multifaceted language and language competence is. In fact, research indicates that a bilingual student's language competencies are influenced by a number of factors, such as environment and motivation, and are constantly evolving and interacting; they are not simple dichotomies that are easily compartmentalized and unchanging. Further, the notion of distinct levels of language proficiency lacks abundant empirical support (August & Shanahan, 2006).

In spite of its limitations, the notion of everyday language versus academic language (the BICS/CALP distinction) enjoys wide popularity among practitioners, primarily because of its applicability to students in classroom situations. It provides a general understanding of students' language needs. Even students who appear to have a good command of spoken English may have difficulty with academic instruction in English.

It is possible to apply the BICS/CALP iceberg analogy to the case of *Luisa,* who is a limited-bilingual student. Because she has lived all her life in the United States, teachers are concerned about her low academic levels in English. Records show that initial assessment results of social and academic language skills in Spanish (done in kindergarten) indicate high levels of social language skills and low preliteracy levels (that is, the ability to recognize rhyming words, sound/symbol relationships, and so forth). Although she was in a bilingual kindergarten, the teacher was not a fluent Spanish speaker. Luisa began first grade with a native-Spanish-speaking teacher, but after her family moved, she was placed in an all-English first-grade class at the new school. In second grade, she received limited native-language support from a bilingual paraeducator, but no such assistance was available in third grade and beyond. Report cards and teacher comments reveal that Luisa has performed poorly in school since kindergarten. She is a popular student, has many friends, and has been quite cooperative in school, which may account for her promotion from grade to grade. Now in high school, Luisa has low academic skills in both English and Spanish.

The iceberg analogy (see Figure 1.5) suggests the following linguistic profile: Luisa has surface features in Spanish and surface features in English, as well. However, she does not fare as well in terms of the more cognitively demanding underlying proficiency. During the critical early developmental period, Luisa did not receive solid, consistent instruction in either language, which restricted her learning. Her conversational proficiency in English does not guarantee academic proficiency.

limited native language support early on...

coverage/support is "spotty" year to year

speaking proficiency ≠ academic proficiency

FIGURE 1.5 Iceberg Representation of Luisa's Language Proficiency

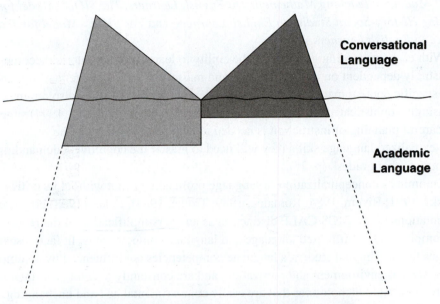

Conversational Language

Academic Language

Broken line indicates areas to be developed for grade-level performance.
Solid line indicates level of proficiency attained.

Source: Based on Cummins, 1994.

The iceberg analogy provides a simple but useful profile for teachers. Of course, a more in-depth assessment of levels of language proficiency is essential if students are to be placed in the proper academic program.

Assessment

The assessment process for English learners ideally begins with a home language survey. The home language survey needs to be in the language spoken by the family. It is completed by the parents or caregivers and is designed to provide information about use of language in family settings and outside of school. If the survey reveals that English is not a student's home language, a native-language proficiency evaluation is the next step.

English proficiency is typically assessed by school personnel who are familiar with second-language acquisition and assessment tools in the area, using an instrument such as the Language Assessment Scales (LAS), the California English Language Development Test (CELDT), the Idea Proficiency Test (IPT), or the Student Oral Language Observation Instrument (SOLOM) (see Figure 1.6 for the SOLOM example). Another assessment, *Teaching Strategies GOLD*® has been found to be valid and reliable for children with disabilities and for those learning English (Kim, Lambert, & Burts, 2013). Along with any of these assessment tools, an evaluation should include informal assessment of oral language, reading, and writing. Informal assessment may be conducted through observation scales, informal writing samples, and informal reading inventories. Typically, a student who is learning English is assigned a proficiency level for purposes of placement. It is far too simplistic to conclude that all students learning English pass through the same stages of learning and through every level of language development in the same way. However, levels of development are commonly referred to in placing English learners in instructional programs. Informal observation scales, such as the SOLOM (Figure 1.6) or some similar

FIGURE I.6 SOLOM Language Observation Matrix

high level ability ✓

Teacher Observation
Student Oral Language Observation Matrix (SOLOM)

Student's Name: _____   Grade: _____   Examiner: _____

Language Observed: _____   Date: _____

LEVEL	1	2	3	4	5
(A) Comprehension	Cannot understand even simple conversation.	Has great difficulty following what is said. Can comprehend only "social conversation" spoken slowly and with frequent repetitions.	Understands most of what is said at slower than normal speed with repetitions.	Understands nearly everything at normal speed, although occasional repetition may be necessary.	Understands everyday conversation and normal classroom discussions without difficulty.
(B) Fluency	Speech is so halting and fragmentary as to make conversation virtually impossible.	Usually hesitant; often forced into silence by language limitations.	Speech in everyday conversation and classroom discussions is frequently disrupted by the student's search for the correct manner of expression.	Speech in everyday conversation and classroom discussion is generally fluent, with occasional lapses while searching for the correct manner of expression.	Speech in everyday conversation and classroom discussion is fluent and effortless, approximating that of a native speaker.
(C) Vocabulary	Vocabulary limitations so extreme as to make conversation virtually impossible.	Misuse of words and very limited vocabulary make comprehension quite difficult.	Frequently uses the wrong words; conversation somewhat limited because of inadequate vocabulary.	Occasionally uses inappropriate terms and/or must rephrase ideas because of lexical inadequacies.	Use of vocabulary and idioms approximates that of a native speaker.
(D) Pronunciation	Pronunciation problems so severe as to make speech virtually unintelligible.	Very hard to understand because of pronunciation problems. Must frequently repeat in order to make him/herself understood.	Pronunciation problems necessitate concentration on the part of the listener and occasionally lead to misunderstanding.	Always intelligible although one is conscious of a definite accent and occasional inappropriate intonation patterns.	Pronunciation and intonation approximates that of a native speaker.
(E) Grammar	Errors in grammar and word order so severe as to make speech virtually unintelligible.	Grammar and word order errors make comprehension difficult. Must often rephrase and/or restrict him/herself to basic patterns.	Makes frequent errors of grammar and word order that occasionally obscure meaning.	Occasionally makes grammatical and/or word order errors that do not obscure meaning.	Grammatical usage and word order approximates that of a native speaker.

The student oral language observation matrix (SOLOM) has five (5) categories on the left: A. Comprehension, B. Fluency, C. Vocabulary, D. Pronunciation, and E. Grammar. It also has five numbers along the top, one (1) being the lowest mark to five (5) being the highest mark. According to your observation, indicate with an (X) across the square in each category that best describes the child's abilities. Those students whose checkmarks (X's) are to the right of the darkened line will be considered for reclassification, if test scores and achievement data also indicate English proficiency.
Reprinted by permission of Nancy Albarrán, San Jose Unified School District

assessing lets us know how well they're progressing!

measure, must include levels on which comprehension, fluency, vocabulary, pronunciation, and grammar are considered. For example, an English learner who is just entering school or is a newcomer to the United States is likely to be at Level 1 or 2, typically speaking very little English and having limited conversational and academic skills. By the time students have progressed to Levels 4 and 5, they are approaching fluency in conversational English. The purpose of assessment and approximate estimates of English proficiency is to provide appropriate instruction.

There have been frequent reports of bias in assessment instruments and in the interpretation of English learners' test results (Artiles et al., 2002). Assessment of English learners' knowledge and skills in English requires consideration of potential bias related to several areas. First, the language proficiency level of the learners needs to be considered in the design and implementation of the assessment because not only the English skills but also the comfort level of the student can impact performance on the test. Second, the amount of time that might be required to obtain accurate information may need to be adjusted, and a number of different assessments are required to obtain accurate information.

Teachers should use ongoing and appropriate classroom assessments (e.g., district benchmarks, textbook assessments, differentiated levels of discussion questions for checking understanding) that enable English Learners to demonstrate their knowledge and skills according to their English proficiency level. Ongoing assessment enables teachers and parents to monitor progress that students are making in each subject and to guide continued differentiation of instruction. Finally, students may have a variety of experiences in home culture that may or may not prepare them for the logic or reasoning required in comprehension questions on a test; hence, multiple sets of information need to be triangulated to provide accurate assessment information. Home-language proficiency should be compared to English-language proficiency and the former should be a central element when assessing learning potential (Baca & Cervantes, 2004).

Instruction

Research suggests that English learners benefit from a separate block of time for ELD or ESL. However, in many urban schools where the numbers of English learners comprise a large percentage of the students, regular classroom teachers provide ELD instruction, sometimes team teaching with an ESL teacher. In their review of research on effective ELD instruction, Dolson and Burnham-Massey (2010) suggest that it consists of learning contexts that:

- Are organized according to recognized developmental criteria such as ELD standards (Dutro & Kinsella, 2010; Snow & Katz, 2010).
- Are appropriate to the age, grade, and English proficiency level of students (Genesee & Riches, 2006; Saunders & O'Brien, 2006).
- Include ample opportunities for English learners to engage in interactive, student-to-student conversations employing the targeted language (Saunders & Goldberg, 1999).
- Have regularly scheduled ELD instruction based on a common curriculum (Saunders, Foorman, & Carlson, 2006).
- Offer instruction provided by highly qualified staff (Kane, Rockoff, & Staiger, 2007).
- Are supported by assessments administered periodically to determine student progress and inform instruction (Dutro & Kinsella, 2012; Snow & Katz, 2012).

The separate block of time for ELD/ESL is not the only part of the school day in which students learn and acquire English. In fact, a substantial amount of progress in English can be attributed to participation in sheltered content instruction because well-designed lessons in content areas (social studies, math, science, language arts) provide opportunities to expand academic language skills.

Stages are often the basis for language development descriptions that are based on some variation of the natural approach (Krashen & Terrell, 1983), which assumes that students acquire a second language in stages, in much the same way that they acquire a first language. According to the natural approach, students have more receptive ability than expressive ability during the early stages of language learning. These programs therefore attempt to create a nonthreatening and motivating language-learning environment. States vary in their terminology, but all essentially follow a process like that shown in Figure 1.7.

In their seminal work in this area, Krashen and Terrell (1983) described the stages as: Preproduction, Early Production, Speech Emergence, Intermediate Fluency, and Advanced Fluency. At present, many states have adopted proficiency levels similar to those in the WIDA (World-class Instructional Design and Assessment) English-language proficiency standards (WIDA, 2013), which extend the stages and expand working definitions:

gestures

- *Entering (Level 1):* Lowest level, essentially no English proficiency. Students are often newcomers and need extensive pictorial and nonlinguistic support. They need to learn basic oral language and literacy skills in English.

At this level, students receive as much native-language support as needed in the academic areas. Content-based ESL instruction focuses on developing English while providing the link between the content areas and their associated English, oral and written language functions, and structures. Time spent developing skills and knowledge in the native language will theoretically provide a foundation for later learning in English. The amount of time a student will spend in a particular stage varies across individuals. Students begin to develop rudimentary literacy skills during these early stages of language learning.

FIGURE 1.7 Stages of English Proficiency Redefined with More Nuanced Descriptions

ENTERING (LEVEL 1): Lowest level, essentially no English proficiency
BEGINNING (LEVEL 2): Second lowest level. Use of phrases and short sentences and are introduced to general content vocabulary and lesson tasks
DEVELOPING (LEVEL 3): Next level of proficiency. Use of general and specific language related to the content areas including basic writing
EXPANDING (LEVEL 4): Akin to an intermediate level of proficiency
BRIDGING (LEVEL 5): Akin to advanced intermediate or advanced level of proficiency
REACHING (LEVEL 6): At or close to grade-level proficiency

- *Beginning (Level 2):* Second lowest level. Students use phrases and short sentences and are introduced to general content vocabulary and lesson tasks.

Agnessa, the Russian student who has exhibited some inappropriate behaviors, is at this level of proficiency. Agnessa and students like her receive academic development in their native language as needed for context-reduced areas such as language arts, reading, math and science concepts, and social science.

- *Developing (Level 3):* Next level of proficiency. Students can use general and specific language related to the content areas; they can speak and write sentences and paragraphs although with some errors, and they can read with instructional supports.

English learners in this developing stage are now beginning to read more widely and are starting to tackle reading and writing tasks that approach grade level, although they continue to need scaffolding and strategy instruction to support their language development. Sheltered instruction is used in subjects where context clues facilitate understanding such as math computation, problem solving, and science labs. Students will have increased opportunities for interaction if they are integrated into classes with fluent English speakers in art, music, and physical education.

- *Expanding (Level 4):* Akin to an intermediate level of proficiency. Students use general, academic, and specific language related to content areas. They have improved speaking and writing skills and stronger reading comprehension skills (compared to the Developing level).

Rahul, the recent immigrant who has grade-level academics in his native language, is at the expanding stage. Students like Rahul are able to speak in longer phrases and complete sentences, although they may become frustrated by not being able to express completely and correctly what they know. For instance, when talking about a familiar topic, such as food or family, Rahul's English may be at an advanced level. Yet in the same hour, when talking about a recent field trip to the Museum of Natural History, Rahul's English may resemble that of the expanding level because of the sophistication of vocabulary required.

Language arts and the social sciences continue to be taught using native-language support as needed. Social science is heavily dependent on language; terms and concepts used are culturally laden, and lessons often draw on a bank of knowledge that may be unfamiliar to English learners.

- *Bridging (Level 5):* Akin to advanced intermediate or advanced level of proficiency. Students use general academic and technical language of the content areas. They can read and write with linguistic complexity. Students at this level have often exited the ESL or ELD program, but their language and academic performance is still monitored.

Students at this bridging level are developing increased academic skills, depending on their age and level of literacy in their native languages. They are often mistakenly thought to be ready for all mainstream classes since their ability to speak and understand English is quite good. However, their ability to understand and complete academic tasks in English may lag behind, especially if they do not have grade-level academic skills in their native language. Therefore, native-language support in language arts continues, providing a strong foundation in literacy, which is necessary for academic success. Sheltered language arts programs are introduced as students begin preparing to transition to the next level.

- *Reaching (Level 6):* At or close to grade-level proficiency. Students' oral and written communication skills are comparable to those of native English speakers at their grade level. Students at this level have exited the ESL or ELD program, but their language and academic performance is still monitored.

No matter which set of language proficiency stages or levels is utilized, the English learner's approximate language level must be determined by formal assessment (using a standardized test such as the LAS, CELDT, or IPT) or informal assessment (through observation, the use of SOLOM, informal writing samples, or informal reading inventories); then this information can be combined with the results of native-language knowledge and skills assessment findings. A comprehensive plan for instruction can then be developed based on the profile of the student, including program options for English learners based on their levels of English proficiency (see Figure 1.8). For example, a student at Levels 1 or 2 on the SOLOM needs extensive focus on listening and speaking English during instruction. Students at Level 3 and higher are able to participate more fully in instruction that includes reading and writing English in the content areas, which is an essential part of advanced English language development and academic learning (see Jill Kemper Mora's award-winning website for more details on levels of English proficiency and matching instruction accordingly at http://coe.sdsu.edu/people/jmora/).

It is important to note that the model presented assumes the availability of qualified bilingual personnel to provide native-language support particularly for students at English proficiency Levels 1 and 2. In many areas nationwide, this is not the case and students at beginning levels of English are in sheltered content classes. This is especially prevalent at the secondary level and in locations where there are only a small number of students from one language group.

Students learning English receive ESL instruction until they reach fluent English proficiency and are re-designated for enrollment in an all-mainstream program. Ideally, the amount of native-language support and the number of sheltered subject areas and mainstream classes vary with each level of English proficiency. Each individual student is likely to learn English in a unique pattern of development (Garcia, 2000). For students at this level, instruction focuses on refining and developing advanced uses of academic English. They are able to participate fully in class discussions; however, it is not uncommon for students to have significant gaps in their academic ability (as was the case with Luisa). Such students need significant intervention, such as specific learning strategies (see Chapter 5), intensive small-group or individualized instruction, or some other interventions. (See the section titled Learning and Behavior Challenges later in this chapter.)

Academic Background and School Experience

The number of years students have spent in school, the quality of their instructional experiences, and the consistency of those experiences are important data. A student like Rahul, who is monolingual/literate in his native language and who has grade-level school experience and an uninterrupted academic background, requires a different academic focus than a student of the same age who has limited literacy skills. For example, the amount of native-language support is based on student need. Students who are developing basic academic skills will require extra time devoted to literacy and will benefit from native-language support (Gutierrez, 2001).

The importance of academic background and school experience increases exponentially with the age of the student. If, like Rahul, a youngster first enters U.S. schools in middle school, prior experience is a critical factor. But for a child enrolling in preschool, prior academic experience is much less relevant. For many English learners,

FIGURE 1.8 Examples of Subjects and Language Instruction

English Proficiency Levels	English-Language Development LEP 2	Core Curriculum for All Students			Mainstream Classes	Self-Image Cross-cultural LEP 5
		Native-Language Instruction LEP 3	Sheltered Instruction LEP 4			
F E P — Fluent English Proficient					All Subjects	
e. Advanced SOLOM 21–25	ESL–Advanced*	Language Arts or other subject for enrichment *Optimal*			All Subjects	*Weave throughout the core curriculum*
d. Early Advanced SOLOM 17–20	ESL–4	Language Arts	Transitional Language Arts, Social Science**		Art, Music, PE, Math, Science, Electives**	
L E P — **c. Intermediate** SOLOM 12–16	ESL–3	Language Arts, Social Science	Math, Science		Art, Music, PE, Electives	
b. Early Intermediate SOLOM 6–11	ESL–2	Language Arts, Math, Social Science, Science (Concepts)**	Math, Science (problems, computation, and experiments)**		Art, Music, PE, Electives	
a. Beginning (non-English) SOLOM 5	ESL–1	Language Arts, Math, Social Science, Science**	Art, Music, PE			

Heading: DISTRICT'S CORE CURRICULUM FOR ENGLISH LEARNERS

*May be provided within the transitional or mainstream language arts curriculum with qualified staff, proper planning, material, and training.

**And career/vocational education (applied academics), especially grades 7–12.

Source: Adapted from Paramount Unified School District Framework.

especially those in upper elementary and secondary grades, lack of school experience affects academic development and English language proficiency. These factors will be considered when deciding on an instructional program.

Accurate information about previous school experience, although often difficult to obtain, greatly helps in instructional planning. When records are unavailable, it is essential to speak with parents, guardians, and the students themselves. Behavior and learning patterns that appear inappropriate may be due to a lack of school experience. Immigrant students need to be given ample opportunity to adjust to their new setting and to learn school procedures. In order to ease the transition, educators need to be sensitive to the situation and willing to make modifications and adaptations as needed.

Assessment

Assessment is critical in all areas of instruction and not just to determine levels of English proficiency. Particularly for students with diverse abilities, assessment in basic skill development and content area knowledge is essential to provide students with instruction that is appropriate, supportive, and nondiscriminatory (Figueroa & Newsome, 2006). For example, Rahul's eighth-grade science teacher may discover that he has not acquired certain skills that are emphasized in U.S. schools, such as outlining, specific study skills, or report writing. The teacher can teach those skills to the class at the beginning of the year and review them as they are used in lessons. (Students who already have these skills would be assigned other tasks.)

If students have already been labeled as having disabilities, assessments would be conducted in the context of the Individualized Educational Plan (IEP) and ideally would provide the vital information necessary to provide differentiated instruction at appropriate levels (Haager, Klinger, & Vaughn, 2007). If students are not labeled as having disabilities but are struggling with academic success, ongoing assessment in the form of curriculum-based measures will provide teachers with consistent information across time, and teachers will use the data to provide differentiated instruction at appropriate levels. Measures such as informal reading inventories, writing probes with grading rubrics, and other resources such as timed tests in oral reading fluency may assist teachers in determining students' level of literacy development (Graves, Plasiencia-Peinado, Deno, & Johnson, 2005).

Instruction

Students with grade-level academic skills in their native languages may move into sheltered classes more quickly than those who lack strong academic preparation. Initially, bilingual support, if available, would ease the transition, as would specific ESL instruction. Sheltered classes that offer sufficient scaffolding, comprehensible input, and contextual support assist students in making steady progress toward attaining standards (see Chapter 3 for a detailed description of sheltered instruction).

Those students with gaps in their education and those who lack strong literacy skills will require much more explicit instruction in the routines and expectations of school as well as procedural, organizational, and academic strategies to enhance academic performance. Often, it is assumed that students understand these aspects of schooling when in fact they must be taught (Chapter 5 includes information on strategy instruction in these areas). Further, instruction needs to be highly contextualized, providing students with opportunities to interact with one another and practice the skills and knowledge presented in lessons.

Learning and Behavior Challenges and Giftedness

Over the past decade there has been a growing concern about the overrepresentation and underrepresentation of minority students in special education classes, especially those who are learning English in school (Baca & Cervantes, 2004; Echevarria, Powers, & Elliott, 2004; Jiménez, 2000; Ruiz, 1995). Once they are labeled as having a disability, students often spend their entire school careers in special education. Carrying the label has a negative impact on social relationships and self-concept (Hallahan & Kauffman, 2004; Pavri & Monda-Amaya, 2001) as well as on long-term outcomes such as graduation and employment (Blackorby & Wagner, 1996). In fact, some advocates for English learners have questioned the quality and appropriateness of special education services for these students (Figueroa, 1989; MacSwan, 2000; Schiff-Myers et al., 1994). An awareness of the controversy around minority students in special education as well as a lack of understanding of cultural and language issues has led some educators to be overly cautious in referring English learners for assessment, resulting in an underrepresentation of some ethnic groups. Students learning English risk receiving no special services or assistance at all. Trends indicate that English learners are less likely than other students to receive special services (Cline & Fredrickson, 1999; Jiménez, 2000) including those individuals labeled as gifted and talented (Bice & Bice, 2004; Fultz, Lara-Alecio, Irby, & Tong, 2013; Kitano, 2003).

While English learners with gifts and talents tend to have a great propensity for resilience, problem-solving abilities, and coping skills, teachers would still follow the same process as already described for assessment to provide supports that students may need. A very bright English learner may show varied signs of language proficiency across a broader range than other students. For example, a student learning English at a very fast rate may be able to "bridge" and "reach" much sooner than other students at their same level. Conversely, the schools have a history of difficulty recognizing gifts and talents when students are not fluent English speakers (Fultz et al., 2013). Language proficiency should be minimally used when gifted and talented qualifications are being determined.

Disproportionate overrepresentation of minority students in special education is most striking among the mild and moderate disability categories. Categories such as learning disabilities, emotional-behavioral disorders, speech and language disorders, and mild mental retardation require subjective judgment because these disabilities do not have a clear biological cause and they are less identifiable than other disabilities such as blindness or Down syndrome. Some argue that the mild disabilities themselves are socially constructed and arbitrary (Barnes, Mercer, & Shakespeare, 1999), leading to extreme variability in identification rates. A number of experts suggest that teachers should view overrepresentation as an indicator of underlying issues that should be addressed rather than focusing on the fact of overrepresentation itself (Artiles, Trent, & Palmer, 2004; Rueda & Windmueller, 2006). High-quality, effective instruction for all students in both general and special education could diminish the significance of overrepresentation.

Given that the estimate of learning disabilities is approximately 15 percent of the school population (National Center for Learning Disabilities, 2006), it is reasonable to assume those estimates would be the same for English learners. Traditional practices with struggling students have been criticized for waiting for the child to fail and then focusing on determining eligibility for special education services. An alternative approach, multi-tiered intervention emphasizes catching the problem early, providing interventions, documenting the student's response to the interventions, and then making data-based decisions about the necessity of more intensive interventions, including special education.

Search for Interventions: A Three-Tiered Model

As seen in Figure 1.9, the first consideration is the quality of instruction in regular education (Batsche et al., 2005; Brown & Doolittle, 2008; Fuchs, Fuchs, & Vaughn, 2008; Klingner , Artilles, & Barletta, 2006). If a student is struggling, then the instructional context is assessed to make sure that the student's needs are being met within that classroom. For English learners in particular, it is important to first look at the appropriateness of the instructional program since the educational system is often insensitive to the issues and stresses surrounding learning English, creating what may be viewed mistakenly as behavioral or learning disabilities (Artiles, Harry, Reschly, & Chinn, 1999; Baca & Cervantes, 2004). Teachers often do not use strategies known to be effective with English learners (Echevarria, Vogt, & Short, 2013; Richards & Leafstadt, 2010).

Although students experience difficulties in school for a number of reasons, sometimes the problems are related to language or learning disabilities. Some common characteristics of students with learning or behavior problems include:

- Withdrawn behavior
- Memory difficulty
- Bizarre behavior
- Poor motor abilities

FIGURE 1.9 Three-Tiered Model of School Supports

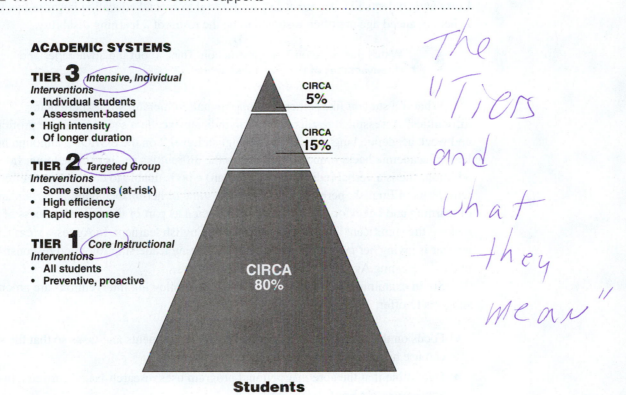

The "Tiers and what they mean"

- Aggressive behavior
- Poor perceptual abilities
- Attention problems
- Poor language abilities
- Hyperactivity
- Poor academic performance
- Low motivation

General educators and special educators share responsibilities for all children, including those with disabilities. The key to helping struggling students is to provide more effective instruction and strong interventions.

Tier 1

As mentioned previously, when behavior or learning challenges appear, classroom instruction is evaluated for a match with learner needs; scientifically based instruction interventions are implemented to help the student within the regular class setting. Individual interventions require consistency and sustained periods of time to facilitate student change. But students who are learning English often experience learning and behavior difficulties that are more associated with the strain of adapting to a new culture and learning a new language than with some type of disability. In the case of Luisa (limited bilingual), who was born in the United States and began school as a Spanish speaker, inconsistent language instruction at critical developmental stages likely contributed to her current poor performance. High transiency rates, the mismatch between school expectations and those of the student's family, insufficient academic background, low English proficiency, inadequate instruction, lack of continuity between instructional programs and a myriad of other reasons may account for the difficulties experienced by English learners. However, Luisa and students like her are at risk for referral to special education because low skills at her advanced age are often assumed to be the result of a learning disability.

 Watch this video on Tier 1 instruction. Think about the advantages and disadvantages of this Tier 1 instruction.

What if a student like Agnessa (monolingual/preliterate) was experiencing difficulties? Assessment results in Russian indicate excellent social language proficiency and weak academic language. She is at English Level 2 on the SOLOM, although her lack of academic background contributes to the difficulties she is experiencing. In addition, she is a verbal individual (in Russian) who is unable to communicate effectively with peers in English, perhaps accounting for some of her misbehavior. A certain amount of learning and behavior problems can be expected as part of the normal process of making the significant adjustments required of English learners. In Agnessa's case, the teacher is giving her positive recognition by assigning leadership roles and responsibilities in class, reducing Agnessa's inappropriate behaviors.

So, in examining the regular class setting, the following interventions are among the supports to offer:

- Focus on the strengths of the student. Adapt assignments and tasks so that the student can use his or her strengths and experience success.
- Determine that the core instructional program uses research-based curricula that are appropriate for English learners.

- Plan specifically around the linguistic characteristics of the learner.
- Identify what the student can and cannot do academically and linguistically based on assessment data. Start teaching at the appropriate level and with techniques that are known to be effective for students who are learning English so that the student can experience success.
- Confer with parents or caregivers regularly to gain their support and involve them in the teaching and learning process.
- Use interactive, engaging approaches to teaching, such as partner sharing, cooperative learning, and cross-age tutoring.
- Provide emotional security for the student by building a positive supportive relationship while maintaining high expectations. This could include providing both native-language support and community support, showing a genuine interest in the life of the student.
- Encourage goal setting and consistent measurement of academic progress with mechanisms for self-report and regular reports to parents or caregivers.
- Make directions clear and simple, and adjust workload and time requirements as necessary.
- Model processes and strategies, since many English learners may not be familiar with U.S. schools' ways of organizing and processing information.
- Plan specific written agreements with students that clarify expectations and emphasize self-regulated learning.

Tier 2

Students in a high-quality instructional program who lag behind other students on measures of performance are identified as those who need further intervention at Tier 2. This group should comprise less than 20 percent of the students in general education.   *< 20%*
Typically, classroom interventions will benefit the student, reducing the learning or behavior difficulties he or she was experiencing (Batsche et al., 2005; Cloud, 1994; Richards & Leafstadt, 2010). However, when students display poor response to high-quality classroom instruction, a school-based problem-solving team decides on supplemental instruction (Baca & Cervantes, 2004; Cline & Frederickson, 1999; Lozano-Rodriguez & Castellano, 1999). The team is typically composed of classroom teachers, including those familiar with second-language acquisition and instruction for English learners, a school counselor, and an administrator. Problem-solving teams (also known by names such as *teacher support teams, multidisciplinary teams, instructional support teams,* or *child study teams*) have resulted in decreased referrals and placement in special education (Hartman & Faye, 1996) and decreased overrepresentation of minorities in special education (Gravois & Rosenfield, 2006). The team defines the problem, determines why it is happening, develops a plan, and evaluates the plan. Tier 2 literacy development consists of small-group instruction with opportunities for students to practice targeted skills.

 Watch this video of Tier 2 instruction. Think about the times that Tier 2 instruction is most beneficial.

Tier 2 interventions have been successful in both elementary and middle school settings (Denton et al., 2008; Graves, Duesbery, Pyle, Brandon, & McIntosh, 2011; Graves, Brandon, Duesbery, McIntosh, & Block, 2011). Areas to examine for informing development of a plan may include the student's home and family situation, school program and language of instruction, levels of native language functioning, English proficiency, attendance patterns, and health issues. By checking records or interviewing the family, the team may discover that the student's academic problems are caused by poor vision or hearing, by a preoccupation over difficulties at home, or by an instructional program that does not meet academic needs. To ensure appropriate evaluation of the whole child (Saunders & Goldenberg, 2010), the following procedural steps are recommended for English learners when learning or behavioral issues are a challenge:

- Talk to parents and learn as much as possible about the student in both community and school activities, including information previously discussed in this chapter: native-language competence, English-language competence, and prior school experience.

- Document progress, or lack thereof, for all interventions implemented. Data-based decisions will be made from records of how the student responded to interventions.

- Ensure that the student who is learning English has teachers who are trained specifically to work with English learners, with professional preparation in second-language acquisition, culture, ESL, and effective sheltered instruction.

- Ensure that the curriculum and the interventions that the teacher uses are those known to be effective for English learners.

- Have various school personnel (including several different teachers) document the student's responsiveness to teaching, including when accommodations and adaptations were made over a sustained period of time.

- Create a home and educational record of the student's accomplishments and challenges.

- Finally, if the student does not respond to intensive interventions, he or she may require more intensive support, such as that provided in Tier 3.

Tier 3

Approximately 5 percent of students will require the kind of intensive interventions offered through Title 1, district remediation programs, or special education (Batsche et al., 2005). These interventions are typically long term and may include a formal referral for assessment to determine eligibility for special education. In the multi-tiered model, eligibility is determined by examining the data that have been collected through the use of multi-tiered practices. More extensive evaluation may be needed to determine eligibility, depending upon the referral questions and developing interventions that will be effective in improving a student's rate of learning. Additional data may include use of formal and informal assessments (curriculum based), observations, and interviews. Ongoing assessment is critical to enable teachers and parents to monitor progress that students are making in each subject and to guide continued differentiation of instruction.

 Watch this video and think about when Tier 3 instruction is needed.

Instruction

The same three-tier model can be applied when considering instruction. For English learners with diverse abilities, Response to Intervention, which is a multi-tiered model is required as part of the identification model for special education (IDEIA, 2004). The intention for utilizing this model is to curtail discriminatory labeling and inappropriate placement of students into disability categories (Klingner, Artiles, & Barletta, 2006). Most RTI models involve implementing the strongest Tier 1 interventions possible (Echevarria & Hasbrouck, 2009; McIntosh, Graves, & Gersten, 2007).

For example, Tier 1 is the instruction delivered by the general education teacher. This instruction involves all we have discussed, including determining English proficiency, level of learning across subjects, and levels of literacy. Tier 1 teachers would engage in best practices to maximize learning progress for English learners. Students who are struggling might be recommended for Tier 2 instruction.

Tier 2 instruction involves small-group instruction to provide intensive practice at the student's level of the learning (Graves, Brandon, Duesbery, McIntosh, & Pyle, 2011; Graves, Duesbery, Pyle, Brandon, & McIntosh, 2011). The goal of interventions is matched to the challenges the student is experiencing such as developing literacy, English proficiency, content area learning (e.g., mathematics), or increasing appropriate behavior. Small-group instruction typically involves students in fairly homogeneous groups from three to eight students (Linan-Thompson, Cirino, & Vaughn, 2008). If students make adequate progress, as measured by specified assessments, they might not need to continue in Tier 2. Tier 2 is offered in addition to Tier 1 and is ideally offered for at least an hour per day at a time in which students miss as little as possible from the regular schedule. Parents and caregivers can be actively involved in Tier 2 by helping students practice skills they are learning at home.

For those few students who do not make adequate progress in Tier 2, Tier 3 services may be recommended. Tier 3 may involve a recommendation for special education. All Tier 3 cases require a problem-solving approach in which teachers and parents or caregivers working as a team decide on a course of action that will result in successful experiences for the individual student (Vaughn, Wanzek, Scammaca, Linan-Thompson, & Woodruff, 2009).

If special education services are to be provided, they must occur in the least restrictive environment, which could be the bilingual, sheltered, or mainstream classroom. The designation ideally provides the student additional support and services with continued and appropriate focus on developing grade-level language and academic competence.

A linguistically appropriate individualized education plan (IEP) should be developed for the student, including the following elements:

1. Assessment in both native- and English-language skills to determine language competence
2. Goals related both to the development of English and the native language, when possible
3. Instructional practices that are known to be effective for English learners, including those that require the active participation of the learner
4. A focus on outcomes, not simply process

The full success of an IEP requires the active involvement of all school personnel and of parents. Accountability is extremely important for designing the best instruction and interventions for learners, as is the establishment of a curriculum-based standard of measurement. Goal setting and a careful look at the possibilities for the year as well as for each month are a critical part of good instruction. In setting annual goals, the teacher must assess the learner's current level of knowledge and skills and their match to the curriculum. In this way, the approximate level of progress that is likely by the end of the year can be estimated. Short-term objectives require the teacher to break down annual goals into approximately 9 or 10 pieces to make a determination of how much progress a student is likely to make on a monthly basis. The system of measurement must be incorporated into both the goal and objective statements as the teacher describes how progress will be determined. Goal setting is essential both for the learner and for the teacher to maximize progress and the sense of urgency for amelioration. Persistent and continued interventions should be implemented until he or she demonstrates success. An IEP should be adjusted if necessary.

If an English learner has been placed in the special education system, the IEP can provide protection and assurances that he or she would not otherwise have had (Baca & Cervantes, 2004). Many students who do not qualify for or require special education services would still benefit from the process of setting individually designed goals and objectives, involving families and other school personnel in the plan, and consistently measuring progress, making adjustments as needed.

Student Profiles Revisited

Rahul—Since he had grade-level academic proficiency in his native language, an instructional plan for maximizing Rahul's potential was implemented. He was placed in sheltered classes for all content areas and received one period of intensive ESL instruction. The ESL specialist monitored Rahul's progress during this year of transition and set goals for the academic skills he was missing. During the ESL class, Rahul was taught procedural, organizational, and academic strategies that are used in U.S. schools. Because of the careful ongoing assessment of his progress, Rahul made excellent academic progress this year and has adjusted well to school. It is anticipated that Rahul will move into mainstream classes next year with the exception of language arts and social studies. He will continue to receive sheltered instruction in those subjects and will continue with ESL as well.

Agnessa—With limited literacy skills in Russian and low levels of English proficiency, Agnessa benefitted from an instructional program that included native-language support and comprehensive English-language development. A bilingual aide worked with Agnessa, devoting two periods a day to developing beginning literacy skills. As Agnessa acquired more English and academic skills, she began to participate more fully, especially when her teacher used sheltered instruction. Many students with behavior issues similar to Agnessa's act out because of a history of academic failure and/or social rejection. The teacher enlisted the support of Agnessa's parents since the instructional program for Agnessa included behavioral contracts and special reading and writing instruction. Parents who are not literate or are semiliterate can still support their children at home by being involved in the program and overseeing it at home. Agnessa's behavior and affect should be carefully monitored, along with her academic performance, to determine if she is making progress.

Ongoing assessment indicated a significant change in behavior. The successes she experienced with the bilingual aide coupled with increased participation in sheltered lessons helped Agnessa relate better to both her peers and the teacher. After the teacher began working with Agnessa's family to have the behavior contract reinforced at home, she was more cooperative at school. Her academic gains were more modest. She acquired some basic literacy skills in Russian and her English proficiency increased through systematic English language development. However, she continues to lag behind her peers in all academic areas. It is anticipated that native-language support will continue next year and at the appropriate time her literacy skills will be transferred to literacy instruction in English.

(3) *Luisa*—After several prereferral interventions were implemented, Luisa's academic struggles persisted. When the multidisciplinary team met with her mother, she mentioned that Luisa was referred for special education services by her fifth-grade teacher as a result of persistent difficulties. At that time, she was not tested or recommended for placement because her parents did not approve of this type of approach. Her family now realized the need for more intensive intervention and approved the formal assessment, qualifying Luisa for special education services. The IEP delineated an aggressive instructional plan for maximizing Luisa's potential, which included work with a resource specialist in the school three times a week, focusing on reading and writing development.

resistant parents

With additional support services, Luisa made significant progress throughout the year. Ongoing assessment of the instructional plan was conducted by collecting samples of her work on a regular basis and tracking progress.

Summary

Many schools have students who represent each of the four types of students mentioned in this chapter. Students have a variety of abilities in different areas such as native-language levels, English-language levels, school experience, academic background, and learning or behavior problems—there is an infinite number of complex, individual profiles for students who are often referred to simply as English learners. Students may have high levels of performance in English but not in their native languages, high levels of performance in both languages (type 1), high levels of performance in their native languages but low levels of performance in English (type 2), low levels of performance in all areas due to lack of school experience (type 3), or low levels of performance in all areas due to inadequate instruction or learning or behavior problems (type 4). Students' abilities can vary within areas and may not fit neatly into types, but this system of analysis assists us in determining how to design appropriate instruction. In order to educate all students appropriately, a systematic process for determining their needs includes gathering data, conducting assessments, and implementing effective instruction in the following areas: (1) native-language knowledge, (2) English-language knowledge, (3) academic background and school experience, and (4) learning and behavior challenges. For students who experience persistent problems that are clearly beyond what would normally be expected for students learning English, a team-based intervention plan should be developed and student progress monitored to determine if multi-tiered instruction is needed.

many "combinations" of possible profiles

Specifically, as a reader you

- contrasted native-language knowledge with second-language knowledge.
  - considered how each should be assessed and what the important considerations for instruction are.
- identified the stages of second-language proficiency.
- described the importance of academic language, and explained why it is **critically important** for school success.
- discussed the types of learning and behavior challenges that a struggling **English learner** could have, and explained why they might occur.
  - listed types of assessment and instructional support that support learning and behavior changes.

The remainder of this book will provide specific theory and instructional approaches for teaching that can improve the performance of individuals who are learning English. Chapter 2 will provide theoretical background for the instructional approaches presented in Chapters 3 to 8.

ACTIVITIES

1. Lupe has lived in a large urban U.S. city for 10 years. She was in bilingual classes in elementary school and is now mainstreamed for all subjects, although her English is not completely fluent. She is friendly and cooperative when she is in class but has high absenteeism. She seems to prefer talking with friends to completing assignments. Teachers think she has academic potential but worry that she will eventually drop out of school because of persistent underachievement. Outline five prereferral interventions that could be implemented with Lupe.

2. Hui came from Vietnam, where he worked with his uncle before emigrating to the United States last year. He had about six years of full-time schooling in Vietnam and two years of intermittent attendance. Now in the tenth grade, he is struggling academically. Draw an "iceberg" representation of Hui's levels of language proficiency, and explain your reasoning.

3. Sara has lived in the United States for six months. She seems withdrawn and does not socialize much with other students. She was educated in her home country and, in fact, studied some English as a foreign language in school. Her teachers are pleased with her work, given the limited time she has been in this country. What type of student is she, and what is an appropriate educational program for her? What do you think the relationship is between an appropriate academic program and her behavior?

4. Lilli has been in sheltered classes for the past two years and is still performing well below grade level. Name at least three ideas for differentiated instruction that might help Lilli.

CHAPTER 2

Theoretical and Historical Foundations

LEARNING OBJECTIVES:

- Analyze the history of students learning English in school and in so doing, identify the ways in which instruction of English learners might be improved in the future.
- Contrast second-language acquisition theory as it relates to the acquisition versus teaching of English debate.
- Describe the importance of contextual support according to Cummins.
- Examine the factors that affect second-language acquisition and consider which are most important.
- Identify the learning theories that most reflect your own teaching style.

Teachers are faced with the unprecedented challenge of teaching students with a wide variety of language and cultural backgrounds, academic preparation, and learning differences. At the same time, educational reforms abound including high academic standards designed to prepare students to be college and career ready. Teachers are best able to meet these challenges when they reflect on their teaching and make adjustments to help students improve their

Darrin Henry/Fotolia

academic performance. Part of this practice involves asking oneself: What approach do I believe has the greatest potential for helping me make the changes needed? To do this, teachers must understand and articulate the theories underlying teaching approaches (Sagor, 2011). Further, teachers are well served to understand and evaluate the theoretical grounding of reform practices and situate them in a historical perspective. In this chapter, we begin with an overview of the history of education for students learning English including those with learning challenges. Since sheltered instruction involves learning both content and language simultaneously we also include a brief discussion of second-language acquisition followed by a presentation of learning theories that addresses how students learn new material and ideas.

History of Education of Students Learning English in School

Immigration

Media coverage, demographic reports, and our own observations of changes in schools contribute to our awareness of the growing numbers of English learners in the United States. How does this current demographic trend align with other periods in our history? In 1965, the United States abandoned its quota system, which had sustained the overwhelmingly Northern European makeup of the nation for nearly half a century. Most of the new immigrants were from developing countries in Asia and Latin America. Large numbers of documented and undocumented immigrants continued to pour into the United States throughout the 1980s, coming from over one hundred different countries and representing a variety of languages and dialects. This trend has been felt acutely in U.S. schools. In fact, the proportion of English learners in U.S. schools continues to grow steadily, and in some states the growth is more rapidly than overall student growth (National Center for Education Statistics, 2013).

Rights of English Learners

Following the Immigration Act of 1965, legislation was passed to assist the public schools in dealing with the influx of non–English-speaking students. Title VII of the Elementary and Secondary Education Act of 1965 supported programs for educating these students, including transitional bilingual education programs. It was ambiguous whether the intent was to develop languages other than English or to simply use the native language as a transition to English as quickly as possible (Gandara, Moran, & Garcia, 2004). The result was that most English learners were placed in English-only classrooms without appropriate instructional assistance. In 1974, a suit was brought on behalf of Chinese-speaking students in San Francisco whose language needs were not accommodated, which thus denied the students equal access to an education. In the ruling, *Lau v. Nichols*, it was made clear that children who do not speak English are entitled to equal access to the school curriculum. The U.S. Department of Education's Lau Remedies advised bilingual education, when feasible, for students in the elementary grades and ESL programs for older students, although other approaches could be used. The *Lau* decision was hailed by many as a victory for language rights advocates but "from the moment that Lau became the law, opponents of bilingual education, immigration rights, and even immigration began a campaign to dismantle any semblance of primary language support" (Gandara, Moran, & Garcia, 2004).

Since 1998, a number of states have asked voters to decide policy for educating English learners. Voters in California, Arizona, and Massachusetts passed anti-bilingual education initiatives, while Colorado and Oregon rejected similar measures. The arguments for both sides of the issue reveal differing attitudes about the changing U.S. demographics. Proponents of the initiatives advocate assimilation and believe that immigrants resist learning English, while opponents view bilingualism as a social, economic, cultural, and academic advantage (Mora, 2009). Educational research indicates that after five years of English-only policies in California, there has not been significant academic improvement for English learners (Parrish et al., 2006) nor for students in the other states that have limited bilingual programs (Zehr, 2008, p. 10).

Students with Disabilities

At the same time that English learners were fighting for access to an appropriate education, families of students with disabilities were waging a parallel effort. A number of court cases and state and federal laws have led to rights for students with disabilities. The landmark law, currently known as Individuals with Disabilities Education Act (IDEA, 2004), resulted in improved services for children with disabilities and their families. The six major principles of the legislation include (1) a free, appropriate public education for all students with disabilities; (2) use of nondiscriminatory evaluation; (3) development of an individualized education program (IEP); (4) education in the least restrictive environment (LRE); (5) implementation of due process procedures; and (6) right of parental participation.

In short, students with disabilities cannot be excluded from school and, in fact, should be educated with their nondisabled peers to the greatest extent possible. Most often this is the general education classroom, with the supports provided to ensure an appropriate education (Taylor, Smiley, & Richards, 2009). These rights apply to all students, including English learners who exhibit learning and/or behavioral problems.

The provisions of IDEA are stronger than those of the Lau Remedies, primarily because IDEA is a federal law while *Lau* is based on the Civil Rights Act but the Supreme Court never did mandate bilingual education. Also, disabilities affect a wider cross-section of the population so supporters who advocate for the needs of students with disabilities tend to be a more influential group, including those who are in positions of power, are educated, and have more resources. English learners with disabilities benefit from these efforts. However, language rights in general remain irregularly enforced across the country due to differing interpretations and implementations of *Lau*.

Programs for English Learners

Historically, programs for English learners, including those with learning challenges, have been uneven in quality and effectiveness. As a result, English learners have experienced persistent underachievement, which has become illuminated significantly by the high-stakes testing and individual accountability enacted through No Child Left Behind. Consider the National Assessment for Educational Progress, also known as "The Nation's Report Card," which revealed that in reading: 71 percent of the eighth-grade English learners (ELs) performed Below Basic, compared with only 22 percent of non-English learners (NCES, 2012b). The performance gap in Grade 8 mathematics was similar: 71 percent of English learners performed Below Basic compared with 24 percent of non-English learners (NCES, 2012a). In fact, on nearly every measure of state and national assessments, English learners lag behind their native-English-speaking peers and demonstrate significant achievement gaps (National Center on Educational Statistics, 2013; Snow & Biancarosa, 2004). These statistics suggest a persistent achievement gap between English learners and their English-speaking peers. The long-term effects of the achievement gap include significantly higher dropout rates among English learners when compared to non-English learners, as found in recent studies in California and New York City (New York State Education Department, 2011; Rumberger, 2011). The quality of educational programs provided for these students has a strong influence on their educational success (Cloud, Genesee, & Hamayan, 2009; Markham & Gordon, 2007).

A review of effective school programs for English learners included several characteristics that were consistent across programs such as putting in place a well-defined plan of instruction that is aligned both with the standards and the language, academic, and cultural backgrounds of students. Another characteristic is having high expectations for all students' performance while at the same time addressing the specific language, academic, and cultural needs of English learners through ongoing assessment. These assessment results are used to inform instruction and make the necessary adjustments for fostering student success. At the school level, strong leadership, highly qualified staff and community involvement contribute to an environment where all staff are accountable for the achievement of English learners (Aguila, 2010).

Widespread implementation of effective programs has been hampered by several factors, including a lack of trained bilingual personnel to deliver quality instruction in the primary language. States with the highest numbers of English learners (e.g., California, Texas, New York) have a shortage of bilingual teachers, and other states where high numbers of English learners are a relatively new trend (e.g., Nevada, Nebraska, South Dakota) are, in many cases, "scrambling to obtain the resources and personnel to adequately serve the newcomers" (Garcia, Jensen, & Scribner, 2009, p. 10). Further, schools may have students that speak dozens of languages, so providing bilingual instruction isn't possible (Agirdag, 2009).

With the dramatic increase in numbers of English learners, schools can no longer rely solely on specialized ESL classes to meet the educational needs of these students, who primarily are placed in mainstream classes. While ESL specialists have an important role in teaching English and overseeing the English language development of these students, general education teachers need to make content area material (e.g., math, language arts, social studies, science) understandable for English learners. Responsibility for the education of these students cannot be relegated to second-language specialists and classroom instruction aides. Also, many English learners are not included in the larger school community and often are not integrated into general education classes socially or academically (Bunch, Abram, Lotan, & Valdes, 2001).

As the number of English learners in schools has continued to grow, many universities across the United States have responded by adding to their teacher preparation programs coursework that specifically addresses issues surrounding the education of these students. All teachers, not just those with ESL certification, must be prepared to meet the needs of this distinct population (Hutchinson, 2013). However, only a handful of states require some degree of coursework about English learners for preservice teachers to receive teaching certification (Echevarria & Short, 2010). In California, these requirements have been extended to special education teacher preparation programs (www.ctc.ca.gov) but many teacher preparation programs still do not provide teacher candidates with information and strategies for teaching culturally and linguistically diverse students. Large numbers of English learners in mainstream classes continue to have teachers who are not prepared to teach them in ways that facilitate their acquisition of language and content.

The situation is all the more critical because the educational reform movement has had a direct impact on English learners, as states have moved to implement high-stakes testing and standards-based instruction for all students. Classroom instruction is guided by standards for core subjects such as social studies, mathematics, science, and language arts. In many mainstream classes, little or no accommodation is made for the specific language needs of English learners, placing them at a deficit when they are expected to achieve high academic standards in English. The Common Core State Standards, adopted by nearly all states, provide a mere two-page document to guide implementation of the standards with English learners. They acknowledge that, "These students may require additional time, appropriate instructional support, and aligned assessments as they acquire both English language proficiency and content area knowledge" (CCSS, 2013). Imagine the difficulty of being expected to perform at grade level in a language you are still in the process of learning. Many times, the difficulties students experience in school are caused by inappropriate modes of instruction that do not take into account their linguistic needs (Wiley, 2008). Moreover, under new state-level accountability measures, all students are expected to pass end-of-grade tests in order to be promoted and graduate, although most states offer an exemption for between one and three years for English learners.

Teachers need to understand the second-language acquisition process and also use teaching practices that are effective for English learners. Sheltered instruction (described in detail in Chapter 3) is an effective way for these students to gain access to content material while acquiring English skills. If English learners are to be successful academically, graduate from high school, be college and career ready, and reach cognitive levels similar to their U.S.-born peers, they must have access to content material and opportunities to practice academic skills and tasks common to mainstream classes (August & Shanahan, 2006; Genesee et al., 2006; Henze & Lucas, 1993; Short, 1999).

Since English language development is an important component of sheltered instruction, the next section will discuss theories of second-language development.

Theories of Second-Language Acquisition

There are a number of important theories of second-language acquisition (see Baker, 1993; Doughty & Long, 2003; McLaughlin, 1987), but some of the most influential work applied to schooling is that of Stephen Krashen. We will begin with a summary of Krashen's work and then address some of Jim Cummins's contributions to understanding the relationship between the development of one's native language and of a second language.

According to Krashen, language is best acquired through natural communication, not through traditional language teaching, which typically involves activities such as memorizing dialogues and conjugating verbs. Large amounts of exposure to comprehensible input (language that is understood) in authentic communicative contexts is critical. Correct language usage is learned through modeling and practice, which leads an individual to internalize rules of the second language and monitor or edit errors. As learners are exposed to abundant amounts of comprehensible input, more complex language forms are added to learners' repertoire of understanding, which moves them to higher levels of proficiency, referred to as i + 1. Since language learning is sensitive to emotions such as anxiety or frustration, these affective variables can block or impede learning of a second language.

In applying these ideas to the classroom, during language-learning lessons, students are not put on the spot to give correct answers but are encouraged to participate at their

welcoming answer

differing opinions

own comfort level. When errors are made, the teacher models correct usage or elaborates on students' comments. For example, a social studies teacher might ask, "What was one of the causes of the Civil War?" A student might answer, "One cause was the differences between farming peoples and city peoples." The teacher would reply, "Good answer, Farook. There were differences in the way people thought, which were influenced by their lifestyles. The South was a farming or agrarian society (teacher writes terms on the overhead projector or white board), and the North was largely an industrialized society. Good answer. So Farook said there were differences between the thinking of farming people (teacher points to 'farming/agrarian') and city people (teacher points to 'city/industrialized'). Good. What else?" Notice how the teacher makes it easy for the student to participate by accepting his answer in the form given. The teacher then models and elaborates on the student's answer. Without the teacher's insisting on correct speech, students are more relaxed and willing to participate, lowering the affective filter

A recent review of research on English learning seems to contradict some aspects of Krashen's hypotheses (Saunders & Goldenberg, 2010). Studies have shown that explicit teaching of English is necessary for students to move to higher levels of proficiency. Students who received focused second-language instruction made more than five times more gains than students who did not receive focused second-language instruction (Norris & Ortega, 2000). So, it appears that second-language teaching is more effective than exposure in comprehensible contexts alone. Time needs to be devoted to explicit teaching to raise students' conscious awareness of aspects of English such as word-order rules and difficult academic vocabulary terms. = *It needs to be more explicit "word work"— modeling isn't enough.*

The Contributions of Cummins

As Crawford (1991) suggests, Jim Cummins's contributions to understanding the relationship between first- and second-language development "shattered a number of misconceptions about bilingualism" (p. 105). In Chapter 1, we discussed one of Cummins's most influential contributions: the concept of two types of language proficiency. The conversational/academic language distinction recognizes that students acquire everyday, conversational English relatively quickly, but the language necessary for school tasks (such as in reading, writing, mathematics, and other content subjects) is cognitive-academic language proficiency, a more complex type of language proficiency that takes longer to acquire. While recognizing the widespread use of the terms BICS and CALP, Cummins now uses the terms *conversational* and *academic language proficiency* (Cummins, 2000).

"vs"

 Watch this video and note how Jim Cummins describes the distinction between everyday language and academic language. Pay particular attention to his guidance for working with English learners.

Two of Cummins's other notions relate to the distinction between language uses: the linguistic interdependence model and the range of communicative demands.

The linguistic interdependence hypothesis (Cummins, 1981a, 1981b, 1994) holds that cognitive-academic skills learned in the native language will transfer to the new language (English) and that such skills are interdependent across languages. For example, once the code of reading has been cracked, an individual can learn to read in other languages without relearning the concept of sound-symbol relationship with each new language. Research evidence supports this hypothesis; studies indicate that many literacy skills "transfer" from one language to another (August & Shanahan, 2006; Genesee et al., 2006). The process of transfer, however, is neither automatic nor inevitable (Gersten, Brengelman, & Jiménez, 1994). It is a process that requires guidance by the teacher, with explicit links made to past learning. For students to draw on previously learned skills or information, they frequently need prompting, reminders, and explicit teaching. This is especially true for students with language or learning difficulties.

Communicative tasks (listening, speaking, reading, and writing) may be easier or more difficult for second-language learners, depending on the task itself and the amount of contextual support provided. The range of communicative demands is conceptualized as a framework with two continua (see Figure 2.1).

1. The horizontal continuum represents contextual support, ranging from contextually embedded communication that provides lots of clues such as gestures, visual clues, and feedback to make the message understood, to context-reduced communication, which relies primarily on spoken messages or written texts, and gives few, if any, contextual clues.

2. The vertical continuum relates to the cognitive demands of the task. For example, a cognitively undemanding task can be performed with little or no conscious thought, such as reciting one's own name and phone number, while listening to a lecture on an unfamiliar topic is a cognitively demanding task.

English learners typically achieve communicative competence more rapidly than academic competence. Therefore, tasks in the A quadrant (Figure 2.1) should be relatively easy for English learners, since they rely on contextual clues and are less dependent on academic language. However, the most common types of instructional tasks are found in quadrant D. They are also the most difficult. These tasks offer few contextual clues and include academic tasks such as reading a text (without pictures or graphics), understanding math concepts, doing math word problems, writing compositions, listening to lectures, and taking tests.

Cummins (2000) summarizes the framework's implications for instruction for English learners: "Language and content will be acquired most successfully when students are challenged cognitively but provided with the contextual and linguistic supports or scaffolds for successful task completion" (p. 71).

FIGURE 2.1 Range of Contextual Support and Degree of Cognitive Involvement in Communicative Activities

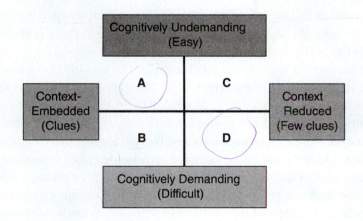

Source: Based on Cummins (1981b).

The goal of sheltered instruction is to take challenging standards-based academic content from the D quadrant and move presentation of information and the activities associated with content lessons into the B quadrant by contextualizing instruction, not watering it down. In that way, English learners are taught grade-level material that is made understandable for them through the kinds of teaching techniques discussed in Chapter 3.

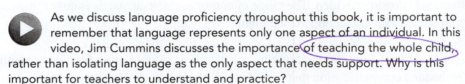 As we discuss language proficiency throughout this book, it is important to remember that language represents only one aspect of an individual. In this video, Jim Cummins discusses the importance of teaching the whole child, rather than isolating language as the only aspect that needs support. Why is this important for teachers to understand and practice?

*F*actors That Affect Second-Language

Second-language acquisition is a complex process; its success or failure will not be explained by a single factor or theory (Gass & Selinker, 2001; Snow, 1992). Many factors can influence acquisition of English, and in an effort to understand some of these factors, we have organized the discussion into two categories: those factors that are inherent in the language learner and those that are influenced by social and academic elements. Some of the factors that encourage or impede second-language acquisition include, but are not limited to those shown in the following table.

Language Learner Factors	Socio-Academic Factors
Motivation	Family
Social Identity	Access to the Target Language
Age	Quality of Instruction
Personality	
First-Language Development	
Cognitive Ability	

Language Learner Factors

Motivation.   Teachers have many different opinions about student motivation, but not all are based on what we know from research. While there is great variation in motivational levels from learner to learner, the importance of high motivation for second-language acquisition is clear. In this regard, Fillmore (1985) asserts that recognizing the need to learn the second language and being motivated to do so are key ingredients for second-language learning.

What are motives for learning a second language? Baker (1992) discusses two types of motivation: integrative and instrumental. When students are motivated to identify with or join another language group—that is, integrate into the group—the process is termed *integrative motivation.* This type of motivation increases the likelihood of becoming proficient in the second language because it involves developing personal relationships that are potentially long lasting. *Instrumental motivation* describes a situation in which individuals learn another language for a practical reason, such as getting a job, enhancing their career possibilities, or passing an exam. This type of motivation may not be as effective in leading to mastery of the second language since it tends to involve short-term goals. Once a goal is achieved—e.g., the exam is passed or the job is obtained—this type

[handwritten: to be part of the culture]

[handwritten: To complete a task/goal]

of motivation may diminish. Some motivation-related issues that are especially relevant for older second-language learners include frustration, anxiety, and embarrassment, which can hamper learning (Carhill, Suarez-Orozco, & Paez, 2008).

Other research on motivation relates to the age-old nature vs. nurture debate, which presents ability as either something one is born with or something that can be developed. In schooling, some teachers believe that each student has an innate ability to learn, whether it is new information or a new language. Others take the position that with proper motivation, teaching, and high expectations, students have unlimited potential. The key appears to be one's mindset. That is, students who believe they can get better at something have a growth mindset and can make dramatic strides in performance. Those with a fixed mindset are not motivated to engage in activities that they are not good at because it challenges their self-image and they do not see the benefit of learning from failure. It appears that one's mindset can be changed. Low achieving students who were trained to adopt a growth mindset about intelligence showed significant improvement in motivation and math grades (Dweck, 2007).

Social Identity.   The way students see themselves in relation to others in school, in their community, and in the larger society has an impact on language learning. Much of the research on second language acquisition does not take into consideration the influence of one's identity on language learning, and it views motivation is a variable that is independent of social context (Norton-Peirce, 1995; Norton & Toohey, 2011). Norton-Pierce (1995) offers the term *investment* rather than *motivation* to depict the relationship between the learner and the target language (e.g., English). Sometimes a learner may be highly motivated to learn English but may nevertheless have little investment in the language practices of a given classroom because it is perceived to be discriminatory, elitist, or a place where there is an uneven balance of power between English speakers and English learners. The resulting resistance of the student impacts his or her language learning. Recognizing the impact of social identity and investment makes a meaningful connection between a learner's desire and commitment to learn a language and his or her complex identity.

Age.   "I'm too old to learn a second language." This statement reveals a commonly held belief that language is ideally learned during childhood. In reality, the optimal age for acquiring a second language is debated widely and there is little evidence that biological factors prohibit language learning at a certain age (McLaughlin, 2000). Younger learners are more efficient at certain aspects of language acquisition related to natural settings, such as the home, playground, and other environments where they interact naturally with native speakers. They tend to pick up the communicative aspects of language more readily. However, since children's language is relatively simple, it may appear to be more fluent. Young learners are also reasonably free from personality issues that can have a negative impact on language learning, such as self-consciousness, mental rigidity, the desire for perfect pronunciation, and so forth. Older learners generally have the advantage of greater experience with language, more well-developed background knowledge, and a variety of social experiences on which to draw. Those who have been schooled may respond better to formal instruction in a second language because of their advanced cognitive abilities and larger repertoire of learning strategies (August & Shanahan, 2010; Collier, 1987; Cummins, 1980; Elkind, 1970; Fillmore, 1985; Genesee, et al., 2006; Scarcella & Higa, 1982; Snow, 1992). However, older immigrant students tend to encounter less support for language learning, more complex academic content, and less time to catch up before encountering high-stakes assessments (Short & Fitzsimmons, 2007).

Overall, children who begin learning a second language and continue over a long sequence will outperform both adolescents and adults who begin later in life and continue their study for the same period (Bialystok & Hakuta, 1994). They will also achieve more native-like pronunciation. However, older learners have the potential to learn second languages to a very high level (Marinova-Todd, Marshall, & Snow, 2000).

Personality. Extroverts may enjoy initial success with the language because they tend to prefer the social aspects of relationships—such as talking, playing, and working with others—and thus have increased opportunities for interaction and access to native-language models. Strong (1983) found that personality characteristics such as talkativeness (initiating interaction) and responsiveness (responding to others' initiations) impacted interaction and that the most successful language learners maintained interaction more effectively than less successful language learners.

Risk taking is a personality characteristic that affects language learning because a risk-aversive individual may miss opportunities to practice using the language. (See the discussion of a growth mindset in *Motivation* above.) A willingness to experiment with vocabulary and forms of the language, along with a desire to draw generalizations from what has been learned will improve proficiency (Fillmore, 1985).

First-Language Development. As was shown in Chapter 1, learning a first language is a complex task, requiring a minimum of 12 years, with certain aspects of development such as vocabulary expansion continuing for a lifetime. Although a tremendous amount of language is acquired from birth to age 5, children from ages 6 to 12 continue to develop more complex forms of semantics, phonology, morphology, and syntax, as well as more elaborate speech acts (McLaughlin, 1987).

Researchers suggest that the level of first-language development significantly influences second-language development (August & Shanahan, 2006; Genesee et al., 2006; Lindholm-Leary & Genesee, 2010). Students who have had solid schooling in "their native languages are more efficient at acquiring a new language since strong oral and literacy skills developed in the home language provide a solid basis for the acquisition of literacy and other academic language skills in English (August & Shanahan, 2010; Genesee et al., 2006). Those who achieve full cognitive development in both languages will gain cognitive benefits, whereas when development of the first language is discontinued, there may actually be negative consequences (Collier, 1989). Native-language instruction enhances the cognitive development of students learning English and raises the status of second-language learning (Bialystok, 2001). For students who have low literacy levels, it is particularly difficult to catch up in the second language, a language they do not yet fully comprehend, so continued native-language instruction is ideal. The deeper the conceptual foundation, the higher the ability to build. Moreover, the practical benefits of continued instruction in the native language are bilingualism and biliteracy. The cases of two immigrant students illustrate the importance of a solid foundation in the primary language.

Jusuf was 6 months old when his family arrived in the United States from Bosnia. The family embarked on this journey into a new land with the promise of a better future for their children. The father decided that in order for his children to learn English and have an edge when they entered school, the family would speak English at home. The father learned some basic English on the job, but Jusuf's mother spoke only a few words of English. Although hindered by lack of proficient English, they were committed to their decision. They limited use of their native language and struggled to use the new language as often as possible with their children.

Melvina's family also made many sacrifices in order to come to the United States to seek a better future. For the first five years of her life, Melvina's father worked long and hard in this new land, while her mother, who spoke no English, stayed home. To keep them from forgetting their homeland, Melvina's mother spent many hours telling Melvina and her baby sister stories of their family and their village in Bosnia. She taught the children traditional songs and rhymes, and Melvina helped her mother prepare the father's favorite meals.

Which child has the advantage when entering school? Although Jusuf's family had the best of intentions, his language will not be as fully developed as that of Melvina. Because native language use was restricted in the home, Jusuf does not have a solid linguistic foundation in either language. He has not had the kinds of preliteracy experiences that Melvina has had. Through her experiences, Melvina has a foundation in preliteracy—she is familiar with word order and patterns, rhyming, vocabulary, and concept development—as well as background knowledge upon which to build. She will not have to relearn acquired concepts when she begins to speak English; the concepts will transfer to the new language.

Cognitive Ability.   Many of the cognitive processes that are important for second-language acquisition are related to general cognitive abilities, such as verbal memory, auditory perception, and categorization. These abilities affect the language-learning process (Fillmore, 1985), although wide variation among learners is expected in this area. Individuals with lower cognitive ability are capable of acquiring a second language, but proficiency levels will be equal to or lower than those in the first language. Further, studies found that students in bilingual programs who had learning disabilities and low academic ability performed as well as equivalent students in English-only programs (Lindholm-Leary & Genesee, 2010).

Socio-Academic Factors

Family.   Students' home environment and family practices impact language acquisition as well as overall academic achievement. Garcia and colleagues (2009) discuss the fact that although English learners vary on a number of characteristics, in general, they come from low income families with limited formal education. Socioeconomic status, maternal educational level, parent English proficiency level, and home literacy experiences all affect a student's acquisition of language (Garcia et al., 2009; Goldenberg, Rueda, & August, 2006). Whether in the native language or English, parental education affects the development of academic English. There is considerable evidence that the linguistic knowledge students acquire in speaking and reading their first language predicts and transfers to learning to speak and read a second language (August & Shanahan, 2006). The language of children's homes is especially critical for schools to build on when children are learning to speak, listen to, write, and read English. In schools where immigrant families are welcomed and considered an asset, parents are encouraged to create a rich linguistic environment at home by using their native language to tell stories, teach songs, read books, and exhibit other literacy practices that are aligned with the kinds of activities of school (Echevarria, Short, & Vogt, 2008). Parents who are unable to read to their children due to low levels of education can still support their children's education in a number of ways, including monitoring homework and television viewing, which are associated with academic achievement (Hoover-Dempsey et al., 2001; Potter, 2006).

Access to the Target Language.   English learners benefit from opportunities to use the language with native English speakers (Snow, 1992). Adolescents who had opportunities to use English in informal settings such as in their neighborhoods, at work, with friends, and in the hallways of school demonstrated stronger English proficiency outcomes (Carhill, Suarez-Orozco, & Paez, 2008). Classrooms where English learners work in groups with native-English speakers and learning environments that encourage student-to-student interaction both foster second-language acquisition. However, simply hearing the language doesn't provide English learners with access to the language. For example, many of us come in contact with speakers of other languages in various settings, but we don't actually learn the language when we hear it spoken. Learning requires contextual clues to make the message understandable, which is why conversational language is more readily developed than academic language. Instruction needs to be meaningful to be accessible for English learners.

Quality of Instruction.   What happens in the classroom is vitally important. The teacher's daily routines, level of lesson preparation, expectations of the students, use of essential teaching practices, instructional strategies, knowledge of the subject matter, understanding of sociocultural factors that affect the student, and techniques for modifying instruction for English learners all impact learner outcomes, including language acquisition. The challenge for teachers of students with diverse abilities is to create classroom conditions in which learners can and will learn by adjusting texts, tasks, and instructional settings to match their needs (Lipson & Wixson, 2002). It has been suggested that many problems experienced by students learning English are pedagogically induced or the result of instructional practices that are not suited to the learner, often resulting in inappropriate placement in special education (Cummins, 1984). The interventions discussed in Chapter 1 are one way of eliminating inappropriate placement of students in special education services. These interventions are used along with instructional practices that reflect effective teaching for second-language learners. If instruction is not made comprehensible and accessible for students, the opportunity to learn both English and content material decreases.

Effective language learning takes place in well-organized classrooms where there are clear learning objectives, systematic instruction based on research-validated practices, and opportunities for interaction with the teacher and peers. Interactive instruction allows students to use elaborated language around relevant topics, building English skills while at the same time developing content knowledge.

Your Turn

You are teaching a class that has six English learners. Three of these students have not made adequate academic progress compared with the other English learners and the rest of the class. Consider the discussion on second-language acquisition. What might be some issues that are hampering the progress of these particular students? What specific steps might you take to assist them in learning?

Teaching English Learners: Theory to Practice

Because one of the goals of sheltered instruction is to teach content—including new concepts, information, and skills—to English learners, it is worthwhile to examine the learning theories underpinning methods and practices. Although many teachers consider theory irrelevant to practice, it is important to keep in mind the theoretical perspective driving a given instructional method or approach. Most teachers have a "folk theory," or implicit theory, that influences their teaching but may be unaware of the established theory underlying it. Teachers benefit from having a decision-making model rooted in theory to assist them in making instructional modifications that meet the learning needs of their students.

Individuals differ in their preferences and learning styles, and one single approach rarely meets the needs of all students. If students are not responding to instruction, teachers need to ask these questions:

1. What are the assumptions underlying the approach I'm using?
2. Do these assumptions apply to my students?
3. Do I obtain my desired outcome using this approach?

change up what isn't working

The process of reflecting on the instructional approach being used, examining the theoretical base for the approach, and appraising student learning needs may yield valuable information for maximizing student learning and performance.

The best teachers we have observed are able to use various approaches, depending on the context and the goals of the lesson, enhancing learning opportunities for students. Examining the components of various modes of instruction helps teachers develop a concept of learning and put into operation new or alternate teaching approaches. Teachers should draw from a continuum of teaching models (Saunders & Goldenberg, 1996).

In looking at the following overview of learning theories, it is important to keep in mind that classroom practices rarely are pure examples of single theories. Rather, effective teachers typically use a balanced approach that includes choices rooted in different learning theories. Many instructional methods and practices make use of aspects of several theoretical approaches. Similarly, sheltered instruction is not driven by a single theory but rather reflects several theoretical perspectives. Instruction for English learners requires attention to their second-language needs; therefore each theory presented will be examined with consideration for second-language issues.

Humanistic Learning Theory

The humanistic teacher is one who desires students to learn to interact well with others and to feel as good as possible about themselves. The affective well-being of students is a central focus of this approach (see Chapter 5) and is always a consideration when planning the school day. Personality development, including cooperation and consideration, is a primary value and is the focus of education.

Ms. Leung believes that student learning is enhanced when students feel good about themselves and the class operates as a community of learners. She frequently uses cooperative learning because it provides opportunities for students to contribute equally and to cooperate with one another (Slavin, 1995). She also schedules a daily sharing time for students to discuss personal interests, share a favorite book, show pictures of family and friends, or tell about a favorite school project or successful school effort. Through this process, Ms. Leung learns a great deal about each student, which enhances her ability to teach in a way that focuses on the strengths of each individual learner.

Ms. Leung's classroom reflects humanistic learning theory. Humanistic learning theory is a general term for those theories that contend that the central focus of human learning is to develop high self-esteem and a healthy personality. Sternberg and Williams (2009) describe it as "a meaningful educational environment in which students are encouraged to see themselves as capable; development of self-esteem; teachers acting warm and supportive; explaining why things must be done a certain way—no rules for the sake of rules." (See Woolfolk [2013] for more information on the affective domain, Maslow's hierarchy of needs, Erikson's stages of psychosocial development, Kohlberg's stages of moral reasoning, and Marsh and Shavelson's structure of self-concept.)

While a humanistic approach makes students feel comfortable, helping to lower their affective filters (see discussion of Krashen's work in this chapter), exclusive reliance on an affective approach may rob students of some of the direct, explicit instruction they need to meet standards. Further, there may be a tendency to lower expectations for English learners, giving the same credit for "trying" as for correct answers.

Developmental Learning Theory

Woolfolk (2013) defines development as naturally occurring stages that take place in an orderly fashion. These stages usually appear gradually and develop at different rates in different people. (See Woolfolk [2013] for more information on Piaget's theory about the development of thinking and Vygotsky's theories on the development of language, general linguistic development, and reading development. Also see Sternberg and Williams [2009] for implications for teaching.)

> Mr. Fleming believes in allowing each student to progress at his or her own pace. He structures class activities so that students can participate at their own levels. He evaluates students' journals according to their ability level. Some students write a few words with an illustration, while others compose whole stories. Mr. Fleming often uses a language experience approach, in which students tell their own stories and he functions as a scribe. Students are taught using Writer's Workshop (see Chapter 5), where they compose at their own levels of functioning.

Teachers whose practices are influenced by developmental learning theory subscribe to stage-like views of development and do not push students into development or force them to skip a stage. These teachers believe that inborn factors largely account for the unfolding of a child's ability over time and allow this unfolding to take place at its own pace when the child is ready.

Strict adherence to a developmental approach may be in conflict with standards-based teaching, which mandates that all students at a given grade level learn certain skills. It may also overlook students' ability to move to a higher level of achievement because their performance may be influenced more by language than by developmental stage. With students learning English, it may be difficult to know with certainty when some students are ready for the next stage, especially when there are gaps in their academic backgrounds and they may have uneven development.

(handwritten margin note: "The students own pace")

Social Interactionist Learning Theory

Influenced by the work of Vygotsky (1978), the sociocultural view of learning recognizes the unique role adults and older children play in learning, emphasizing the importance of modeling and the use of language to facilitate learning. These "more capable others" provide the child with the information and support necessary for intellectual growth by listening to the child and providing just the right help to advance his or her understanding. Assisted learning in the classroom involves giving prompts, reminders, and encouragement at the right time and in the right amounts to foster understanding.

According to this view, the social side of learning is important because interaction with teachers and peers has both cognitive and affective consequences. Through social interaction, students confront other points of view and discover how other people respond in various situations. This process of understanding others' points of view and learning to explain and defend one's own view gives students new information; in addition, the social interaction adds a verbal level to their understanding. Social interaction, according to Vygotsky, contributes to the development of language.

Vygotsky viewed language as a child's first tool for social interaction. As children mature, they internalize speech and use it in their own private interactions with the environment. Children can often be seen talking aloud during play and directing their own actions, which eventually leads to language directing thought. One example of an instructional approach that facilitates this type of learning is the instructional conversations approach (see Chapter 4).

> In Ms. Nelson's class, a lot of student-to-student and teacher-to-student interaction can be heard and observed. As a teacher, Ms. Nelson sees her role as providing students with the right amount of information and support necessary for intellectual growth. During a lesson, Ms. Nelson listens to the children and provides the right help to advance the children's understanding. She does this by giving prompts, reminders, and encouragement at the right time and in the right amount to foster understanding. Rather than dominating the lesson and seeking specific correct answers, she is careful to ask questions that will draw out the children's ideas and assist them in constructing meaning from the text based on their own experiences and backgrounds. You will hear questions and comments like "Why do you think he will do that?", "Tell me more about that," and "Would you react that way under the same circumstances? Why?" in her classroom.

[handwritten note: No "Yes/No" questions]

Sometimes English learners may need more explicit instruction and the type of repetition that is not typically a part of a social interactionist approach. For example, some information or vocabulary may be more effectively presented in lists, graphic organizers, or repetitive exercises (e.g., drill and practice) than through discussion.

Cognitive Learning Theory

Although there is no one cognitive learning theory, cognitivists tend to focus on such factors as kinds of knowledge; the information-processing model of learning, including perception, attention, memory, and metacognition; discovery learning; learning strategies; and problem solving (Woolfolk, 2013). They also tend to explore internal mental processes such as memory, reasoning, and strategies for acquiring facts and concepts. Most cognitive theorists do not try to explain all learning through a single theory but instead share a generally agreed upon philosophical orientation. Generally, cognitive psychologists believe that people are active learners who initiate experiences, seek out information to solve problems, and reorganize what they already know to achieve new insights.

Perhaps the major contribution of cognitivists has been in the area of memory as it relates to learning theory. For example, confirmation of mnemonic strategies (procedures that facilitate memory) has been gained through research into such subjects as verbal rehearsal, chaining, and the keywords strategy (see Chapter 6). Instructional choices focused on cognitive theory are those that encourage students to think about their own learning and those that focus students on their own learning. For example, when the teacher says, "Let's repeat this a few times so we can remember it," he or she is using verbal rehearsal to enhance knowledge gained and relying on cognitive theory. Or a teacher may insist that each time students solve a problem in class, they use the following steps: (1) define and clarify the problem; (2) experiment, reflect, and apply examples; and (3) solve the problem or draw conclusions.

> Discovery learning is an instructional approach that Mr. Gimplin uses often in his class. This is an intuitive approach in which students are provided with pieces of the knowledge "puzzle" and encouraged to induce the principle or rule. For example, in one lesson, Mr. Gimplin gave students 20 Popsicle sticks and told them to make groups of 2. He asked how they would find out how many sticks they had. Some students said they would count them ("1, 2, 3 . . ."). But one or two of the students said they would count by 2s to make it easier. These students had essentially discovered multiplication. The teacher pointed out to the students that some of them had found an easier way to find out "how many": Counting by 2s or 3s is multiplying, which is an easier way to add. Mr. Gimplin also uses mnemonic strategies to help students learn and retain information.

This approach may prove difficult for English learners if they lack the vocabulary needed to participate as fully as the approach intends. Many English learners, because of lack of English proficiency and gaps in their education, do not benefit from routines and structures that clue them into the teacher's expectations. In order to seek out information and initiate experiences, English learners would most likely need some structure or a minimum level of English proficiency.

Behavioral Learning Theory

While cognitivists are concerned with knowledge and how it is gained, saved, used, and lost, behaviorists believe learning is manifested through behavioral changes that can be observed and measured. (See Woolfolk [2013] for elaboration.) For behaviorists, language is a skill like any other behavior that we learn. Language is learned by presenting language with attractive experiences in the environment and by rewarding the learner once language occurs.

The best-known approach to behavioral learning is operant conditioning. The goal of the operant learning approach is to change behavior by manipulating antecedents and consequences. Modern behaviorists tend to focus on antecedents of behavior more than on its consequences, realizing that setting up the environment for success can do more to change behavior than waiting to enforce consequences. According to behaviorists, teachers can modify antecedents and assist learning by (1) demonstrating skills and asking students to imitate them; (2) walking students through an organized series of steps in a process; (3) clarifying concepts by providing examples and nonexamples; (4) providing clear, simple wording that is easy to imitate and that can be reinforced easily when reproduced; and (5) involving students actively throughout the learning process to provide ample practice.

Ms. Bobkowski begins most lessons by writing objectives on the board that indicate the step-by-step process students should follow to be successful. Usually, the behaviors, or steps of the tasks, are sequenced from simple to more difficult, and instructional activities are carefully planned to increase learning. She also focuses on consequences in the form of positive reinforcers for increases in appropriate behavior, such as positive teacher affect, verbal praise, privileges such as computer time or free time, and any other reinforcers that are effective with the students. Students are dealt with individually, with target behaviors reflecting the needs of the student. New behaviors are taught through continuous reinforcement. Ms. Bobkowski reduces inappropriate behavior by ignoring it and attending to appropriate behavior.

Behaviors are discussed in observable terms ("What are you going to do first?" "Where will you put it?" etc.), and learning is measured by the acquisition of new behaviors. For example, Ms. Smith asked students to write reports about their trip to Sea World. She specified that each student was to write a paragraph with a main idea and three detail sentences about the field trip. She also specified that students should indent, punctuate, and use capital letters correctly. She required a handwritten first draft; a self-corrected second draft, to be signed by a peer editor and the teacher; and a final version printed from the computer. After each phase, students were to take notes home to parents explaining their accomplishments. The teacher walked around class during each phase, giving support for participation and hard work. She assessed the results of each student's efforts and set goals for each accordingly. Over time, students were required to become more and more independent, with a focus on generalizing or using the newly learned skills in many different situations, with increasingly reduced teacher supervision.

The behaviorist approach tends to be teacher directed and controlled. Many English learners develop language proficiency and understanding of concepts through interaction and discussion. It is difficult for students to learn a new language when they lack significant opportunities to practice using the language in authentic ways. Further, inquiry or discovery learning opportunities are lost when lessons are teacher dominated.

An understanding of learning theory can become a decision-making model when a teacher realizes that certain educational goals are more likely to be accomplished using specific approaches. If a teacher finds that some students are struggling in a given learning environment, it may be wise to think about which approaches are currently in use, which are missing, and what changes might be implemented to yield a balanced approach to support student learning and positive behavior supports.

Summary

A variety of language backgrounds and language proficiency levels are represented in U.S. classrooms today. Teachers can use their knowledge of theories that underlie practice to reflect on and adjust instruction in order to better meet the individual needs of students. This chapter demonstrated how knowledge of the second-language acquisition process helps teachers design lessons that are appropriate for English learners and that facilitate learning for these students. For example, strong literacy skills in the native language facilitate English-language acquisition, as we saw with the students profiled in Chapter 1. When teaching in English, the cognitive and linguistic demands of academic tasks should be considered and instruction modified to meet the needs of the students.

Specifically, as a reader you

- analyzed the history of students learning English in school and identified ways to improve teaching of English learners in the future.
- contrasted the acquisition versus learning debate in second-language acquisition theory.
- described the importance of contextual support according to Cummins.
- identified the factors that affect second-language acquisition that you consider most important.
- identified the learning theories that most reflect your own teaching style.

ACTIVITIES

1. The school's ESL teacher has been asked to work with an English learner who receives special education services (has an IEP). She is unfamiliar with the legal rights of English learners with disabilities. What would you tell her about the student's rights?
2. Select three instructional approaches with which you are familiar (for instance, cooperative learning, the language experience approach, direct instruction, or thematic teaching). Identify the theories that influence each approach.
3. Using Cummins's grid (Figure 2.1), discuss what level of cognitive demand and context (quadrant A, B, C, or D) is represented by a student who performs each of the following activities:
   a. uses the text as evidence for a position during debate
   b. acts out a historical event
   c. points to items in the classroom
   d. writes short paragraphs
   e. watches a movie with academic content
   f. uses the computer for finding information
   g. listens to a lecture on the atom
   h. plays "Steal the Bacon"
4. Discuss how the activities in quadrant D of Figure 2.1 can be changed to fit quadrant B. What specific techniques or approaches would you use to contextualize instruction and make it understandable for English learners?
5. In a science class, the teacher sets the room up with a variety of objects such as tubs of water, aluminum foil, and clay. The question on the board is: What makes objects float? Students enter the class and, in small groups, explore the materials, make decisions regarding what data to collect, and discuss the data's meaning. Students are urged to think, ask questions, and draw conclusions on their own. What theory drives this teacher's practices?

CHAPTER 3

Sheltered Instruction in the Content Areas

LEARNING OBJECTIVES:

- Define sheltered instruction and explain common misperceptions about this type of teaching.
- Practice applying the 8 components of the SIOP® Model of sheltered instruction to your teaching.
- Identify key similarities and differences between sheltered instruction and effective instruction.
- Describe specific considerations for students with learning disabilities.

"Sheltered instruction is nothing more than good teaching—and I already do that." This statement is commonly heard from teachers who have English learners in their classrooms. True, sheltered instruction shares many of the characteristics of effective instruction, but it is more than simply good teaching—much more.

This chapter begins by presenting a definition of sheltered instruction and introducing the Sheltered Instruction Observation Protocol® (SIOP) Model of instruction. We then examine a social studies unit that illustrates the distinction between effective and sheltered instruction. We conclude with a discussion of the needs of students with learning difficulties.

Annie Pickert Fuller/Pearson Education

Definition of Sheltered Instruction

Teaching to high academic standards, including the Common Core State Standards (CCSS), presents challenges for English learners who are learning rigorous content in their second language. It is more important than ever that teachers use a research-based instructional approach with these students. *Sheltered instruction* is a means for making grade-level content, such as science, social studies, and math, more accessible for English learners (ELs) while also promoting English development. The term *sheltered* indicates that such instruction provides refuge from the linguistic demands of mainstream instruction, which, unless modified, are beyond the comprehension of many English learners. Sheltered instruction, called SDAIE (Specially Designed Academic Instruction in English) in some regions, provides assistance to learners in the form of visuals, modified texts and assignments, and attention to their linguistic needs. The term *sheltered* is used widely in schools across the United States to speak of content-area classes for English learners, such as sheltered math, sheltered science, and sheltered social studies (Echevarria & Short, 2010).

While sheltered instruction utilizes and complements sound instructional methods and strategies recommended for both second-language and mainstream classes, a number of features make sheltered instruction more than good teaching. Some of those unique features, illustrated in Figure 3.1, include adapting academic content to the language proficiency level of the students (differentiated instruction); using supplementary materials

FIGURE 3.1 A Comparison of Sheltered Instruction and Effective Instruction: Unique and Shared Features

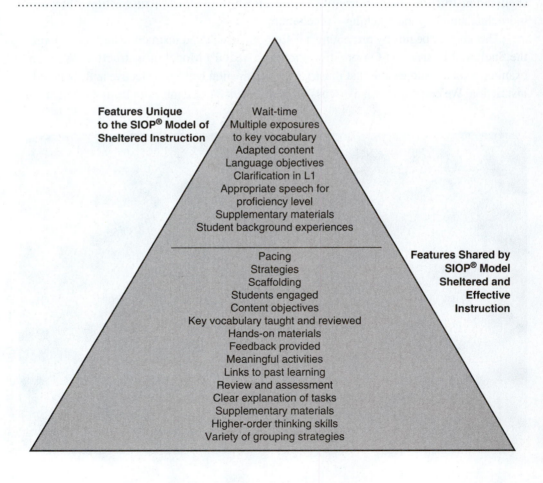

Features Unique to the SIOP® Model of Sheltered Instruction

Wait-time
Multiple exposures to key vocabulary
Adapted content
Language objectives
Clarification in L1
Appropriate speech for proficiency level
Supplementary materials
Student background experiences

Pacing
Strategies
Scaffolding
Students engaged
Content objectives
Key vocabulary taught and reviewed
Hands-on materials
Feedback provided
Meaningful activities
Links to past learning
Review and assessment
Clear explanation of tasks
Supplementary materials
Higher-order thinking skills
Variety of grouping strategies

Features Shared by SIOP® Model Sheltered and Effective Instruction

to a high degree; emphasizing key vocabulary through repetition and multiple exposures to words; and using speech that makes information comprehensible to students. As you can see, nearly all students would benefit from the features of sheltered instruction, but teaching for English learners differs more in degree than in kind. For instance, effective teachers may highlight key vocabulary, but in sheltered classes, highlighting and practicing key vocabulary is a critical part of every lesson and is emphasized throughout the lesson.

not just key words -- every word

For many years, sheltered instruction (or SDAIE) consisted of a set of techniques and activities that made the content understandable for English learners. However, because there was not an agreed-upon model, teachers tended to pick and choose among the techniques and activities. Also, there wasn't adequate focus on language development. As a result, implementation was uneven and some sheltered classes were not as effective as they could have been.

 Think about your own notion of sheltered instruction as you watch this video describing effective sheltered instruction operationalized in the SIOP® Model. As you watch, list those features that you are least familiar with and think of ways you might begin to incorporate them in your teaching.

*T*he SIOP® Model

In the mid-1990s, researchers set out to develop a model of sheltered instruction that would guide teachers in how to use effective practices systematically and to give teachers a tool for reflection and improving their teaching. The Sheltered Instruction Observation Protocol, or SIOP (Echevarria, Vogt, & Short, 2000, 2004, 2008, 2013), has been highly effective in improving practice for teachers of English learners and is currently used in schools in all 50 states and multiple countries (siop.pearson.com). It differs from other sheltered instruction approaches because of its solid research base and proven results (Short, Echevarria, Richards-Tutor, 2011).

The SIOP® Model is composed of 30 features organized around the eight components shown in Figure 3.2: Lesson Preparation, Building Background, Comprehensible Input, Strategies, Interaction, Practice & Application, Lesson Delivery, and Review & Assessment. In SIOP classes, language and content objectives are woven into the lessons in a particular subject area so that the teacher develops both subject matter competence and students' English language abilities.

 Consider both the language development your students need as well as the content information as you watch this video about content and language objectives. Why are both important?

Teachers use the SIOP as both a lesson-planning guide and a way to reflect and improve upon the effectiveness of their teaching. The psychometrically reliable SIOP observation protocol is useful in providing feedback to teachers as well as for teacher self-reflection (Guarino et al., 2001).

The SIOP® Model is not a step-by-step process for teaching, but is a framework that offers teachers a way to be sure that the features of effective teaching for English learners are present in their lessons. It is aligned with the Common Core State Standards and provides teachers with a systematic way of assisting students in meeting the standards. The SIOP Language Arts lesson (Figure 3.3) shows one way of implementing the features of the SIOP® Model in a first-grade lesson on building content vocabulary, but there are a myriad of other ways as well and many different types of activities that fit within SIOP

FIGURE 3.2 The Sheltered Instruction Observation Protocol (SIOP)®

The Sheltered Instruction Observation Protocol (SIOP)® (Echevarria, Vogt, & Short, 2000, 2004, 2008, 2013, 2014a, 2014b)

Observer(s): _____ School: _____
Date: _____ Teacher: _____
Grade: _____ Class/Topic: _____
ESL Level: _____ Lesson: Multi-day Single-day (circle one)

Total Points Possible: 120 (Subtract 4 points for each NA given) _____
Total Points Earned: _____   Percentage Score: _____

Directions: Circle the number that best reflects what you observe in a sheltered lesson. You may give a score from 0–4 (or NA on selected items). Cite under "Comments" specific examples of the behaviors observed.

	Highly Evident		Somewhat Evident		Not Evident	
Lesson Preparation	4	3	2	1	0	
1. **Content objectives** clearly defined, displayed, and reviewed with students	☐	☐	☐	☐	☐	
2. **Language objectives** clearly defined, displayed, and reviewed with students	☐	☐	☐	☐	☐	
3. **Content concepts** appropriate for age and educational background level of students	☐	☐	☐	☐	☐	
4. **Supplementary materials** used to a high degree, making the lesson clear and meaningful (e.g., computer programs, graphs, models, visuals)	☐	☐	☐	☐	☐	N/A
5. **Adaptation of content** (e.g., text, assignment) to all levels of student proficiency	☐	☐	☐	☐	☐	☐
6. **Meaningful activities** that integrate lesson concepts (e.g., surveys, letter writing, simulations, constructing models) with language practice opportunities for reading, writing, listening, and/or speaking	☐	☐	☐	☐	☐	

Comments:

	4	3	2	1	0	N/A
Building Background						
7. **Concepts explicitly linked** to students' background experiences	☐	☐	☐	☐	☐	☐
8. **Links explicitly made** between past learning and new concepts	☐	☐	☐	☐	☐	
9. **Key vocabulary** emphasized (e.g., introduced, written, repeated, and highlighted for students to see)	☐	☐	☐	☐	☐	

Comments:

	4	3	2	1	0
Comprehensible Input					
10. **Speech** appropriate for students' proficiency level (e.g., slower rate, enunciation, and simple sentence structure for beginners)	☐	☐	☐	☐	☐
11. **Clear explanation** of academic tasks	☐	☐	☐	☐	☐
12. **A variety of techniques** used to make content concepts clear (e.g., modeling, visuals, hands-on activities, demonstrations, gestures, body language)	☐	☐	☐	☐	☐

Comments:

FIGURE 3.2 Continued

	Highly Evident		Somewhat Evident		Not Evident	
Strategies	4	3	2	1	0	
13. Ample opportunities provided for students to use **learning strategies**	☐	☐	☐	☐	☐	
14. **Scaffolding techniques** consistently used assisting and supporting student understanding (e.g., think-alouds)	☐	☐	☐	☐	☐	
15. A variety of **questions or tasks that promote higher-order thinking skills** (e.g., literal, analytical, and interpretive questions)	☐	☐	☐	☐	☐	

Comments:

	Highly Evident		Somewhat Evident		Not Evident		
Interaction	4	3	2	1	0		
16. Frequent opportunities for **interaction** and discussion between teacher/student and among students, which encourage elaborated responses about lesson concepts	☐	☐	☐	☐	☐		
17. **Grouping configurations** support language and content objectives of the lesson	☐	☐	☐	☐	☐		
18. Sufficient **wait time for student** responses consistently provided	☐	☐	☐	☐	☐	N/A	
19. Ample opportunities for students to **clarify key concepts in L1** as needed with aide, peer, or L1 text	☐	☐	☐	☐	☐	☐	

Comments:

	Highly Evident		Somewhat Evident		Not Evident	N/A
Practice & Application	4	3	2	1	0	N/A
20. **Hands-on materials and/or manipulatives** provided for students to practice using new content knowledge	☐	☐	☐	☐	☐	☐
21. Activities provided for students to **apply content and language knowledge** in the classroom	☐	☐	☐	☐	☐	☐
22. Activities integrate all **language skills** (i.e., reading, writing, listening, and speaking)	☐	☐	☐	☐	☐	

Comments:

	Highly Evident		Somewhat Evident		Not Evident
Lesson Delivery	4	3	2	1	0
23. **Content objectives** clearly supported by lesson delivery	☐	☐	☐	☐	☐
24. **Language objectives** clearly supported by lesson delivery	☐	☐	☐	☐	☐
25. **Students engaged** approximately 90% to 100% of the period	☐	☐	☐	☐	☐
26. **Pacing** of the lesson appropriate to students' ability level	☐	☐	☐	☐	☐

Comments:

	Highly Evident		Somewhat Evident		Not Evident
Review & Assessment	4	3	2	1	0
27. Comprehensive **review of key vocabulary**	☐	☐	☐	☐	☐
28. Comprehensive **review of key content concepts**	☐	☐	☐	☐	☐
29. Regular **feedback** provided to students on their output (e.g., language, content, work)	☐	☐	☐	☐	☐
30. **Assessment of student comprehension and learning** of all lesson objectives (e.g., spot checking, group response) throughout the lesson	☐	☐	☐	☐	☐

Comments:

Teacher: Joanne Monroe
SIOP Lesson: Difference between Fantasy and Realty
Subject: English Language Arts
Unit: Character Analysis
Grade Level: 1st

Content Standards: Common Core Standard—ELA—Literacy RL
Retell stories, including key details and demonstrate understanding of their central message of lesson.

English Language Arts: Word Analysis, Fluency, and Systematic Vocabulary Development
Acquire and use new vocabulary in relevant contexts.

ELD Standard: Building Content Vocabulary

Key Vocabulary:	**Supplementary Materials:**
Content vocabulary frogs: smooth, moist, slimy, narrow toads: rough, powerful, striped	Book—Frog and Toad Are Friends by Arnold Lobel
Academic Vocabulary: fantasy, reality	Word-Definition-Picture Chart (teacher made)
	Word Web with the words Characteristic of a frog, Characteristics of a toad
What do you think is the difference between a fantasy story and a reality story? Do you think the characters in the story could be real? Why? Why not? Do you know any other examples of stories that are fantasies but have real life characters?	Sentence Strips
	Chart with the following sentence frames:
	The frog's skin is _____.
	The toad's skin is _____.
	The frog lives in _____.
	The toad lives in _____.
	The fantasy frog lives in a _____.
	The fantasy toad lives in a _____.

Connections to Students' Background Experiences and Past Learning:
Links to students' background experiences—SW orally share information they know about frogs and toads.
Links to Prior Learning—Students are familiar with the format and have ample practice in use of both the Word-Definition-Picture chart and the word web. Show students the Word-Definition-Picture chart. Review and discuss all of the vocabulary words on the chart. Add these words to a Word Web with the word *Characteristics of a Frog and Characteristics of a Toad* in the middle.

Content Objective:	**Meaningful Activities Lesson Sequence:**	**Review/Assessment:**
1. Students will identify characteristics of a real toad and a real frog by looking at pictures of frogs and toads.	• Post and orally explain content and language objectives.	Ask students to volunteer adjectives, but give opportunities to share with a partner before adding to the chart. Observe students as they share.
Student Friendly CO: Your job today is to look at pictures and describe a real frog and a real toad.	• TW ask if students have ever seen pictures, read about, or seen a cartoon or movie about frogs or toads (e.g., *Frog and Toad* Movie).	
Language Objectives:	• Show pictures of real frogs and toads and pictures of fantasy characters and tell students that their job is to describe the real frog and toad and the fantasy frog and toad to their partner.	Monitor students and promote discussion beyond their statements for those who have the language ability.
1. Students will orally describe characteristics of a real frog and a real toad to a partner in a complete sentence.		
Student Friendly LO: Your job today is to describe a real frog and a real toad to your partner in a complete sentence.		

2. Students will write 2 sentences each describing the characteristics of a real frog and a real toad. **Student Friendly LO:** Your job today is to write 2 complete sentences about a real frog and a real toad. **3.** Students will write 2 sentences each describing the characteristics of a fantasy frog and a fantasy toad. **Student Friendly LO:** Your job today is to write 2 complete sentences about a fantasy frog and a fantasy toad.	• Add adjectives produced by students on Characteristics of a Frog and Toad Word Web. • With a partner, students will orally complete the following sentence frames using the word web. The frog's skin is _____. The toad's skin is _____. The frog lives in _____. The toad lives in _____. The fantasy frog lives in _____. The real frog and real toad are similar because _____. The fantasy frog and the fantasy toad are similar because _____. • Students will volunteer to read their descriptive sentences or their partner's descriptive sentences. • They write a description of their favorite frog or toad either real or fantasy using the following frame: • My favorite frog is the real frog because _____.	Allowing students to read their partner's sentence relieves the anxiety that many students have when speaking in front of the class, but at the same time gives them practice in doing so. Collect the sentence frames for evaluation and then place them in a pocket chart for further reading by the students.

Closing:
Students read their descriptive sentences to a partner. Teacher places sentence strips in pocket chart and revisits periodically.

Review key vocabulary as well as content and language objectives with students.

lessons (Vogt, Echevarria & Washam, 2015). The important point is to make sure that lessons provide students with optimal learning conditions that include the characteristics shown in Figure 3.2. When teachers use the features of the SIOP® Model consistently in lessons, student achievement in content areas improves (Echevarria, et al., 2011) and English learners acquire academic English (Short, Fidelman & Louguit, 2012).

In addition to providing language and content objectives, SIOP lessons are characterized by teachers modeling tasks, using assessment to guide instruction, providing opportunities to use and practice academic language, and using supplementary materials to make lessons clear and meaningful. Information that is embedded in context allows English learners to understand and complete cognitively demanding work, building the skills that prepare them to be college and career ready.

The features of the SIOP® Model are effective with all students, but are critical for English learners (Echevarria, et al., 2011). While a school may not have designated sheltered classes, the SIOP should be used regardless of how many English learners are present in a class. Research indicates that it benefits English-speaking students and English learners alike (Echevarria & Short, 2011).

A hallmark of the SIOP® Model is its emphasis on language development. Specifically, having a language objective in every lesson reminds teachers of the important role language plays in learning in all subject areas. It also allows for systematic attention to language teaching in every lesson and opportunities for students to learn and practice English skills in all classes throughout the day. In Chapter 4 we provide suggestions for writing effective language objectives.

The importance of academic language for all students is acknowledged in the CCSS Standards for Listening and Speaking. These standards emphasize that students need solid communication skills to be college and career ready, and the SIOP® Model provides a forum for integrating language into content teaching.

As mentioned previously, SIOP teaching differs from effective instruction mostly in the degree to which certain instructional features are implemented. Some of the following characteristics show the distinction between SIOP teaching and effective instruction.

A Well-Planned Lesson

Effective instruction calls for well-planned lessons; however, it is critical that SIOP teachers make sure that lessons are planned and delivered in a way that ensures English learners will be able to participate fully. Having content and language objectives that are shared with students is important for focusing the lesson and informing students about what they will learn. Making sure the features of the SIOP® Model (Figure 3.2) are represented in the lesson increases English learners' comprehension of the content and develops their English proficiency. Formative assessment throughout the lesson informs the planning of subsequent lessons.

Sometimes teachers express concern about the amount of time it takes to plan SIOP lessons. Initially, it does take time to incorporate SIOP features in lesson plans, but with practice it becomes an automatic way of teaching so planning time is reduced.

Another feature of SIOP teaching that sets it apart from effective instruction is the extent to which the text is adapted to meet students' language and learning needs, while still reflecting high expectations. The level of text used in content areas and in English language arts tends to be challenging for English learners to read with comprehension. These students need exposure to complex texts so that they can become familiar with the sentence structure and vocabulary of grade-level text. However, they also need experience with texts that are right at their reading and language level so that they can read independently. (Chapter 6 details ways teachers can make subject-area curriculum, including textbooks, understandable for English learners.)

Because the SIOP® Model is student centered, students are assigned more real-life activities (for example, completing surveys, writing letters, engaging in simulations, or constructing models) with lots of opportunities for listening, speaking, reading, and writing. In a lesson on values, for instance, students could get into small groups and be given scenarios to discuss and write about. One might be "You come across the answer key to the upcoming science test. Do you put it on the teacher's desk, keep it and study from it, or give it to friends so you'll all do well on the test?" Another might be "Your grandmother is ill and you agree to stay with her for the weekend while your parents work. Later you get an invitation to a party that the most popular kids will attend. What do you do?" The students spend time discussing the dilemma and then write down their solutions to the situation.

In a SIOP lesson, the teacher selects key academic terms that are critical to understanding the lesson, writes them for students to see, and discusses each one at the outset of the lesson. Vocabulary instruction is most effective when words are explicitly taught and also used in context, providing a balanced approach. Vocabulary words can be brainstormed, mapped, and clustered, or a mnemonic strategy could be employed. Review and practice is an important instructional "habit" to develop because repeated exposure to vocabulary increases retention.

Vocabulary words may also be added to individual personal dictionaries or to word banks posted around the room. These resources become reference points for students to remember definitions and relationships between terms and to model correct spelling. To boost recall, students may draw a picture with which they associate the word next to it, write a definition of the word, or write a sentence using the word. As students encounter these words throughout the lesson (and in subsequent lessons), they can recall the definition or can infer meaning from the context. In both cases, students are exposed to new vocabulary and see its application within the text.

Another unique feature of the SIOP® Model is reducing the linguistic load of teachers' speech. Natural but slower speech, clearly enunciated, can increase comprehensibility, particularly when effort is made to use shorter sentences with simpler syntax, especially for beginning speakers. Take, for example, the sentence "To add or subtract numbers with exponents, whether the base numbers are the same or different, you must simplify each number with an exponent first and then perform the indicated operation." A preferable delivery might be (pointing to examples on the board), "To add or subtract numbers with exponents, you must complete two steps: (1) simplify each number with an exponent and (2) perform the operation. This is true whether the base numbers are the same or different."

Just numbering the steps/tasks helps a lot.

The use of more pauses between phrases allows students time to process what has been said before the next utterance begins. Although many teachers of English learners believe they are consciously making an effort to pause between phrases, audiotaping of lessons usually yields surprising results. One method for ensuring that pauses are long enough for students to process the information is to count two seconds between utterances—for example, "An equation is a mathematical sentence, a relationship between numbers or symbols. (The teacher counts silently: 1001, 1002.) Remember that an equation is like a balance scale, with the equal sign being the fulcrum, or center (1001, 1002)." Naturally, this technique will be more effective when the teacher employs other techniques simultaneously, such as showing a visual of a balance scale, pointing to the fulcrum when reference is made to it, and writing an equation and equals sign on the board or an overhead transparency.

more pauses slows it down a bit

Another way to increase the comprehensibility of the message is to use consistent vocabulary and appropriate repetition. Repetition, or natural redundancy, reinforces language. Songs, chants, raps, and patterned stories give students opportunities to practice using the language and can provide reinforcement of vocabulary, language structures, and intonation (Richard-Amato, 2010). During instruction, use consistent vocabulary as much as possible. To expand vocabulary, communicate the same idea repeatedly using different words. In the example above, the term *mathematical sentence* was elaborated upon and the synonym *center* was given for the term *fulcrum*. It may be useful to emphasize the original expression by repeating it, giving students the opportunity to hear the same idea expressed in more than one way.

One of the most important components of SIOP lessons that also sets them apart from effective instruction is the extent to which students interact with one another and with the teacher. While an opportunity for student interaction is also a characteristic of effective instruction, it is especially important for English learners to practice using the new language in meaningful ways. How can students become proficient in English if they lack opportunities to practice the language? How can they meet high academic standards without using and practicing the academic language needed to do so?

Typically, teachers dominate linguistic interactions in the classroom. Studies have revealed the extraordinary paucity of opportunities for students to participate in meaningful discussions and question-and-answer sessions. (For more discussion of interaction, see Chapter 4.) SIOP lessons provide ample opportunity for discussing and questioning between teacher and students and among students in a variety of group configurations. Grouping becomes more critical when working with students with a variety of language and learning abilities. Flexible grouping, moving students among groups strategically, gives students the opportunity to clarify key concepts in their primary languages as needed, by consulting an aide, peer, or primary-language text. One of the benefits of sheltered instruction is that students are exposed to good models of English language as well as provided with the opportunity to practice using English in academic settings. However, English learners are in the process of acquiring a new language and will benefit from clarifying concepts in their native languages when needed.

There is a high correlation between student achievement and the amount of time students are actively engaged in learning tasks. With the SIOP® Model, the goal is to have students engaged 90 percent to 100 percent of the lesson through the use of SIOP features such as interaction, meaningful activities (where students practice and apply skills and concepts), and the use of techniques for making the lesson's information understandable. Too often, important academic time is wasted on noninstructional events, such as taking attendance and passing out papers. Highly engaging lessons start immediately after the bell rings and usually begin with a review of past learning. The class then reviews both content and language objectives. Presentation of lesson content begins, maximizing student interest and involvement. The key issue is keeping students actively engaged in learning. The lesson ends by refocusing students on the lesson's objectives and reviewing what was learned.

Academic engaged time and lesson preparation are interrelated because it takes planning to keep students engaged throughout the period. Students, particularly English learners, cannot afford lost academic time. Finally, SIOP teaching is distinct in the extent to which instruction is contextualized so that English learners have ample "clues" for understanding lessons. The following are some features that help increase comprehensibility of lessons.

SIOP Techniques for Making Lessons Comprehensible

1. *Modeling.* The teacher models what is expected of students. Before students begin solving word problems in math, the teacher takes them through a word problem step by step, modeling useful strategies and think-alouds for solving such problems. Students with diverse levels of ability benefit from concrete, step-by-step procedures presented in a clear, explicit manner.

2. *Realia.* For a unit on banking skills, students might practice filling out actual bank deposit slips, ATM forms, and check registers. When learning about geology, students might be given samples of rocks and minerals. For consumerism, students might read actual labels on products. The idea that products costing the same may vary in quality (last longer or work better) can take on more meaning when students have the products to examine and compare. A textbook discussion of the idea is more easily understood when students are actually looking at the items.

[handwritten marginal note:] You have to prepare for these students cannot afford the luxury of wasted time.

3. *Pictures.* There are a variety of photographs and drawings available commercially or on the Internet that depict nearly any object, process, or topic covered in the school curriculum. Many of these are part of curriculum programs or are options in the programs.

4. *Technology.* With the burgeoning number of device and equipment options available, technology can be an effective way for making content more understandable and meaningful for students. For example:

- As information is introduced, technology such as an interactive white board, document reader, or an overhead projector can be used to give constant clues to students. Teachers jot down words or sketch out what they are presenting. The written representation of words gives students learning English a chance to copy the words correctly, since certain sounds may be difficult to understand when presented orally. Students with learning problems often have difficulty processing auditory information and are helped with the visual clues offered through use of technology. For example, rather than relying solely on verbal presentation of the water cycle in a biology class, the teacher uses an overhead projector or interactive white board to write the basic terms as they are being discussed (see Figure 3.4). These additional visual clues help students understand the spoken words and the meaning of the word *cycle*. In the consumerism lessons, the sheltered teacher frequently used the overhead projector to visually reinforce the words and ideas presented orally. Transparencies may be filed and kept accessible for review or when a question about a topic is asked. Using the same transparency for clarification or review can be effective for retention of information. The same is true for saving computer-generated illustrations.

- *Multimedia.* Media options range from something as simple as listening to a audio recording of Truman's announcement of the dropping of the atomic bomb to an

FIGURE 3.4 | Water Cycle as Displayed by Overhead Projector

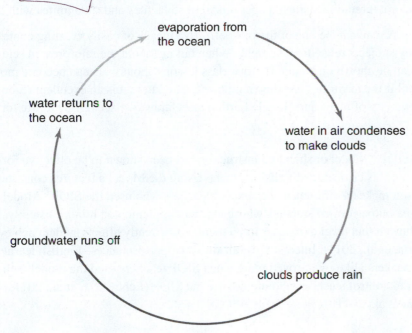

interactive laser computer display. Videos, DVDs, audio recordings, and online websites are examples of multimedia that can enhance comprehension for English learners.

5. *Demonstration.* In a middle-school class studying archeology, a student asked how artifacts get buried deep underground. Rather than relying on a verbal explanation, which would have been meaningless to many of the students learning English, the teacher demonstrated the process. First, he placed a quarter in a pie plate and proceeded to blow dirt on the quarter, covering it slightly. He then put dried leaves on top, followed by a sprinkling of "rain." Finally, he put some sand on top, and the quarter was then underneath an inch or so of natural products. Although the process was described in the text, most students did not have the reading skills or English proficiency to understand it. The demonstration made a much greater impression on the students and was referred to later when reading about and discussing the earth's layers and other related topics.

6. *Timelines.* These are particularly useful in the social sciences. As one lesson progressed through Western civilization, a timeline was mounted along the length of a wall that visually represented each historical event as it related to other events and periods in history. As an event was studied, the teacher made some visual representation on the timeline and continued adding to it throughout the course of the year.

7. *Graphic depiction.* Information represented visually often makes greater impact and is easier to remember. Graphing the students' weekly consumption of junk food, fruits and vegetables, and milk products is more interesting and meaningful than simply reading about the various food groups and recommended servings. The text becomes more understandable when the graphing activity is completed before reading the text. Many of the terms and concepts will then already be familiar to the students. Graphic organizers also provide an effective way to graphically depict text, ideas, or information in a lesson. They are easier for English learners to read than dense text and they highlight the main points of a lesson.

8. *Bulletin boards.* Although technology abounds, bulletin boards remain an effective method for posting visual representations of lesson information for reference, such as an example of a business letter, some friendly letter formats, steps for solving math problems, or a three-dimensional paper model of stalactites and stalagmites with labels.

9. *Maps.* A map can be one of the most effective means of easily creating context, since many subjects relate to geography. When talking about the rainforest in science, its location can be shown on a map. History class lessons about wars can become more meaningful if the territories are shown on maps. The Internet is an excellent resource for finding a variety of maps and Google Earth makes faraway places come to life for students.

The SIOP® Model of sheltered instruction has been shown to be effective for all students, but it is critical for English learners. Using the Model's features consistently in every lesson makes a difference. Students of teachers who used the SIOP® Model to a high degree outperformed students whose teachers implemented it inconsistently. This finding showed that level of teacher implementation directly affects student achievement (Echevarria, et al., 2011). Interestingly, all students' performance—English learners and English speakers alike—improved more when SIOP teachers used the model well compared to control teachers who did not use the SIOP (Echevarria, et al., 2011; Echevarria et al., 2011b).

Your Turn

Please read the following classroom scenario and analyze how better planning would have made the lesson more effective.

Scenario:
In a sheltered science class where middle school students were studying the function of arteries and veins, the lesson began with a display of the following review questions on an overhead transparency.

1. Why do you think we need both arteries and veins in order to live?
2. Why do you think arteries need to be thicker and heavier than veins?

Students were given 5 minutes to answer the questions. After the students gave their answers aloud, the teacher told the class to form work groups so they could do an activity that involved creating a model of arteries and veins in the body. Although the students complied, they did so slowly, taking 5 minutes to form groups. The teacher then gave each of the 5 groups a large sheet of butcher paper and told them to trace one group member's body on the paper. A couple of the groups began the assignment, but 9 minutes passed before one group began tracing, according to observational notes. The students' next step was to go to the front of the class, where there were drawings of the heart and spools of red and blue yarn. Students were told to cut out the paper drawings of the heart and cut several lengths of yarn to represent veins and arteries. However, there were no instructions as to which group member was to do which job. The result was that one person from the group went up and waited in line to get the items while the other group members sat around talking. It took 15 minutes to get the items needed to complete the project. Students then worked together to glue yarn from the heart to various places in the body. When students had questions, such as which color should be used for which veins, they asked the teacher. After approximately 50 minutes, students cleaned up. Finally, the teacher concluded the period by asking the students what they had done. They replied that they had traced the body and glued yarn. At the end of the period, only one group was near completion of the project. The teacher told them that they would complete their work the following day.

This was a creative, interesting lesson, but it lacked sufficient planning. How could it have been improved with more preparation?

Sheltered Instruction and Effective Instruction: A Comparative Case Study

Effective instruction and sheltered instruction share many characteristics but English learners require modification for instruction to be comprehensible for them (August & Shanahan, 2006). A series of middle school social studies lessons can demonstrate the similarities and differences. These lessons were part of a pilot study (Echevarria, Greene, & Goldenberg, 1996) in which three teachers taught the same content to English learners, two using a sheltered approach and one using effective instruction. Note the types of

FIGURE 3.5 Contrasting Sheltered and Effective Instruction Lessons: Chronology of 4-Day Unit

Effective Instruction

1. Individual, independent vocabulary work
2. Wrote definitions
3. Read silently to themselves
4. Class discussion
5. Completed worksheet about purchases
6. Review and closure
7. Reviewed vocabulary orally
8. Teacher-centered: text and paper-and-pencil tasks
9. Review and closure
10. Introduction of lesson with review
11. Teacher-led discussion
12. Read text, using independent, silent reading
13. Completed worksheets individually, then compared scores with partners

Sheltered Instruction

1. Vocabulary work done in small groups
2. Reported definitions aloud, paraphrasing
3. Read aloud in groups with support
4. Class discussion with visuals (realia, writing on board)
5. Hands-on activity
6. Review and closure
7. Reviewed vocabulary orally with words written for reference
8. Student-centered, hands-on activity
9. Review and closure
10. Introduction of lesson with review
11. Discussion in pairs, teacher wrote conclusions on overhead transparency
12. Read text using a variety of reading options and checked for understanding
13. Completed worksheets as a game, compared scores across groups

modifications the sheltered teachers used to make the lessons more understandable for their students, seen in Figure 3.5.

The lessons were part of a four-day unit on consumerism. The first day's lesson introduced key vocabulary: *brand name, ingredient, consumer, false advertising, effective,* and *myths*. The content objectives of the unit were:

1. What health values to look for in products and services consumers buy or use
2. How product labels can help consumers
3. How advertising can help consumers

The language objective was to use key vocabulary in context. Students read the textbook definition of *consumers:* "those who buy and use products." In the effective instruction group, each student looked up vocabulary words individually in the glossary and wrote his or her definitions. In the sheltered group, each word was assigned to a group of five students to look up in the glossary, and each group then reported its definition to the class and paraphrased the definition of the word.

The objective of the second day was to learn how consumers could make informed decisions. The lesson began with all groups reviewing the definition of *consumer* and other vocabulary words. Students then began reading a section in the text titled "You Can Make Good Decisions." The effective instruction students read the section silently to themselves; the sheltered students read as a group, with the teachers providing paraphrasing and clarification as needed. After reading, both groups discussed the need for consumers to examine the quality of the item as well as the price. Teachers in both groups mentioned that cheap prices sometimes indicate poor quality, but some brand name prices are based on the name, not the quality. In the sheltered group, teachers showed a sample of cheap shoes and well-made shoes, writing the cost of each pair on the board. Then the shoes were passed around for students to compare. They discussed cost and quality.

The effective instruction group was given a worksheet containing these four questions:

1. You want a new jacket. The Lakers jacket is almost twice the price of a similar jacket sold by Sears. Do you buy the expensive Lakers jacket or the Sears brand? Why?
2. Two cameras are the same price, but one comes with a zoom lens. Which would you buy? Why?
3. An 8-ounce tube of toothpaste costs $3.00, and a 4-ounce tube of the same type costs $2.00. Which would you buy? Why?
4. Shasta Cola costs $2.50 for a six-pack, and Coke costs $3.25 for a six-pack. Which do you buy? Why?

The sheltered instruction group participated in a hands-on activity in which items were arranged in stations around the room. At each station, students compared two items and decided if the quality was the same and if the difference in price was worth it. Students completed worksheets at each station (see Figure 3.6), rotating from one station to the next. All groups had the same closure at the end of the lesson: "Today you learned

FIGURE 3.6 Activity Worksheet

1. Are these two items of the same quality?

no

2. What is the cost of each?

Item	Cost
crayons	$.99
crayola Crayons	$1.99

3. Which would you buy? $1.99 crayola crayons

4. Why? Because they would last longer and, their better kinds

that consumers should make informed decisions. What are some things you should consider before buying something? Tomorrow we'll find out how we can be more informed to make better decisions."

The third day of the unit followed a similar format: The sheltered instruction lessons were more student centered, providing more context and hands-on activities, while the effective instruction lessons were paper-and-pencil oriented, relying on the teacher and textbook as sources for learning. Again, both groups reviewed what a consumer is and why consumers should make informed decisions. Review of vocabulary was oral for the effective instruction group; the sheltered group benefited from having the words on an overhead projector. All teachers opened the lesson by saying, "Today we're going to learn about how product labels help consumers."

Both groups began by reading a section in the textbook about reading labels and the important information they give consumers. In both groups, students were asked, "Can consumers believe the information they read on health product labels?" Students were assigned either to a group that argued yes or a group that argued no. Each group was required to defend its answer using information from the textbook.

After the brief debate, the effective instruction group answered questions posed in the textbook about labels, while the sheltered instruction group participated in a hands-on activity to further their understanding of the concepts presented in the textbook. The teacher brought in a variety of food containers, medicine containers, and clothing with labels, and the students formed groups. Each group was given one food container, one medicine container, and one clothing item. As a group, they completed a worksheet about reading labels (see Figure 3.7). All the teachers closed the lesson by saying, "Today you learned how a consumer can learn about products and make good decisions. Why would you not buy a sweater that has to be dry cleaned, even if the price is good? Why would you not buy vitamins where the first ingredient labeled is sugar? Tomorrow we're going to see how advertising affects our choices."

On the final day of the unit, both groups reviewed the definition of *consumer* and the things they had learned about being more informed consumers, such as considering cost and quality and reading labels. The objective of the final day was to show how advertising can help consumers and how it can trick consumers.

Students in both groups were directed to look at a shampoo ad in the textbook depicting an attractive couple riding bikes. The teachers asked if the ad had useful health information about the shampoo. The effective instruction teacher led students in a question-and-answer session about the ad and what it communicated. The sheltered students formed pairs and were given 2 minutes to write down words that described the people in the ad (*happy, healthy, fun, pretty, handsome*). Students were asked to share some of their words. The sheltered teachers wrote the words on the overhead transparency as students said them. Teachers in both groups pointed out that ads give consumers the impression that using the product will make them resemble the people in the ad. Teachers further asked students, "If the people in the ad were smoking, would you think that the brand being smoked was healthful?"

Both groups then turned to the textbook to read and discuss. The sheltered teachers used a variety of reading options, such as having students read with a partner, read aloud, or read in groups, with the teacher paraphrasing, clarifying, discussing, and checking for understanding frequently. The effective instruction group relied more on independent silent reading. Checks for understanding consisted of brief teacher-student interactions with fewer opportunities for elaboration and discussion than the sheltered format. In the textbook passage, students were directed to the term *brand name* and asked to give examples based on their experiences. The sheltered teachers wrote students' responses on

Medicine

1. What are the **directions** for using this product?

The directions are that you only have to use
a small amount, spreading and rubbing in well.

2. What can you learn from the **warning**?

that we have to keep out of reach of
children.

Food

1. What is the major ingredient of this product? Sugar is a major
ingredient

2. What other health information is on the label?

Nutrition information. Calories & vitamins

Clothing

1. What material is the clothing made from?

It is 55% Ramie   45% cotton

2. According to the label, how should it be cleaned?

Hand wash cold water

overhead transparencies. Students were asked questions such as whether consumers have any protection from false health information in advertising. Next, a variety of laminated magazine and newspaper advertisements were distributed to students. Effective instruction students individually completed the worksheets and then compared their scores with those of their partners. Teachers modeled how students were to score each ad. Sheltered instruction students, preassigned by the teacher in groups of three, rated each ad (see Figure 3.8). A timer was then set for 4 minutes. When the timer went off, the group had to have the ad scored and move on to the next ad. When the timer went off again, groups exchanged ads with another group for scoring. After 8 minutes (4 minutes per ad), the groups compared their scores. Sheltered teachers directed this portion of the lesson by asking questions such as "How did group 1 score this ad? and group 2? Group 1, why did you give it a score of 9? Group 3, how did you score this ad? Compare your score with group 4." The class discussed how some people like certain things while others like different things. The teacher pointed out that this distinction is what advertising is about: targeting certain groups (young mothers, teenagers, senior citizens) and trying to put together an ad to which that particular group will respond.

FIGURE 3.8 Advertisement Activity

Score each ad in this way:

0 = No useful information
5 = A lot of useful information

Circle the score you give to each ad.

Ad #1   1   2   3   4   (5)

Why?   Becous It has how your hear will loke and
the vitamins will make your hear beter and
its beter for your hear

Ad #2   1   2   3   4   5

Why? _____

Circle the score you give to the other group's ads.

Ad #1   (1)   2   3   4   5

Why?   I think that is not good becous it
doesnt say If your lips will be dry.

Ad #2   1   2   3   4   5

Why? _____

Your group members:

1. Francisco

2. Eric

3. Joel

All teachers ended the lesson with this statement: "Today we have seen how advertising can help consumers and how consumers can use ads to get important information. We've also seen how advertising is used to influence consumers. How does advertising differ from the information you get on labels?"

On the final day, students in both groups were also given a test that included multiple-choice items, definitions of vocabulary items, and short-answer questions. This social studies unit gives an idea of the modifications sheltered teachers make. Effective sheltered lessons are the result of thoughtful planning done at the beginning of the year. Teachers typically plan together by grade level by reviewing the Common Core State Standards (or other state standards), textbooks, state framework guides, curriculum guides, and teachers' manuals to determine the essential content for a specific grade level or course. Planning involves weaving critical concepts and ideas related to each standard into meaningful, connected units that build upon each other. Once the most important concepts have been determined, the nonessential details can be eliminated and the broad range of students' academic needs can be addressed through careful unit planning. This type of big-picture planning assists teachers in formulating a vision for the students that translates into cohesive lessons that build upon one another, providing English learners with continuity and reinforcement of major concepts and vocabulary.

In the social studies class just described, the theme was an individual's power to make choices. With thematic teaching, the teacher selects a concept or theme and weaves it across the curriculum. When presenting the key concepts from the unit, the teacher emphasizes an individual's ability to choose between products and make wise decisions. Students could be asked about products available in their home countries and whether they were able to choose from among several brands. In the discussion on advertising, students learned that they could choose whether or not to buy a product. Using recurrent themes when introducing new learning provides linkages that render the material more understandable. The extent to which teachers use sheltered elements is difficult to capture in a written description because the high level of student interaction, the student-centered focus of the instruction, and the many ways the teacher uses visuals and other means to create a context for information and discussions are not evident. Further, many features are unique to sheltered instruction, not so much in their essence but in the degree to which they are used. For example, tapping into students' background knowledge is useful in most instructional situations, but when working with English learners it is essential to make the connection between students' knowledge and experience and the lesson at hand.

Finally, not every feature of sheltered instruction is present in each lesson, but most should be implemented throughout a series of lessons. In other words, one day's lesson may be a hands-on cooperative activity designed as a follow-up to the previous day's lesson that involved reading from the text. In this case, modifying the text would not be applicable, but many of the other components would be evident.

Discussion of the Case Study

In the unit on consumerism, the content level of the sheltered instruction and effective instruction lessons were the same; both were based on the core curriculum. Since lesson objectives must always reflect grade-level content (although it is permissible to cover background information that the student needs for understanding), it would be inappropriate to teach English learners a curriculum intended for younger students simply because they are in the process of acquiring English. In both the sheltered and effective instruction lessons, the objectives were clearly supported by lesson delivery. Each lesson had a focus that was easily identified as the lesson unfolded. In addition, major concepts were explicitly identified. In the sheltered and effective lessons, the teacher wrote the major concepts on the board or overhead transparency, discussed each one, and referred back to each as it was covered during the lesson. Both teachers in the consumerism lessons told students they were going to learn about how product labels help consumers and tied information back to this concept throughout the reading and discussion.

Concepts are also reinforced by linking them to students' backgrounds. This benefits English learners in two ways: It taps the students' previous knowledge on the topic being studied and ties it to the lesson, and it validates students' cultural background and experiences by providing opportunities for students to talk about their lives and relating them to the topic.

By bringing in students' cultural backgrounds, the teacher explicitly draws parallels between the topic and the students' experiences. The teacher might ask, "How many of you have bought something and had it break right away? How many of you have wanted something because you saw a commercial, but when you got it, it wasn't as good as you thought?" Using their own experiences to introduce new learning is a good way to engage students in a topic. Also, when discussing myths associated with products, such as the myths that mouthwash prevents colds or that protein shampoo feeds hair, students are encouraged to share cultural beliefs about certain products. In preparation for the lesson on advertising, immigrant students may be asked to bring in newspapers or magazines in their native languages to compare their ads to American advertising styles.

Content material is organized so it relates to previous lessons. English learners need to have the relationships between new learning and past lessons explicitly stated in order to clarify the connection between lessons. Timelines and word banks facilitate this process, since events, previous vocabulary, and terms are posted for students to see and remember. For example, prior to the unit on consumerism, students had studied about pollution and about household items that contain dangerous chemicals. That information could be revisited when students study the value of reading labels. The presence of chemicals in products may affect consumer decisions. The unit following consumerism should be a topic that logically follows. Using state curriculum frameworks and curriculum guides facilitates the creation of connected lessons that build upon one another.

Another feature that is common to both sheltered and effective instruction is that the teacher consistently varies delivery modes. A recitation or lecture mode is possibly the least effective way of teaching students who are learning English (Cazden, 2001; Tharp & Gallimore, 1988). It relies heavily on comprehending verbal input and provides limited contextual clues for the learner. Effective instruction offers a variety of learning opportunities for students, including explanation, modeling, demonstration, and visual representation. Sheltered instruction does the same, but to a much higher degree. When students are acquiring a new language, modeling is essential, and varying delivery modes assists in comprehension and helps keep students engaged in learning throughout the lesson. What they may not understand presented one way may become clearer when it is presented in a different fashion. The importance of academic engaged time was discussed previously and cannot be overstated. Teaching is not going on unless students are learning. In order to learn, the student must attend to and be cognitively engaged in the task.

Frequent checks for understanding characterize both effective instruction and sheltered instruction. These checks can be done individually or by asking group questions, such as "Everyone who thinks a consumer is only a person who buys goods and services, raise one finger; everyone who thinks a consumer is someone who buys and uses goods and services, raise two fingers."

Ample variation in reading options is a feature of both approaches, with sheltered lessons using variation more frequently. Options include teacher read-aloud, buddy reading, choral reading, and silent reading. Listening to a reading on tape is effective for English learners and is used more commonly in a sheltered class. Reading for meaning is one of the more challenging activities for students learning English. Students' reading fluency is limited, since many do not have the vocabulary necessary to read with ease, while others lack the advantage of a strong academic background on which to draw. Students with learning problems often have comprehension difficulties as well. Varying the reading format allows students to have reading experiences that are assisted or scaffolded by others. Scaffolding is the process of providing support as needed, with less support required as students move toward independent functioning. As the teacher reads aloud, he or she can pause at natural breaks. During sheltered lessons, paraphrasing and clarification are a routine part of the reading process.

With both approaches, lessons are designed to provide opportunities for students to use higher-level skills, including problem solving, hypothesizing, organizing, synthesizing, categorizing, evaluating, and self-monitoring. In a lesson on economics, a teacher showed the covers of several weekly news magazines with headlines about massive layoffs. She then asked, "How do you think workers feel when they see these headlines? Why does it make them nervous?" Students were asked to work with partners and come up with three ways that massive layoffs affect everyone. Opportunities for higher-level thinking such as this should be presented throughout a lesson.

Scaffolding is used with both sheltered and effective instruction. However, the implementation differs in that effective instruction teachers typically use questioning techniques to guide students, prompting and prodding verbally to get students to the correct answer. In sheltered instruction, scaffolding is used frequently throughout the lesson, since the varying levels of English proficiency and academic backgrounds of students necessitate doing so. The teacher accepts the students' ideas without correcting their form but instead adds clarification and elaboration as needed. The teacher does not rely on verbal scaffolding alone but may use context clues to clarify meaning and promote understanding. When conducting whole-group lessons in sheltered or effective instruction classes, students participate by giving signals such as thumbs-up or thumbs-down to indicate their opinions or answers.

Specific Considerations for Students with Learning Disabilities

As we discuss best instructional practices for English learners in sheltered classes, we would be remiss not to mention that in nearly every class a variety of English learners are represented, including students who are gifted, those who are typically achieving, as well as students with learning disabilities. In this section, we offer a brief discussion of sheltered instruction for students with learning disabilities who need extra support in acquiring English.

English learners with identified learning disabilities most likely will not learn at the same rate as other English learners, and they may need additional techniques employed to help them comprehend the lesson and develop targeted skills. These students often need more repetition and clarification, and they may require more time to complete assignments. Many of the features of the SIOP® Model of sheltered instruction are considered best practice for students with learning difficulties since the emphasis of the SIOP is to differentiate instruction and create a learning environment that promotes student success, including providing students with explicit, high-quality feedback and modeling. In one study, English learners identified as having learning disabilities were included in sheltered classes whose teachers implemented the SIOP® Model. Using pre- and post-test data, these students made significant overall improvement in writing and specifically in the areas of language production, support/elaboration, and mechanics (Echevarria, 2001).

These research findings indicate that the features of the SIOP® Model align with practices that work with students with learning disabilities. A focus on specific objectives, displayed and reviewed with students, along with an emphasis on acquisition of vocabulary provides the kind of instruction that these students need. Using supplementary

FIGURE 3.9 Considerations for English Learners with Learning Disabilities

- Provide abundant guided practice for acquisition of concepts.
- Adjust the pace of instruction according to students' needs.
- Use assistive technology to enhance learning.
- Allow extra time to complete assignments.
- Set students up for success and use positive reinforcement.
- Partner students with others sensitive to their learning needs.
- Provide alternative activities when a task may draw undue attention to students' disabilities (e.g., reading aloud, a task that requires fine motor skills or sustained periods of attention).
- Plan and use appropriate positive behavior support techniques.
- Employ learning strategies known to be effective with students with disabilities (see Chapter 6).

Source: Based on J. Echevarria (May 1995), Sheltered instruction for students with learning disabilities who have limited English proficiency, *Intervention in School and Clinic*, 30(5), 302–305.

materials to make lesson concepts clear and meaningful and adapting the content to the students' academic and linguistic levels are also important features of instruction for English learners with learning difficulties.

Further, many English learners with learning disabilities have difficulty with oral presentation of information. The use of extra linguistic clues such as gestures and body language assists students in understanding the message and focusing their attention. For example, in the consumerism lesson, the teacher pointed to the words *cheap* and *expensive* on the board as she said, "Would you rather buy the cheap pair of shoes (holding them up) or the expensive pair (holding them up)?" The process of stating the terms while holding up the items may need to be repeated to ensure comprehension, particularly if the terms are more difficult academic terms than the ones used in the consumerism example. Figure 3.9 provides additional suggestions for adapting sheltered instruction lessons to meet these students' needs. For an excellent resource on teaching students with learning disabilities see www.ncld.org.

SUMMARY

Sheltered instruction is designed to teach English learners content area material in a way that makes it understandable to them and also develops their English language proficiency. The SIOP® Model is a scientifically tested model of sheltered instruction for English learners that offers a lesson planning and delivery system to teachers for planning and carrying out best practices for English learners. While sheltered lessons clearly share some of the characteristics of effective instruction, they expand on others to meet the needs of English learners and include some characteristics that are unique to these individuals because of their levels of English proficiency. Further, many of the characteristics of a sheltered lesson will enhance the ability of students with learning difficulties to make sense of the content and develop their English proficiency. Therefore, sheltered instruction is good instruction, but it involves insight into the needs of English learners.

Specifically, as a reader you

- defined sheltered instruction and explained common misperceptions about this type of teaching.
- practiced using some of the 8 components of the SIOP® Model of sheltered instruction in your teaching.

- identified key similarities and differences between sheltered instruction and effective instruction.
- described specific considerations for English learners with learning disabilities.

ACTIVITIES

1. Using a textbook from a given subject area, develop a lesson using the features of sheltered instruction outlined in Figure 3.2.
2. In small groups, brainstorm ways to make a sheltered lesson more comprehensible.
3. Indicate which of the features of the SIOP® Model of sheltered instruction in Figure 3.2 are not part of your current teaching repertoire and which ones you use frequently.
4. Take a look at your analysis of the lesson in the Your Turn feature. Now, compare it to our analysis that follows. How many points were aligned with our analysis? Which points we made might you disagree with? Why?

   Our Analysis: The goal of every lesson needs to be student learning, not simply the completion of activities. The lesson should have started with a more thorough review of concepts learned in previous days about the human heart. The teacher might have even shown a brief video clip of blood flowing through arteries and veins. There was little accountability in terms of how well students understood and answered the two questions posted. She might have had students compare answers and report out what they had written in their notebooks to ensure that each student had the correct information in his or her notebook. As the lesson got going, the teacher should have planned specific tasks for each member of the groups by having two students trace, one get the heart paper, and another get the yarn. What took 15 minutes could have taken 2 to 3 minutes. Also, the teacher should have precut the yarn so that students would not have to stand in line for 5 to 10 minutes waiting for the spools. The teacher could have instructed students to bring their notebooks with them to the group and use their notes to answer questions that arose before asking the teacher questions. The wrap-up should have been planned to reinforce the concepts and vocabulary of the lesson. Unfortunately, lack of focus and poor planning resulted in a lesson that included little more than having middle school students tracing and gluing, as the students mentioned at the conclusion of the lesson.
5. List at least five different ways a teacher can check for students' understanding.

CHAPTER 4

Understanding, Adjusting, and Teaching the Language of the Classroom

LEARNING OBJECTIVES:

- Explain the ways that knowing about academic language improves teachers' effectiveness in working with English learners.
- Analyze the language demands of a lesson and create meaningful language objectives to advance students' language proficiency.
- Reflect on some techniques for developing oral language proficiency.
- Identify some key ways that a sheltered teacher's discourse will be different from that of a mainstream teacher who is unaware of second language issues.
- Compare the elements of instructional conversations to typical instruction and note how they differ.

For English learners to be proficient and productive students, and learn the language skills necessary to be college and career ready, they need lots of opportunities to use language in social and

Woodapple/Fotolia

72

academic settings. However, in many classrooms, not just those for English learners, students are severely limited in their opportunities to use language in a variety of ways (Cazden, 2001; Goodlad, 1984; Mercer & Hodgkinson, 2008; Sirotnik, 1983). In a study of bilingual education and English immersion programs, researchers reported that each program type reflected traditional transmission or recitation teaching, which is dominated by teacher talk. When students are given a chance to respond, their responses typically are limited to simple information-recall statements. The study concluded that teachers tend to offer a "passive language-learning environment, limiting student opportunities to produce language and develop more complex language and thinking skills" (Ramirez, Yuen, Ramey, & Pasta, 1991). This traditional approach to interaction retains a strong presence in classrooms today (Myhill, Jones & Hopper, 2006).

73

CHAPTER 4

*Understanding,
Adjusting, and
Teaching the
Language of the
Classroom*

 Think about and write down ways you can reduce the amount of teacher talk and promote more student to student interaction as you watch the video on classroom interaction.

Understanding the Language of the Classroom: All Teachers Are Language Teachers

Language is used in many ways, depending on the setting, audience, and purpose. In academic settings we often use a variation, or *register,* of English different from the informal register encountered in everyday settings that is used when talking with family and friends or interacting on social media. Academic language uses more sophisticated vocabulary, more complex sentence structures, and rhetorical forms applied primarily in academic settings. This type of language use is not something that comes easily to most students—and even less so to English learners who likely have had little exposure to it. Because their literacy and language backgrounds differ from those of mainstream students, English learners benefit from modeling, practice, and feedback in using academic English in ways that are consistent with the expectations of school (Valdes, Bunch, Snow, Lee & Matos, 2005).

The Common Core State Standards call for students to be college and career ready by demonstrating a wide range of skills that require the proficient use of academic language. Specifically, some of the skills required include the ability to:

- evaluate a speaker's point of view, reasoning, and use of evidence and rhetoric.
- participate effectively in a range of conversations and collaborations with diverse partners, building on others' ideas and expressing their own clearly and persuasively.
- present information, findings, and supporting evidence such that listeners can follow the line of reasoning.
- adapt speech to a variety of contexts and communicative tasks, demonstrating command of formal English when indicated or appropriate.

It is clear from these standards that academic language is something that needs to be taught and modeled by teachers and recognized and understood by students. The emphasis on standards-based instruction and accountability makes it all the more critical that English learners engage in meaningful lessons where teachers encourage authentic student contributions and provide opportunities to express, interpret, and negotiate meaning in English.

74

CHAPTER 4

*Understanding,
Adjusting, and
Teaching the
Language of the
Classroom*

Academic language is often thought of as vocabulary, and vocabulary does comprise a large part of what makes up academic language. There are general academic language terms that are used across content areas as well as content-specific terms used in math, science, history, and other subjects. However, for English learners to be proficient in academic language, they also need explicit instruction that gives attention to the grammatical, morphological, and phonological aspects of the English language (Harper & de Jong, 2004).

The specific language demands of each academic content area require every teacher to be a teacher of English to a certain degree. All teachers need to integrate language instruction into their content lessons. This can be done most effectively by having both content and language objectives in every lesson.

$\mathcal{T}$eaching Language through Objectives

Lesson planning involves developing content objectives to guide lesson delivery but teachers must also incorporate objectives that support students' academic language development.

 In reality, all teachers are language teachers because of the specific language demands of each content area. Think about the language used in the lessons you teach as you watch a video describing linguistics and its importance for all teachers How can understanding linguistics help teachers?

To enhance language learning, the objectives should represent an aspect of academic English that students need to learn or master. Language objectives should be stated clearly and simply, and they should be presented to students both orally and in writing. Mostly importantly, the objectives should represent an aspect of academic English that students need to learn or master.

Language objectives compliment the content objectives of a lesson. In a history class, for example, students are reading about the Iranian hostage crisis of 1979. A content objective might be: Students will distinguish between fact and opinion in the text. A language objective might be: Students will use past tense forms of verbs when citing facts and opinions. In this example, students are meeting a history/social science standard (distinguishing fact and opinion) and learning about a historical event. At the same time attention is being paid to the grammatical form of past tense so that students are explicitly taught verb forms that will advance their English proficiency.

This lesson might begin with a review of fact and opinion, a skill that has been taught in previous years. Then the teacher would remind students that the past tense is used when we talk about events that have already happened. English-proficient students might spend a few minutes writing to a prompt while the teacher works with a small group of English learners on regular and irregular past tense forms. (The words can be added to students' personal dictionaries for reference.) After the teacher "jumpstarts" the lesson for students, the teacher and students read the history text and the lesson unfolds. At the point when students are asked to indicate fact or opinion, the English learners may be provided sentence frames such as "This statement is a fact because ___(use past tense)___." "This statement is an opinion because ___(use past tense)___." In this way, students are learning the content of the lesson while reviewing and practicing a grammatical form. Language objectives may come from a variety of sources such as state English language development

(ELD) standards, English language arts standards, and TESOL standards. The idea is to make sure that features of language development are introduced, practiced, and reviewed in a systematic way so that English learners get enough exposure to master English skills and do so in an organized rather than arbitrary way. Many English learners reach intermediate proficiency and plateau there, in part because they lack explicit, systematic instruction and practice in the grammatical aspects of English that will propel them to higher levels of academic language proficiency.

Language objectives provide students with strategic instruction around what academic language sounds and looks like within the context of content instruction. Language objectives may be developed for lessons based on four categories of language skills (Echevarria, Vogt, & Short, 2013): academic vocabulary (key terms for understanding the lesson); language skills and functions (the way students are expected to use language in the lesson); language structures or grammar (structures such as passive voice that are difficult for English learners); and language learning strategies (the practices that help students learn on their own such as self-monitoring and pre-reading or re-reading strategies). Specific language objectives might involve having students:

- present math problems and explain how they reached their answer.
- write a comment on a class blog using at least one new vocabulary word.
- question, debate, agree or disagree, state an opinion, ask for clarification.
- identify root words and affixes (prefixes and suffixes).
- argue a position using evidence from text.
- distinguish similar terms such as *expression* and *equation* in math or *graph* (verb) and *graphic* (noun) in social studies.
- determine a speaker's point of view.

Language objectives benefit teachers and students alike. Developing language objectives makes teachers aware of the language demands of the lessons they plan and teach. Having explicit language objectives written and reviewed at the outset of a lesson makes English learners aware of the lesson's expectations and assists them in learning the language skills they need for the lesson. Without explicit language objectives, the language skills required for a lesson are opaque and typically unrecognized by both teachers and students. For practice writing language objectives, see the Your Turn feature.

Your Turn

Every lesson should have language objectives that support the lesson's learning goals and prepare students for the type of academic language they need to understand the lesson's content and perform the related activities. These objectives should be written in student-friendly language such as, "Today you will . . ." or "Students will be able to . . ."

Verbs used in language objectives might include: retell, describe, persuade, compare, or write. For your own practice in writing language objectives, select a topic for lesson planning. First determine what your content objectives will be so that the language objectives support the key concepts of the lesson. Then write several language objectives that will promote students' academic language growth. Be sure that you write them clearly and simply enough so that students can understand.

76
....

CHAPTER 4

Understanding,
Adjusting, and
Teaching the
Language of the
Classroom

Developing Oral Language Proficiency

The importance of oral language development is well established (August & Shanahan, 2006). In their comprehensive review of research on the oral language development of English learners, Saunders and Goldenberg (2010) and Saunders and O'Brian (2006) reveal several benefits of oral language proficiency:

- Oral proficiency is strongly related to reading achievement.
- More proficiency encourages interaction with native-English speakers, which in turn provides language models and improves proficiency.
- A cycle develops where improving English proficiency leads to more English use, which leads to subsequent gains in oral proficiency.
- With improved oral proficiency, English learners tend to use more complex learning strategies.
- As oral proficiency develops, English learners demonstrate a wider range of language skills including use of higher-level questions, more academic use of language, and increased capacity to define what words mean.

In addition, oral English proficiency contributes significantly to the acquisition of sight words for young English learners, a skill that is an important component of reading (Helman & Burns, 2008).

The evidence is clear about the importance of oral language proficiency, but the challenge is to create learning environments that encourage English learners—and all students—to practice using academic English.

For these students to be taught in a language-rich environment in which they interact with important ideas and discuss lesson content, the structure of content classes needs to be altered so that instead of teachers talking and students listening, students are interacting in their collaborative investigation of a body of knowledge. We have found that substantiative student-to-student and teacher-to-student interaction is an essential component of effective sheltered instruction (Echevarria, Vogt, & Short, 2013)

Adjusting Language with Sheltered Instruction

Effective sheltered teachers structure their lessons so that students have ample opportunities to use academic English. In doing so, they make adjustments to their own speech that facilitate understanding for English learners and encourage active student participation. Many of these modifications are specifically addressed in the chapters on sheltered instruction (Chapter 3) and differentiated instruction (Chapter 7). These modifications have been shown to improve student achievement (Echevarria, 2012; Echevarria, Short, & Powers, 2006), and they are consistently recommended by experts on second-language acquisition. The degree of modifications should be adjusted to students' level of English proficiency, with intermediate speakers receiving fewer modifications than beginning speakers of English. Modifications include:

1. Sentence length and complexity of sentence structure (syntax) should be controlled.
2. Speech should be at a natural but slower rate than normal, and enunciation should be clear.

3. Use of idioms should be avoided, or meanings should be made clear.

4. High-frequency vocabulary should be chosen when possible, and vocabulary range should be controlled.

5. Full referents should be used rather than pronouns.

6. Emphasis should be placed on key words, phrases, and concepts by intonation or by using pauses to set them apart from surrounding material.

7. The same words and phrases should be repeated several times instead of using a variety of expressions.

8. Direct rather than indirect questions should be used.

9. Instructions should convey one idea or action each and should be presented in correct, temporal sequence, preferably written for students to see and refer to.

10. Repetition, restatements, and redundant grammatical structures should be used.

How should these features be integrated into lessons? In a study comparing the language used in a mainstream science class and a sheltered science class (Pritzos, 1992), the following transcripts were included, which show a sheltered science teacher using several strategies that he did not use with mainstream students.

Mainstream Class

Teacher: Dustin, read Chris's answer for me.

Student: An insulator holds electricity in, and a conductor lets energy flow through.

Teacher: Very good. An insulator does not allow electricity to pass through. And a conductor allows electricity to pass through. Write OK beside the answer if they've done that, and then pass it back to them.

Sheltered Class

Teacher: I won't tell ya' any names 'cause I've seen a whole bunch of students—where the student writes this: Says, "A conductor conducts things." (Writes on board) Does that tell me anything? Does that tell me about this word?

Student: Yeah.

Teacher: It's in here (points to the word *conductor*). No (shakes head). So I would say: "Conductors . . ." We said—and they told me "pass through" (writes on board). Eh, now . . . better answer. So we say, "A conductor allows things to pass through (points to written words). Insulator does not allow things to pass through (points to insulator, pass through and shakes head) or stops things." And in this case it stops electricity. Conductor allows electricity to pass through (points to conductor). Now, look at your paper and at your partner's paper. Did they write something that tells you "Things pass through is a conductor, does not pass through is an insulator"? If they wrote that, then write OK. If they had that idea, write OK.

Although the two excerpts are comparable in content, in the sheltered class the teacher makes several modifications to increase student understanding. For example, the teacher writes the words *conductor, conducts things, insulator,* and *passes through* on the board and refers to these terms with gestures at least seven times, providing visual clues to supplement his speech. In addition, he uses some metalinguistic analysis when he asks the students whether it is appropriate to use *conduct* to define *conductor*. In the mainstream class, the teacher says, "A conductor allows electricity to pass through." In the sheltered class, he initially uses the hypernym *thing* ("A conductor allows things to pass through") and then later uses the word *electricity*. Pritzos points out that this strategy could be used to lessen the cognitive load of the definition, allowing more attention to be placed on the ideas *insulator, conductor, pass through,* and *not pass through*. Further, when electricity is introduced, the teacher overtly identifies *things* as *electricity* for clarification and then restates the definition for *conductor* using the word *electricity*.

Paraphrasing provides another strategy for increasing comprehensibility. The teacher first says, "does not allow things to pass through" and then paraphrases with the synonymous phrase "or stops things." Other kinds of strategies that teachers in this study employed were reducing the rate of speech and using more careful pronunciation when addressing the sheltered classes.

In another example, we transcribed discourse from the consumerism unit presented in Chapter 3. The first example is the transcript of a portion of a typical lesson found in a mainstream class, and the second is the transcript of the sheltered teacher teaching the same portion of the lesson.

Mainstream Class Lesson

Teacher: Look at the piece of clothing at the bottom. It says (he reads), "This shirt is flame-resistant," which means what?

Student: Could not burn.

Student: Won't catch fire.

Teacher: It will not burn, won't catch fire. Right. (Continues reading.) "To retain the flame-resistant properties"—what does it mean "to retain"?

Student: (unintelligible)

Teacher: To keep it. All right. "In order to keep this shirt flame-resistant (he reads), wash with detergent only." All right (he reads). "Do not use soap or bleach. Tumble dry. One hundred percent polyester." Now, why does it say, "Do not use soap or bleach"?

Student: 'Cause it'll take off the . . .

Teacher: It'll take off the what?

Students: (fragmented responses)

Teacher: It'll take off the flame-resistant quality. If you wash it with soap or bleach, then the shirt's just gonna be like any old shirt, any regular shirt, so when you put a match to it, will it catch fire?

Student: No.

Teacher: Yes. 'Cause you've ruined it then. It's no longer flame resistant. So the government says you gotta tell the consumer what kind of shirt it is and how to take care of it. If you look at any piece of clothing: shirt—it doesn't come on off on your underwear or your socks—but on your pants, your shirts, um, your skirts, anything. There's always going to be a tag on these that says what it is made of and how you're going to take care of it. OK. And that's for your protection so that you won't buy something and then treat it wrong. So labeling is important. All right. Let's review. I'll go back to the antiseptic. What did we say *indications* meant? Indications? Raise your hands; raise your hands. Robert?

Student: What's it for?

Teacher: What is it for, when do you use this? OK. What do directions, what is that for, Victor?

Student: How to use . . .

Teacher: How to use. OK, so indications is when you use it (holds one finger up), directions is how you use it (holds another finger up), and warnings is what?

Students: (various mumbled responses)

Teacher: How you don't use it. This is what you don't do.

Close inspection of this teacher's discourse patterns indicates some practices that do not facilitate learning or English acquisition. The first ineffective practice is complete teacher dominance. He talks for lengthy periods of time, with students often losing interest, judging by their looking away, engaging in quiet conversations with each other, and being inattentive. He does not give students much opportunity to interact—either with him or with other students.

The second ineffective practice is cutting students off and answering his own question, even when he does ask for student input. The first time this happens, a student says, "'Cause it'll take off the . . ." and the teacher responds, "It'll take off the what?" Prompting the student to finish the sentence is a good teaching strategy; some researchers believe a brisk instructional pace is desirable. However, this teacher consistently cuts students off and answers questions himself, stifling student participation. A more productive behavior for English learners would be for the teacher to wait for the student to think of the word. Alternately, he could direct the students to the text for the word. Instead, he waits a mere split second each time before answering the question himself.

The third ineffective practice is not providing opportunities for elaborated responses. He tends to ask for single-word answers, and when he does ask a question that requires a complete sentence, rather than validating students' responses by saying, "Tell me what you mean" or "So you're saying . . .?" he moves ahead with the lesson. He asks questions but does not listen to the students' answers or try to encourage them to elaborate.

Here is the same lesson using a sheltered approach.

Sheltered Instruction Class

Teacher: Most clothing must have labels that tell what kind of cloth was used in it, right? Look at the material in the picture down there (points to picture in text). What does it say, the tag right there?

Student: The, the, the

Teacher: The tag right there.

Student: Flame-resis

Teacher: Resistant.

Student: Flame-resistant. To retain the flame-resistant properties, wash with detergent only. Do not use soap or bleach. Use warm water. Tumble dry.

Teacher: One hundred percent.

Student: Polyester.

Teacher: Now, most clothes carry labels, right (pointing to the neck of her sweater), explaining how to take care of it, like dry clean, machine wash, right? It tells you how to clean it. Why does this product have to be washed with a detergent and no soap or bleach?

Student: Because clothes . . .

Teacher: Why can't you use something else?

Students: (Several students mumble answers.)

Student: (says in Spanish) Because it will make it small.

Teacher: It may shrink, or (gestures to a student) it may not be . . . what does it say?

Student: It's not going to be able to be resistant to fire.

Teacher: Exactly. It's flame resistant, right? So if you use something else, it won't be flame resistant any more. How about the, uh, look at the antiseptic (holds hands up to form a container), the picture above the shirt, the antiseptic?

Student: Read it?

Teacher: Antiseptic. (Teacher reads.) And other health products you buy without a prescription often have usage and warning labels. What can you learn from this label? Read this label, quietly please, and tell me what you can learn from the label. Read the label on that antiseptic. (Students read silently.)

Teacher: What can you learn from this label?

Student: It kills—oh, I know.

80
....

CHAPTER 4

*Understanding,
Adjusting, and
Teaching the
Language of the
Classroom*

Teacher: Steve?

Student: It kills germs.

Student: Yeah, it kills germs.

Teacher: It kills germs. You use it for wounds, right? What else?

Students: (various enthusiastic responses)

Teacher: One person at a time. OK, hold on. Veronica was saying something.

Student: It tells you in the directions that you could use it, that like that, 'cause if you use it in another thing, it could hurt you.

Teacher: It could hurt you. OK, what else? Ricardo?

Student: If you put it in your mouth. Don't put it in your mouth or your ears or your eyes.

Teacher: Very good. Don't put it in your mouth, ears, and eyes. OK, for how many days should you use it? No more than what?

Student: No more than ten days.

Student: Ten days.

Teacher: So don't use it—you have to follow what it says so don't use it more than ten days. Now, the next activity you're going to do . . .

(The teacher explained that they would be doing an activity in which they would read labels for information.)

The sheltered lesson differs from mainstream instruction in two distinct ways: (1) the balance of teacher to student talk and (2) the level of student participation. The sheltered teacher asked questions, waited for student responses, and restated or elaborated the responses. The transcript shows a more even balance between teacher talk and student talk. The videotape reveals substantially more student participation in the sheltered lesson, with students enthusiastically responding to questions, while during the effective instruction lesson, students were more passive. Further, the sheltered teacher used the text as a referent during the lesson, pointing to terms and illustrations.

The teacher effectively implemented components of sheltered instruction to enhance comprehension of the subject matter while delivering whole-group instruction. Small-group instruction can provide even more individualized engagement in meaningful discourse. One such interactive approach is the use of instructional conversations.

*U*sing Instructional Conversations for Language and Concept Development

Instructional conversations (ICs) use a small-group format (five to seven students) to create opportunities for students to engage in thoughtful, reflective, and sometimes provocative discussions about ideas, texts, and concepts (Goldenberg, 1992–93; Tharp & Gallimore, 1988). As the teacher seeks to improve comprehension and develop language, ICs provide a forum for developing new understandings and constructing meaning from the text. Together, the group discusses possible interpretations or predictions, and constructs meaning and ideas jointly. Instructional conversations entail less direct transmission of knowledge and understanding from teacher to student and more opportunities for students and teachers to reach new levels of understanding together. During an IC, both teacher and students are responsive to one another, with no one person dominating the discussion, although the teacher does serve as the primary facilitator. The goal of ICs is to create rich language opportunities for students during which they can think, reflect, express ideas, and argue positions as they develop new understandings around a text.

81
....
CHAPTER 4

Understanding,
Adjusting, and
Teaching the
Language of the
Classroom

Most of the work with ICs has been with students who have characteristics that are associated with poor academic performance and school failure: poor families, immigrant status, or limited English proficiency. Research conducted with ICs has shown several positive effects. Echevarria (1995b) found that students, even those labeled language and learning disabled, used higher levels of discourse and had greater participation during IC lessons than during lessons taking a more conventional basal approach. Further, ICs promoted higher understanding of concepts than a recitation or basal-like comprehension lesson (Saunders & Goldenberg, 1999).

The role of the teacher in an IC lesson is one of facilitator—assisting students in joint activity, helping them construct meaning from texts, and promoting their understanding of ideas and concepts they otherwise would not understand on their own (Vygotsky, 1962, 1978). In other words, an IC is more than a good discussion. It involves a movement in understanding so that by the end of the IC, students should have a greater understanding of the theme or concept than when it began.

In an effort to create a model for conducting ICs in a tangible, systematic way, 10 elements that characterize an IC were developed (Goldenberg, 1992–93; Goldenberg & Gallimore, 1991). These elements provide a framework for teachers as they plan and implement ICs in their classrooms.

   1. Every lesson should have a theme around which the discussion centers. The theme is determined by what new understanding the teacher wants students to gain through the discussion.

To assure that the theme is carried throughout the lesson, some IC teachers have written questions on sticky notes and affixed them to the pages of the book. For example, when the theme is courage, the teacher might have a question posted on the page for reference, such as "In what ways do you think the main character showed courage here?" With this strategy, the teacher is reminded to link the discussion to the theme consistently, enhancing the students' understanding of the concept or the theme. The theme has been described as the glue that holds the lesson together, and without it, the lesson may be fragmented. In every IC lesson, there should be a larger point or issue that drives the direction of the lesson rather than a simple series of questions and answers that are often disconnected.

In order to have an interesting discussion, the theme should be something that is relevant to the students. For instance, in a textbook story about a girl who is uninterested in reading but gets turned on to books when she goes with her brother to the library and hears the librarian reading aloud to a group, obvious themes might be reading or learning to like something. Or the teacher might select a theme about caring for or being cared for by siblings. This might lead to a lively discussion of students' own experiences. By the time the teacher explains that they are going to read a story about a girl who is in the care of her older brother, so she has to accompany him to the library, they will be eager to hear about the character's experience. A rather mundane story from a basal reader comes to life when the students can read it from this thematic perspective. If they can relate to the situation, their interest will be held during the lesson, as the theme or concept is woven through it.

   2. Teachers actively tap into and use students' background knowledge and experiences. The teacher either elicits what students know or provides students with pertinent background knowledge and relevant schemata necessary for understanding a text. Background knowledge and experiences are then woven into the discussion.

82
························

CHAPTER 4

*Understanding,
Adjusting, and
Teaching the
Language of the
Classroom*

Instructional conversations provide a format for activating prior knowledge or building requisite knowledge through discussion. As discussed in other chapters, English learners bring to the classroom their own set of experiences and knowledge, as well as their unique views of the world. Instructional conversations explicitly capitalize on what the students bring. A lesson about a pioneer girl making friends with some Native Americans might seem irrelevant to the lives of urban middle school students, but if the teacher draws upon the students' experiences with friends, these experiences can then be tied to the character and to her new friends.

If students have a rudimentary understanding of a concept or idea, it can be used to move them to greater levels of understanding. Even if they have no prior exposure to a topic or idea, students will explore what they do not know and their thoughts and ideas will be validated through the IC discussion. Simply put, ICs provide a bridge between their knowledge and experiences and new concepts.

Teachers elicit students' prior knowledge and learning by asking questions such as these:

- What have you experienced that is similar to the character's experience?
- How do you think the settlers felt? Where in the text can you show evidence of it?
- How would a situation like this be handled in your native country?
- If you were the character, what would you do? Why?
- Would your parents allow you to do that?

Questions such as these that relate the text to the students' experiences are skillfully presented throughout the discussion, providing a continuous link between the students and the story.

3. When called for, the teacher provides explicit teaching of a skill, fact, or concept. When a student does not understand a vocabulary word, concept, decoding skills, or process, the teacher provides specific, direct instruction. For instance, "Add the numbers in this column and then the numbers in that column." As the student progresses and becomes more independent, the teacher adjusts the amount and type of assistance provided, perhaps asking questions such as, "Where do you think you could start?" Within the context of an IC, direct teaching may be simply defining a term and moving on, or it may require more in-depth teaching of a skill or concept.

4. During an IC, the teacher actively encourages students to use more complex language and expression. The teacher encourages more extended student response by using a variety of elicitation techniques. For example, the teacher invites students to expand ("Tell me more about . . ."), asks direct questions ("What do you mean by . . .?"), offers restatements ("In other words, . . ."), and makes frequent pauses.

As mentioned previously, there is abundant evidence that teachers tend to dominate lessons linguistically, without being aware of the need to elicit elaborated student utterances and authentic student responses. Such opportunities are created by using comments like "Tell me more about that" or "Tell me what you mean by that." If the student gives a one-word answer, the teacher may ask, "Why do you think that?" or "What basis do you have for that?" After asking the question or making a request for elaboration, the teacher then remains quiet—even for an extended period. With practice using these strategies, the students become acutely aware that the expectation is for them to fill in and that the teacher is not going to jump in and paraphrase or finish the thought for them.

Increasing wait-time gives students the opportunity to formulate their ideas. As one special education teacher using ICs explained:

> I found that my expectations of what the students could produce and the kinds of ideas that they could come up with are very different than they used to be. . . . Allowing them wait-time and asking them to explain why they feel the way they do and to relate it to something we've read . . . I'm more willing to give them more opportunities to speak and explain themselves in a variety of situations.

5. Students are expected to provide evidence or a basis for their statements, opinions and positions. The teacher asks students' to use the text, pictures, and reasoning to support an argument or position. For example, the teacher probes for the basis of students' statements by asking, "Where in the text did you find that?" "How do you know?" or "What makes you think that?" or "Show us where it says . . ."

This element of IC is consistent with the Common Core State Standards and their emphasis on using text evidence as a basis of discussion and writing.

6. The teacher asks fewer "known-answer" questions. Much of the discussion centers on questions and answers for which there might be more than one correct answer. This type of questioning promotes high-level thinking and problem solving. A teacher mentioned that when she is not getting the responses she wants from the students, she does a self-evaluation. She usually finds that her questions are of the type that elicit a yes-no response or a predictable answer. The kinds of questions that generate a good discussion are those for which there may be more than one correct answer. Open-ended or prompting questions encourage students to think, express opinions, and construct meaning. Here are some examples of open-ended questions:

- By looking at the page, what do you think the chapter will be about?
- What can you learn from reading this label?
- How are these plants different?
- How does your idea differ from what we read in the text?
- What else can you tell me about that?
- On what basis would you group these objects?
- Why might that be?
- What makes you think this might be different?
- Why would the colonists do that? Show where it indicates that in the text.

These questions call for opinions, inferences, or predictions. However, teachers have reported that asking such questions consistently is difficult, since literal recall questions are easier to formulate. Nevertheless, higher-order questioning is critical in encouraging students to really think about the material and to give more elaborated responses to questions.

7. The teacher adjusts the discussion to follow opportunities provided by students' contributions. While there is an initial plan for the discussion based on the theme and "chunking" of text, the teacher also responds to students' comments and adjusts the discussion accordingly.

In an eighth-grade language arts class with a group of English learners who were labeled as having learning disabilities, the teacher was discussing a story about a young

84

....

CHAPTER 4

*Understanding,
Adjusting, and
Teaching the
Language of the
Classroom*

man reading a magazine on the bus (Echevarria, 1995a). The students read the next part of the story as a group. It described how some men speaking Russian boarded the bus and how when the main character, Mike, reached his stop, he exited the bus and said a quick greeting in Russian to the men. The story explicitly stated that Mike's brother-in-law spoke Russian, which is how Mike learned the phrase. The next part of the story describes how Mike realizes that the men have gotten off the bus at the next stop and are running after him, firing a gun. He quickly escapes from the men and arrives safely at his second-story apartment. Sometime later, he hears noise outside, looks out the window, and sees that the men have found where he lives. The teacher pauses in the reading and asks, "How do you suppose the men found out where Mike lived?" The correct answer was that they got his address from the subscription label on his magazine, which he'd left on the bus. However, one student said that the Russians probably asked other Russian people in the neighborhood who Mike was. The teacher reported later that she was tempted to skip over the student's response, which seemed to be at best implausible and at worst "out in left field." Instead, she was responsive to the student's contribution and probed to clarify his point. She said, "Tell me more about that. How would they do that?" The Latino student explained that in their predominately Latino community, everyone knows where the few Samoan families live, and if anyone wanted any information about a Samoan-speaking person, everyone would know where to go. By being responsive and encouraging the student to elaborate and clarify his meaning, the teacher said she learned an important lesson: that there are connections between students' seemingly "off the wall" comments and the point being discussed, which will become clear if students are given the encouragement to explain their ideas.

8. Rich discussion involves multiple related comments or **connected talk**. The discourse pattern of an IC resembles that of any good conversation. Multiple participants interact, taking turns and making relevant comments. Comments often build on another speaker's and extend the conversation. Students are explicitly taught how to politely agree or disagree with other points of view and contributions using evidence from the text to support of defend their position.

9. The atmosphere of an IC is **rigorous but not intimidating** for students. The teacher creates a zone of proximal development, which means that he or she provides just the right amount of assistance the students need until they are able to function independently. The rigor of the setting is balanced by a positive affective climate.

The teacher conducting an IC strives to engage students in a good conversation but does not lose sight of the instructional intent of ICs. It is not enough simply to have an interesting discussion. The discussion needs to be linked to the instructional goal (content and language objectives) of the sheltered lesson. Students should be engaged intellectually in ways they might not be otherwise. In a videotape of a series of ICs (Echevarria & Silver, 1995), the teacher pushes her students to go farther in their thinking by asking questions such as "How could that be? Why would that be?" "What gives you the idea that the buffalo could be the woman?" "How can you just accept that? Would that happen in our lives?" or "How would the author show us that?" Without intimidating the students, she challenges them to think about and discuss the story at higher levels of understanding.

10. The teacher encourages **general participation by all students.** Students and teacher are collaborators in the endeavor thus nobody controls who speaks when. Students do not raise their hand to be called on but contribute to the conversation spontaneously. The teacher functions more as a facilitator than an authority "in charge" of the discussion.

Typically, quality interaction does not automatically happen once the teacher begins using an IC approach (McIntyre, Kyle, & Moore, 2006). Students must overcome the conditioning of schooling, where the discourse patterns typically found in both elementary and secondary classrooms involve the teacher asking a question (initiate), a student responding, the teacher evaluating the response (IRE) or providing feedback (IRF), followed by another teacher-asked question (Cazden, 2001). Often students who are not called on disengage and are not involved in the discussion. With practice using instructional conversations, students begin to realize that the teacher is genuinely interested in their ideas and opinions and will give them the time they need to formulate and express their thoughts.

An example of the type of discourse used during an IC can be seen in the following transcription of a lesson with Latino fifth-graders in which the teacher encouraged meaningful discourse by guiding students' thinking (Echevarria & Silver, 1995).

Teacher: There was a word that came up: *respect*. You said he had respect. Why did he have respect for her instantly like that?

Student: 'Cause he . . .

Student: Love.

Teacher: He had love? How did he have that instant love for her?

Student: 'Cause she came from the buffalo nation.

Student: She, she was nice. She dressed not like them.

Student: She dressed . . .

Student: Differently.

Teacher: But he still felt this love and respect for this different, this person from a different kind of a culture?

Several: Yes, uh-huh.

Teacher: How can that be? Why would that be? (Students remained quiet.)

Teacher: You know, what that brings me to this that Rolando brought up his idea about the author's purpose—why this is going on. Okay. And I'd like you to remind us what you said about the author's purpose, Rolando, and we're gonna check out what we think about that, okay? What was it that you thought might be the author's purpose?

Student: That, like, 'cause the man, he fell in love with the woman, and the woman's a buffalo and the man likes hunting buffalo, he might kill her. And the author's purpose means never to kill buffalo 'cause they're a great part of nature.

Teacher: What do you guys think about that? Why would you agree? Why do you think that's a good idea?

Student: 'Cause they're almost 'stinct.

Students: They're not very much.

Teacher: Okay. So not killing them, what would that serve?

Student: That would make more and then the buffalos make little ones and they're an endangered species and soon they, they won't be endangered species anymore.

Teacher: Okay. That would be a good author's purpose. Any other author's purpose that is a possibility? . . . Cynthia brought up a different idea in her prediction. It wasn't about killing buffalo—do you remember? Could you tell us what you said?

Student: It's like, killing a buffalo is like killing a beautiful woman.

The teacher provided assistance to the students, guiding them to higher levels of understanding. The students undoubtedly couldn't have reached this level of discussion on their own, but with the assistance of a skilled teacher, they came to understand some complex ideas.

86

CHAPTER 4

*Understanding,
Adjusting, and
Teaching the
Language of the
Classroom*

An added benefit of this type of classroom discourse is that it allows teachers to get to know their students in ways they might not have otherwise. Through discussions, teachers tap into students' knowledge and experience, listen to their ideas, and encourage them to express themselves. As a result, teachers develop a sensitivity to and an awareness of learners' needs and are better able to support their learning (Dong, 2009).

SUMMARY

The academic language used in classrooms is not the type of language English learners learn incidentally through exposure alone. It needs to be acknowledged by teachers and explicitly taught to students. Further, teachers need to adjust their own discourse so that it is understandable to English learners. In this chapter we discussed the importance of academic language and ways it can be developed to provide English learners with the skills they need to be successful in school.

Specifically, as a reader you

- explained the ways that knowing about academic language improves teachers' effectiveness in working with English learners.
- analyzed the language demands of a lesson and create meaningful language objectives to advance students' language proficiency.
- reflected on some techniques for developing oral language proficiency.
- identified some key ways that sheltered teachers' discourse differs from that of a mainstream teacher (ne who is unaware of second-language issues).
- compared the elements of instructional conversations to typical instruction and noted how they differ.

ACTIVITIES

1. Using a textbook from any subject area, select a section of text or a topic to teach. Analyze the academic language that needs to be taught to English learners. Write at least two language objectives for the lesson.
2. Using the same text or another, write a brief outline of how you might teach the selected section or topic. In a small group, role-play teaching the lesson, focusing on using discourse that encourages linguistically balanced student-teacher interaction. Be sure to develop questions that allow students to use elaborated answers (not yes-no responses), as well as other features that encourage meaningful academic language use by students.
3. Select a video of any teaching situation (for instance, on YouTube). Transcribe a segment of the lesson and discuss the aspects of sheltered discourse addressed in the chapter. Pay particular attention to the ratio of teacher talk to student talk, and opportunities for elaborated speech versus phrases and single-word answers.
4. Select a lesson plan you've recently used to teach a lesson. With a partner, brainstorm practical ways that you might adapt the lesson plan so that it encourages English language development. Be sure to add a language objective.

CHAPTER 5

Promoting Affective
and Cultural Connections

LEARNING OBJECTIVES:

- Discuss the principles of setting up a successful reading and writing instructional environment.

- Identify the important considerations for emotional and motivational support to second-language learners.

- Demonstrate an understanding of the purpose of native-language instruction and the potential benefits it has for students.

- List four examples of cultural and emotional support of the individual differences of students and their families.

When students experience challenges in school, their affective, or social-emotional, reactions are often counterproductive. Coupled with the general diversity of society, challenges in learning English or in performing well in school can often produce intensification of racial and ethnic tensions (Artiles, Rueda, Salazar, & Higareda, 2002; August & Shanahan, 2006; Baca & Cervantes, 2004; Gay, 2000; Graves & Rueda, 2008; Jimenez, 2003; Obi, Obiakor, & Algozzine, 1999; Pang, 2001). The purpose of this chapter is to provide readers with information about how to create a learning environment that is emotionally and culturally responsive to learners. A good learning environment can enhance self-esteem

Woodapple/Fotolia

Describe cultural diversity in the United States. Why is it important for you as a teacher to strive to understand and support cultural diversity?

and motivation in all learners (Fitzgerald & Graves, 2004; Johnson & Nieto, 2007; McIntosh, Graves, & Gersten, 2007; Ruiz, 1995a, 1995b). There is a parallel in this chapter to the standards for teachers of English learners in many states. For example, the California Teachers of English Learners (CTEL) Domain 3: Culture and Inclusion, establishes the importance of the connections between cultural relationships and academic achievement.

 Watch this video and summarize the information presented about cultural diversity in the United States.

Emotions and feelings of inadequacy tend to be stronger when students are simultaneously trying to learn English and meet other school responsibilities (Genesee, et al., 2006; Genesee, Lindholm-Leary, Saunders, & Christian, 2005). Beginning English learners are in a new cultural setting and do not have their usual support systems (Haager & Windmueller, 2001; McIntosh et al., 2007). The students are in a survival mode; they are unable to simultaneously consider others' feelings, plan for their own futures, and function outside an egocentric concern for their own survival (Baca & Cervantes, 2004). The new culture is practically inaccessible to these students, because they draw extensively on first-language strategies and resources (Harry & Klingner, 2005). The students typically encounter new information or processes in school that are unfamiliar and therefore difficult to learn. Many theories about affective issues indicate that a student who is trying to learn English may experience extraordinary school challenges (Cloud, Genesee, & Hamayan, 2009; C. C. Torres, 2000; M. N. Torres, 2001). The English learner may experience ridicule or rejection by peers and teachers when trying to use English. He or she may also experience challenges and perceive failure in communicating effectively with peers and school personnel. After encountering these challenges, the student is likely to resist learning English and may experience emotional blocks or trauma when trying to speak English (Cummins, 1992). Students like with behavioral issues or learning difficulties are likely to experience a greater sense of belonging, feel more supported emotionally, and have higher self-esteem when teachers take the following steps (Graves, 1998):

1. Provide activities that promote success in reading and writing.
2. Provide ample practice and careful corrections.
3. Focus on relevant background knowledge and cultural connections.
4. Actively involve learners.
5. Use alternate grouping strategies.
6. Provide native-language support.
7. Focus on content and activities that are meaningful to students both emotionally and culturally.
8. Create roles in the classroom for family and community members.
9. Hold high expectations for all learners.
10. Be responsive to cultural and personal diversity.

Providing Reading and Writing Activities That Promote Success

Students have a more positive feeling toward school when they are successful. We wrote extensively in Chapter 3 about strategies for teaching English learners in the content areas. Activities such as language experience approaches are thought to promote language development (Artilles et al., 2002). In one third-grade class with approximately 85 percent English learners, the teacher had weekly individual conferences with students. In these conferences she would ask the student to either retell a part of a narrative the class was reading or retell a part of a content-area chapter. The words spoken by the student were written in his or her notebook. The student was then to read that text to a peer, all the while editing and revising with peer input. Although the teacher wrote the words, the student was aware of his or her own intellectual ownership of the text. The teacher was just a scribe. The students could edit and revise the text and confer with peers to "fix it up." Once a week students would read aloud their summaries or stories and post them on the "work this week" bulletin board. This teacher kept a portfolio of each child's work, and each week a new piece was added. At the end of the year all of the students had quite a book of their own writing to take home. In their book, entitled *Scaffolding Reading Experiences for English Language Learners,* Fitzgerald and Graves (2004) assert that when students read their own words and have an opportunity to edit and revise, language learning is intensified.

Literature-based instruction in reading and writing typically provides rich and exciting activities for students in the early grades. As students move to middle school, the same type of language experience approaches are increasingly important. Abundant information is available regarding this type of instruction for secondary students (Graves & Liang, 2005; Waldschmidt et al., 1999).

Ruiz and her colleagues have investigated the effects of the optimal learning environment (Ole) program on literacy development in several studies of English learners with learning disabilities (Ruiz, 1995a, 1995b). The work on Ole was later validated and extended by Graves, Valles, and Rueda (2000). The Ole program includes an integration of oral language, listening, speaking, reading, and writing with a combination of writing-as-a-process and strategy instruction. The learning environment is designed in a way that facilitates this development by including the following elements:

- interactive journals, in which the teacher responds to students' daily entries in writing to provide modeling of written dialogue
- Writer's Workshop based on writing-as-a-process, in which students go through planning, drafting, editing, revising, final drafting, and publishing each time they produce a written product
- patterned writing and reading, in which students read and copy key phrases from children's literature, such as the works of Eric Carle
- creating text for wordless books
- shared reading with predictable text
- literature conversation with read-alouds
- literature study with response journals
- student-made alphabet wall charts

> *Your Turn*

> How does Writing as a Process facilitate literacy development in English learners?
> What language development could possibly occur when it is part of written
> expression?

Ruiz in her earlier work and Graves et al. (2000) found that the use of Ole improved
the writing performance of bilingual individuals and provided a mechanism for non-writers
and readers in both English and Spanish to develop improved performance in both
languages.

 Watch this video of a Readers and Writers' Workshop and make a list of the
benefits you see in facilitating literacy development.

Several additional studies of Spanish-speaking youngsters with learning disabilities
have provided information about the Ole project and its effects on writing outcomes
(Graves, Valles, & Rueda, 2000; Ortiz & Graves, 2001). The first was a descriptive case
study comparison of writing instruction in four bilingual special-education settings
(Graves et al., 2000). The second study was a quasi-experimental study of two groups of
Spanish-speaking students in special education settings that compared the effects of Ole
with those of traditional writing instruction. Studies indicate significant progress for
students who were part of the Ole projects. The important benefit of the Ole method is
to allow students to read and write natural language that they find important and that
they produce themselves. The inclusion of publishing perfect final copies of their spoken
language that has been converted into written language yields a mechanism for learning
standard Spanish and English. This creates an opportunity for students to integrate
personal language knowledge and experiences into the broader framework of written
Spanish and English. Saunders and Goldenberg (1999) also confirmed in their research
that when beginning writers are encouraged to write journal entries in their native
languages, these writers are more comfortable in school and gain English skills faster
than those who do not have native-language opportunities for writing.

Research has consistently found that progress on meaningful tasks tends to promote
positive affect in the learner (Baca & Cervantes, 2004). In one eighth-grade class,
97 percent of the students were Latino, and the majority of them were not born in the
United States. The students had varying levels of English and Spanish proficiency. The
teacher used English reading materials about young children on a farm in Iowa that were
far below the students' grade levels. Some of the phonics-based materials had mundane
story lines. One young man in the class sat with a scowl on his face and constantly sought
attention from his peers through inappropriate behavior. The teacher reported that this
student and many others were frustrated and that their parents were concerned about their
lack of progress. It was recommended that this teacher start to use a more meaningful
approach by providing constructivist activities relevant to the students' lives. The teacher
devised practice exercises to develop vocabulary, spelling, sequencing, and identification
of main ideas and developed other activities based directly on student-generated work.
When the teacher used this approach, the behavior problems virtually vanished and
the troubled students became happier and more cooperative. Providing constructivist
activities to students can change their attitudes and their performances. Students with

behavioral or learning difficulties can enhance feelings of belonging at school because they are able to bring their own ideas to the task. These types of activities are also likely to enhance students' self-esteem, as they begin to take pride in their work and to experience success.

 Connections between reading and writing promote vocabulary and language development. Watch this video and state two ways that writing facilitates reading and vice-versa.

Journal writing is another example of a meaningful writing assignment that can both yield assessment information about the writing of students and be added to the daily routine with ease. At the beginning of each class day or at the start of each unit, writing practice appears critical for the development of secondary students' writing skills. It can also reinforce positive feelings toward school when the task can be personalized (Guthrie & Wigfield, 2000).For example, one middle school math teacher had students use a binder as a journal. The teacher assigned various types of writing throughout the year. For three minutes at the start of each math period, the students made journal entries about their thoughts and feelings concerning the math homework. At other times, the students wrote for three minutes about how the concepts they were learning applied to their lives. The students were asked to share their writing in small groups or to read journal entries to the class without disclosing the student writer. Each week, the teacher collected the journals, read the entries, and provided written comments in the journals. The comments created a written interaction, or dialogue, with each student and established an opportunity for language development, even in a math class.

 Watch this middle school teacher and reflect on why small group instruction is effective here.

Written expression is a common method used to assess subject matter knowledge. However, written expression is often problematic for English learners. Allow students to demonstrate knowledge in other ways, such as speaking into a tape recorder, to a peer, or to the teacher. Students can work in pairs to complete writing assignments or express their ideas in graphic or pictorial forms rather than in words alone.

Providing Ample Practice and Careful Corrections

Students remember and reuse information better with ample practice. Successful students generally feel better about school and have higher self-concepts. Teachers can provide successful experiences by giving abundant practice and applying new knowledge in ongoing, authentic experiences. Consider an example of a unit on Coastal Native Americans, in which students practiced report writing, finding main ideas, and sharing writing in the context of the unit. Students continued to practice these skills within the context of future units. In order to minimize anxiety, teachers must approach correction during practice cautiously (Graves & Rueda, 2008). In particular, students who have experienced school failure or who are learning to speak English as a second language often need encouragement, and they need to be told when they have responded correctly. For example, teachers are advised to approach error correction indirectly as follows:

Enrico: When animals move from place to place, they midrate.

Teacher: Did you say *migrate*, Enrico (with emphasis on the *gr*)? That's right, Enrico. When animals move from place to place, they migrate. Good. (The teacher writes the word on the board once again.)

The teacher responds positively to the correct content and models the correct pronunciation by repeating the word.

*F*ocusing on Relevant Background Knowledge and Cultural Connections

Connecting culturally with students can be defined as having acceptance and respect for each unique individual and recognizing individual differences, including race, ethnicity, gender, sexual orientation, socio-economic status, age, cognitive abilities, social abilities, physical abilities, religious beliefs, political beliefs, or other ideologies. The exploration of these differences in a safe, positive, and nurturing environment is important for empowering students to embrace and celebrate diversity. In this context, educational theories and research from many different perspectives indicate that students learn better when teachers include relevant student experiences and culture in instruction (Woolfolk, 2013). Other researchers have posited that necessary background knowledge must be built because the experiences often simply do not exist in the students' repertoire (Beck, McKeown, & Kucan, 2007).

Tapping into existing knowledge involves asking students to generate questions or tell what they know prior to studying a unit or chapter. For example, students with disabilities could be culturally recognized in a study of chapter books such as *Freak the Mighty* (Philbrick, 1993) or the sequel, *Max the Mighty* (Philbrick, 1998). If either of these were selected for instruction, students could relate their own background knowledge and experiences to the themes of self-reliance and self-determination in the context of disabilities. Critically important is student analysis of disability and society. These chapter books tell the stories of boys with disabilities who explore their issues and challenges both socially and in school, with an emphasis on their relationships with others. Books like these assist students in understanding terms like *ableism* and the damage having this bias inflicts on individual empowerment. Reading about the definition of *ableism* and empowering individuals with disabilities to lead discussions about their perceptions and thoughts would be excellent prereading activities to prepare for the reading of these books. Prereading activities can also involve asking students to skim the text and write their questions or telling students the title of the chapter and asking them to write all that they know. In addition, research on and discussion of relevant background knowledge assists the students in finding "hooks" within their thinking to facilitate memory and learning.

 Watch this video and note the ways that students use prior knowledge to prepare for new learning.

In another example, one high school teacher we observed showed students portions of the movie *Lady Sings the Blues* (the story of Billie Holliday's life) to illustrate what life was like in the South prior to the civil rights era. For their research on a history unit on the civil rights movement, students were shown video clips and involved actively in projects in which they compared life today to that before the civil rights era (Gersten, Baker, Smith-Johnson, & Dimino, 2006).

Using connections and associations from the lives of students serves the dual purpose of bringing the learners consciously and actively to the task at hand and validating their own life experiences. This addition to a lesson maximizes the amount students learn by linking new knowledge to existing knowledge. This focus on relevant background knowledge lowers anxiety and heightens motivation. Students are more interested in school and more likely to experience positive feelings toward school and themselves as learners (August & Shanahan, 2006).

Teachers can ask students for relevant background knowledge about a topic. A brainstorming session can produce student examples in association with the topic. These student-generated examples can then be used to help establish relevance to the topic. For example, when asked for a direct application of a geometry lesson in math class, students might say that it could be used to build a bridge, cut a pizza, build houses, or install a carpet. The teacher needs to plan daily activities that center around these student-generated applications of knowledge (Graves & Rueda, 2010).

 Watch this video and list the cultural connections in the context of language experiences.

In a study of mathematics and middle school students of Mexican descent, Henderson and Landesman (1992) found that students had better success in mathematics when they were involved in student-formed construction companies. Each student group named its own construction company and assigned roles within. Each company was allotted $1.5 million to purchase supplies and pay the workers for the construction of a bridge. Purchases from the "school warehouse" required bookkeeping and double-checking of math skills. All math skills on the scope and sequence for middle school were encountered during the project. Students learned adult responsibilities such as budgeting, check writing, and accounting. Each company was required to file tax returns each year and budget for state and federal tax assessments.

In another example, a fifth-grade teacher presenting a math unit on fractions began by showing pieces of pie that when put together made one whole pie. On another occasion, she used a cut-up egg crate and then put it together to make a whole crate. Students talked about whether they ate eggs or pie. Students were then asked how many pieces of pie would need to be cut in their house to serve their families. The teacher further provided opportunities for students to develop knowledge of and experience with fractions by giving each student squares of material and telling them to cut their squares into five equal pieces. They were asked to survey family members about their use of fractions. They were provided with different classroom experiences, such as folding a piece of paper into four equal parts to make a card for family members or determining how many parts or chapters were in a whole book. This allowed students to develop some background knowledge by way of their own recent experiences (Gay, 2000).

Actively Involving Learners

Learning theorists and researchers from many perspectives concur that active learning produces the greatest success (Jiménez, 2003; Woolfolk, 2013). Successful learning enhances positive emotional feelings and self-esteem. When a student is highly active, greater student involvement is even more crucial for maximizing learning opportunities (Henze & Lucas, 1993). A student like with behavioral problems and learning disabilities benefits when teachers give students a number of choices to actively involve them in the learning process. A teacher can use routine questioning, small-group and cooperative-group activities, partner and individualized sharing opportunities, and role-playing to keep students physically active and involved in their learning. Teachers who actively engage students meaningfully often are more successful than teachers who do not (Jiménez & Gersten, 1999). Successful teachers ask many questions, including many high-level questions, of all students (Linan-Thompson, Cirino, & Vaughn, 2007). Approaches in which teachers ask many questions that do not have specific answers, such as instructional conversations (see Chapter 4), improve the language skills of learners and the comfort levels of students in school (August & Shanahan, 2006). When a teacher decides to use concise wording to define a concept such as that in the lesson on animals that migrate, a short segment in which the students repeat "Animals that migrate move from place to place" is recommended. Such segments are likely to facilitate memory and long-term use of the information. When teaching students who are learning English, the opportunity to repeat and at times rehearse terminology and sentence structure has been shown to improve English language skills.

Individualized sharing opportunities such as talking, reading, and role-playing contribute to language development in students (Genesee et al., 2006). Teachers can use segments of time for individualized sharing. For example, in a high school class of 30, three students a day are asked to present 5-minute oral reports. In two weeks, each student in the class will have presented a report and the teacher will have used only 15 minutes of the 50-minute period each day.

Some excellent tools for promoting physical learning are manipulatives for teaching math (for instance, Popsicle sticks or dice). An example not as obvious is the use of a timeline for teaching history. Students can learn to understand a timeline by charting their own lives. After timelines are introduced, students can mark the time period being studied in the history lessons.

Personal timelines can be displayed in the classroom, and the historical timeline can be displayed on a larger scale and updated regularly. Other examples of techniques that can keep students actively involved in a history lesson are role-playing, displaying actual objects from a historical time period, and videotaped reenactments.

Using Alternate Grouping Strategies

Partner sharing, peer tutoring, and cooperative grouping are important activities in which students can participate and feel valued (Chambers et al., 2006; Greenwood, Arreaga-Mayer, Utley, Gavin, & Terry, 2001). However, several researchers advise that alternative grouping should be approached with caution (Beaumont, 1999; Greenwood et al., 2001). One strength of partner sharing and cooperative grouping is the engaging nature of the activities. Students of different cultural and academic backgrounds work together. Another strength is that teachers can pair individuals who have different academic strengths so that students can learn from each other. Partner sharing and cooperative grouping can guarantee an equal opportunity for all to participate actively. Peer tutoring works best when structured and thus requires careful planning by the teacher. Specific and pointed instruction can be provided by peer tutors, and both the tutors and students often show academic benefits from their interaction. (See Greenwood et al. [2001] for a full review.) Cooperative groups promote problem solving by allowing students to share among themselves (Arreaga-Mayer, 1998; Klingner & Vaughn, 1996; Slavin, 2004).

Teachers typically structure cooperative group activities so students know exactly what is expected, how much time they have to complete a task, and the exact role for each member of the group. For a history lesson called "Looking at the Revolution from Different Points of View," the teacher divided students into cooperative groups. Each group represented a different cultural element in America. The cooperative groups (Native American, African American, Spanish, French, English, and Loyalists) considered how their assigned cultures felt about the Revolutionary War. The teacher indicated that the group designated as Native Americans reported pro-independence attitudes. The group thought independence would allow the Native Americans to make their own laws and to be free again. The students were able to think like eighteenth-century Native Americans without letting the actual historical events affect their answers. Regarding grouping, teachers can choose many different grouping structures during instruction to maximize active involvement and success (Reyes, 1992). Rigid, consistent ability grouping is not recommended. Research, however, indicates that forming small groups of students with similar needs can be very beneficial (Reyes, 1992). When all the students in a group need the same information but the instruction requires more teacher attention than can be offered in a large group, the teacher can choose small-group instruction. Teachers can often save time by grouping three to nine students together. Each small student group recites the same information at once, and the teacher can efficiently monitor performance. The teacher can usually provide more active student involvement in small groups by asking individualized questions and requiring group responses. When compared to large-group instruction, the teacher can move at a faster pace and provide more individual attention within a small group. Continually changing student groups should prevent any stigmas associated with fixed-group structure.

Recent studies and theory about practice yield a reiteration and support for the previous work cited above. In the context of a response-to-intervention framework as discussed in Chapters 1 and 7, Tier 2 intervention can provide small-group intensive instruction for added support in literacy, math, or behavior management (Graves, Brandon, Duesbery, McIntosh, & Pyle, 2011; Graves, Duesbery, Pyle, Brandon, & McIntosh, 2011; Klingner, Artilles, & Barletta, 2006; Linan-Thompson, Cirino, & Vaughn, 2007).

Providing Native-Language Support

When a student's native language is included in the classroom, students learn that their languages are respected and valued. The students, in turn, tend to feel respected and valued because their native languages and cultures are recognized (Howard, Sugarman, Christian, Lindholm-Leary, & Rogers, 2007; Jiménez, 2003). Respect for and utilization of a student's native language and culture are integral to responsive teaching and can improve the transfer and comprehension skills necessary for learning a new language (August & Shanahan, 2006; Chang, 2004; Grant & Gomez, 2001). In addition, development and engagement of native language skills allow for students to draw on the skills they have already acquired.

A case study shows how a limited-Spanish-speaking science teacher became a role model for English learners. The teacher spoke Spanish with his pupils to demonstrate the value he placed on the learners' native language and became a role model regarding the learning of a new language (Pease-Alvarez & Winsler, 1994). Although his knowledge of Spanish was quite limited, he sought help from students in using Spanish properly. He taught all the scientific terms in the lesson in both Spanish and English. Each class started with a Spanish translation of the key vocabulary for the topic. Students responded well to this teacher, and their English skills improved.

The important benefit of Ole method was described earlier in this chapter (Graves, Valles, & Rueda, 2000). Based on a writing-as-a-process model, Ole is unique in that it allows students to read and write native language that they find important and that they produce themselves. The inclusion of publishing perfect final copies of their spoken language that has been converted into written language yields a mechanism for literacy development in native language, if that is deemed appropriate for the student. This creates an opportunity to integrate personal language knowledge and experiences into the broader framework of written Spanish and English. Saunders and Goldenberg (1999) found that when beginning writers are encouraged to write journal entries in their native languages, the writers are more comfortable in school and gain English skills faster than those who do not have native-language opportunities for writing.

In another situation, a history teacher provided key words about the Pilgrims and Thanksgiving in both Spanish and English (Hornberger & Michaeu, 1993). She conducted a discussion in which she wrote the key words in both languages (for example, Thanksgiving = Día de Gracias) to facilitate understanding and interest. In terms of communication skills and academic progress in English, native-language instruction seems to improve the performance of students. Sioux children receiving weekly instruction in their tribal language outperformed students who did not (Franklin & Thompson, 1994). In this school, tribal members came to assist teachers with the delivery of instruction. The students who received the native-language instruction participated for several hours a week. When compared to other Sioux students who had not received native-language instruction, those who received native-language instruction learned more English and did better in school.

Teachers who are not fluent in languages other than English have numerous sources for assistance and support. Other school personnel and community members can assist even when multiple languages are represented in a class (Graves & Rueda, 2008; McIntosh et al., 2007). There are a number of ways to incorporate native languages in the classroom when the teacher does not speak a language other than English (Graves, Gersten, & Haager, 2004). The teacher can use bilingual dictionaries, library books in native languages, or ask students, other teachers, or the school staff for help. Students can assist or tutor other students, ask questions or write in the native language, and interact socially with students to learn more language (Lucas & Katz, 1994). An excellent source of native-language help is parents. Parents can communicate with other parents in the native language, encourage other parents to read to the students in the native language, and volunteer in the classroom to provide additional native-language interaction.

One monolingual teacher found a useful way to show value and respect for native languages while also empowering students. The teacher organized a Translation and Bridging Committee of students in grades 2 through 6. The committee was responsible for preparing notes for parents and programs for school assemblies in Tagalog and Spanish. This gave students a sense of pride about the role of their native languages in the school environment.

Focusing on Content and Activities That Are Meaningful to Students Both Emotionally and Culturally

Theories about language acquisition generally support native-language instruction to facilitate underlying academic proficiency. The instruction can later be "transferred in" and applied to English language learning (August & Shanahan, 2006; Baca & Cervantes, 2004; Chang, 2004; Jiménez, 2003). However, native-language instruction is not always available in schools (Aguila, 2010). To help native-language speakers, teachers can create a nonthreatening atmosphere where students can share information about their own cultural and ethnic backgrounds. For example, the teacher can arrange partner sharing and cooperative group activities to facilitate feelings of safety and comfort. The students in each group can learn how problems are solved or how stories are told within each unique cultural and linguistic perspective.

Gonzalez, Moll, and Amanti (2005) write extensively about the value of the "funds" of knowledge that students bring to the classroom from their own experiences. These funds of knowledge can be tapped through daily journal entries. The knowledge the teacher gains about the students should be incorporated into lessons and coursework. For example, in an American history lesson on the design of the first American flag, students can be instructed to draw a picture of any flag with which they are familiar. They can be assigned to study and draw flags representing their countries of origin for either themselves or for family members. This might also be a good parent-involvement activity; parents might be asked to bring in or send in a real flag or to draw pictures of the flags of their countries of origin. Activities like these may foster an environment that is inclusive and comfortable for students from diverse cultural backgrounds, including those who may have disabilities.

 Watch this video and think about how you might learn about the cultures of your students. Why is this important?

Another type of cultural diversity is disability culture. Students with disabilities could be culturally recognized in study of chapter books such as *Freak the Mighty* (Philbrick, 1993) or the sequel, *Max the Mighty* (Philbrick, 1998) as mentioned earlier in this chapter. The themes of self-reliance and self-determination in the context of disabilities are essential to the successful transition of all students to post-secondary life. Recognition of personal culture is also critically important for all students to reflect upon. This helps students understand and avoid perspectives such as ableism and the damage of this way of thinking to individual empowerment.

Creating Roles in the Classroom for Family and Community Members

The celebration of cultural and linguistic diversity in the schools is not likely to feel authentic to parents and community members until a comfortable place is created for the families of all students (Baca & Cervantes, 2004; Gay, 2000; Goldenberg, Gallimore, Reese, & Garnier, 2001). Teachers must establish relationships with family members and should invite families to serve in the classroom. Family members in the classroom might help students learn about other cultures and can serve as role models for all students (Torres-Burgo, Reyes-Wasson, & Brusca-Vega, 1999). In one class, a parent who claimed to have made more than 100 piñatas was asked to guide a piñata art project. Classroom service does not have to be culturally specific, though. It is designed to bring parents and community members into the class on a regular basis to provide a multiplicity of cultural leadership. For example, any parent could be asked to share life experiences or job-related experiences (Hildebrand, Phenice, Gray, & Hines, 2000). Parents and family members can be encouraged to volunteer for many different roles in the classroom. Volunteers can read stories to students or work with small groups. They can help students with science projects or memorizing math facts or participate in field trips. Parents or community members with special skills can speak or teach in class. For example, one teacher invited a father who works on a fishing boat to speak to the class about ocean animals. The student assisted his father with English and they worked together to present fish stories and pictures to the class. In another example, a fifth-grade teacher planned a unit entitled "Viva San Diego." The teacher invited parents to participate. Each student was to pick an area of the city he or she wanted to learn more about, such as Balboa Park or San Diego State University. Students and parents were to do research and to visit their chosen areas to learn as much as they could about them. In the end, each student wrote a report and made a model of the area selected. All of these models and reports were displayed in the school showcase.

Family Literacy Nights

Recommendations from the National Literacy Panel (August & Shanahan, 2006) point to the importance of family involvement in education and the important roles that families play in the development of literacy. Ji Mei Chang (2004) describes a research project that aimed to establish an after-school support group for low-achieving Asian American English learners in middle school. Teachers and parents participated to assist students in the sheltered instruction program by attending workshops and forming a support team. The teams were composed of general education, special education, and English-language development teachers and parents. After a year of inservices, "Family Literacy Nights" were launched. The goals of the project were (Chang, 2004) (1) for students to use classroom knowledge at home; (2) to use activity teams of peers, parents, and teachers to complete projects at home that are similar to projects received in the classroom; (3) to use teams to gain knowledge through various methods of teaching and learning like vocabulary development and role-playing; (4) to have parents create lists for supervising student learning at home.

Parents were taught to follow strategies for home use developed by Chang (2001) in her work at the Center for Research on Education, Diversity & Excellence (see: www.cal .org/crede/pubs/ResBrief9.htm). They are paraphrased here.

1. Help your child produce what she really knows.
2. Model language used at home and in school.
3. Provide opportunities to use new vocabulary words at home.
4. Help your child relate what was learned in school to home each day.
5. Give positive feedback.
6. Help your child think of questions and see how ideas and concepts are related.

7. Talk about lifelong learning.
8. Value your child's abilities in multiple ways; help your child learn through multiple paths.

The Colorín Colorado website (http://www.colorincolorado.org) offers free online information for bilingual families who seek resources for reading and language activities at home. The recommendations are for parents to sing to, talk to, read to, and encourage their children, to honor their gift of two languages, and it provides suggestions for books to read. The website also recommends strategies for ways parents can build strong relationships with teachers.

Holding High Expectations for All Learners

Research over the past 20 years consistently indicates the importance of holding high expectations for learners (Artilles et al., 2002; August & Shanahan, 2006; Baca & Cervantes, 2004). However, Treuba, Jacobs, and Kirton's research (1990) showed that high school English teachers had low expectations of Latino students. The teachers interviewed felt that Latino students were incapable of completing higher-level projects. As part of an experiment, the teachers assigned students higher-level projects with topics relevant to their own lives. The students conducted authentic research from their own experiences and from the community. The results of the experiment indicated that they could complete high-quality projects. Trueba and colleagues (1990) concluded that Latino students could produce relatively high-level work when they understood the connection between schoolwork and out-of-school experiences. August and Shanahan (2006) point to practices that have the effect of lowered expectations for English learners and the problems associated with those practices such as lowered self-esteem and increased dropout rates among Latino students. In order to create an environment with high expectations for all learners, teachers must make a concerted effort to challenge all students at the highest levels.

The Common Core State Standards and college and career readiness standards in other states emphasize text complexity and language, increased emphasis on building knowledge from informational text, and an expectation that students will produce and use evidence in text to justify their views (Santos, Darling-Hammond, & Cheuk, 2013). This is an example of a task that promotes critical thinking and the higher expectations of the Common Core. The newly adopted standards' focus on meaningful activities, problem-based learning, and the enhancement of critical thinking creates higher expectations for all learners. An example of a project that one tenth-grade history teacher assigned was to create a PowerPoint® presentation on one of the *caudillos* of South and Central America. Teams of students were to select one caudillo by a certain date to assure that each team selected a different caudillo. Students were to find all the information they could about the particular caudillo, making sure to find at least one primary source, three library sources, and only one Internet source, but not an encyclopedia-type source. Students were to write their own version of history in the context of a PowerPoint® about their caudillo. One group prepared their PowerPoint® on Jos Monagas of Venezuela. Students were instructed to include information about the timeframe, politics, economics, society, and religious influences at the time. Given a week to prepare and two meetings with the teacher, each team of students created wonderful and very creative PowerPoints® that were very informative.

In another example, to create high expectations of students, a fourth-grade teacher set a goal to ask each student a higher-order question at least once a week. The teacher composed at least six higher-order questions for each 50-minute period. He kept a box containing each student's name on a piece of paper and drew five names from the box each day. He wrote those names on the board and checked them off as he asked each student one of the higher-order questions. The names drawn one day were taken from the box so that the remaining names for the next days of the week were those of students who had not yet been asked questions. The questions were not necessarily asked in succession but were spread throughout the period, coupled with different parts of the plan for the day.

Students are more likely to perform well when asked and expected to answer higher-order questions. For example, one middle school science teacher designated a weekly problem solver for the classroom. Any class problem during the week was assigned to the problem solver. The problem solver could work independently or use a self-selected committee. Students responded well to the responsibility and to their new roles in the classroom. One week, the student problem solver was faced with a situation in which the teacher had scheduled a field trip to the beach as part of a marine biology unit, but the school could not supply enough adult supervision. The field trip was not approved. The principal told the teacher that if the class members obtained adult supervision, the class could still make the trip. The student of the week proposed sending notes home to all the parents and to community members asking for supervisors for the field trip. The effort was entirely student initiated, and the notes were handwritten by the problem solver and her committee. The students were successful in obtaining enough adult supervision, and the field trip was approved. The students were pleased with their efforts and their new responsibilities in the classroom.

Teachers can create challenging environments for students by arranging activities in which the students form collaborative or cooperative problem-solving groups. For example, during the unit on marine biology, the science teacher asked a student group to list how they thought an oil spill had affected sea life. The teacher then had the students pair off and write reports on how an oil spill would affect grey whales.

Being Responsive to Cultural and Personal Diversity

Teachers have a responsibility to promote cross-cultural understanding throughout the school (Baca & Cervantes, 2004; Gay, 2000; Harry & Klingner, 2005; Jimenez, 2003; Pang, 2001). Students from ethnolinguistically diverse backgrounds may have experienced ignorance, prejudice, or disrespect, and also may have been targets of abuse. A teacher plays an important role in promoting a positive social climate at school. Schoolwide implementation of rules for appropriate ways of interacting in a democratic, pluralistic community is essential. Rules created with student input and facilitated by student mediators can enhance students' understanding of democratic processes. School personnel and teachers must conscientiously provide classrooms and school grounds where learning and respect are primary values. Successful teachers know each of their students and take an active interest in them. For example, a sixth-grade teacher of students who were designated as English learners was also the faculty advisor for the Homework Club. The teacher encouraged students from all cultural and linguistic groups to join the Homework Club. During the daily lunchtime meetings, the students were allowed to eat lunch, play music, and receive help with their homework. The teacher created a safe atmosphere for fun and learning. Parents could attend the meetings as well.

In their work on learning environments for English learners, Jong, Harper, and Coady (2013) concluded that teachers of English learners need enhanced expertise. They describe this expertise along three primary dimensions: (1) understanding English learners from a bilingual and bicultural perspective; (2) understanding how language and culture shape school experiences and inform pedagogy for bilingual learners; and (3) having the ability to mediate a range of contextual factors in the schools and classrooms where they teach. Added to this is the layer of empowerment that teachers may be able to create for all students, by incorporating opportunities for self-reliance and self-determination as they learn content information in school.

These dimensions need to be present in each teacher. A good example of this is a high school teacher of students who were in sheltered English classes. She spent time in class explaining campus activities and assisting the students in filling out applications for campus programs and activities. The teacher became an advocate for the students by ensuring decisions about campus clubs, programs, and after-school activities were fairly made. This seemed to help students feel as much a part of school as everyone else. When the students learned that the teacher was their ally and that she was always facilitating their participation in school activities, students were more motivated to learn from her. From time to time in class, this teacher would raise questions about school issues that may have involved prejudice or stereotyping. She encouraged open discussions in which students were challenged to think about interpersonal conflicts from a variety of perspectives. The teacher wanted the students to understand that actions have consequences. They were encouraged to see the benefits of nonviolent, logical, problem solving when interpersonal conflicts arise.

Summary

This chapter discussed the importance of promoting affective and cultural connections through various means. It is important to understand that affective issues enhance the learning capabilities of English learners and any student who may be struggling in school, including those with identified disabilities. Students that are identified as struggling or identified with disabilities must be considered when arranging the classroom environment. Teachers should provide emotional support and encourage students with their progress.

Specifically, as a reader you

- Discussed the principles of setting up a successful reading and writing instructional environment.
- Identified the important considerations for emotional and motivational support to second-language learners.
- Demonstrated an understanding of the purpose of native-language instruction and the potential benefits it has for students.
- Listed four examples of cultural and emotional support of the individual differences of students and their families.

ACTIVITIES

1. Outline ways in which a teacher might help a student with behavioral problems and learning difficulties feel like a vital and respected member of his class.

2. Interview someone for whom English is not a first language. Probe deeply into the types of school experiences he or she has had. In particular, inquire about any desirable school experiences. Ask the person about the 10 recommendations for teachers in this chapter.

3. Ponder the following statement made by a teacher: "I tried to learn Spanish in college, but it's just too difficult. I don't know how anyone learns to speak a second language." With a classmate or in a small group, discuss the ramifications for students and teachers if this type of statement is acceptable. Discuss the ramifications for students and teachers if this type of statement is unacceptable.

4. Suppose Cambodian American and Vietnamese American students were engaging in physical fights at school. What are some possible strategies for resolving problems between the groups and fostering nonviolent interactions?

5. Plan a Family Literacy Nights Program for your school. List three topics for discussion with parents. Plan a series of steps for parents to follow with students during homework completion.

6. Describe how Common Core State Standards or revised standards in your state are different from the standards for history, language arts, math, and science (you can choose just one content area) from 5 years ago.

Learning Strategies

LEARNING OBJECTIVES:

- Define the term *learning strategy* and delineate types of learning strategies.
- Present examples of specific strategies for reading, writing, and content areas that you think would be useful when teaching. State why they might be useful.
- Restate the guidelines for selecting learning strategies.
  - Explain why these guidelines are important.
- Describe five implementation considerations when teaching learning strategies.

Sheltered instruction is a process by which subject matter instruction is made more meaningful and accessible to English learners. As Chapter 3 indicates, effective sheltered lessons include many features, and while every content lesson may not include all features, teachers need to incorporate each feature into weekly planning and instruction. For example, use of higher-order thinking skills is an important feature of sheltered instruction that should be a part of lessons each week. In addition, learning strategy instruction may be a part of the daily planning and instruction cycle depending on the needs of the students.

 Watch this video clarifying the difference between instructional and learning strategies. Summarize the difference between the two.

Monkey Business/Fotolia

Teachers must be sensitive to the fact that English learners have extraordinary cognitive burdens when learning new information in English. Students with learning and behavioral challenges also experience cognitive overload when learning new information. Hence, English learners with learning and behavioral difficulties can have exceedingly taxing cognitive burdens when instruction is in English. Students can be so overwhelmed by the process of deriving meaning from a second language that they do not spontaneously generate the strategies needed for efficient and effective learning (Lee, 1986; Ortiz & Graves, 2001; Yang, 1999). Teachers can facilitate learning by directly teaching strategies. Explicit instruction of learning strategies increases the comfort and learning potential of students needing support, and it has a long history of research supporting its efficacy in the fields of educational psychology, special education, and general education, including instruction of English learners (August & Shanahan, 2006; Dutro & Kinsella, 2012; Fitzgerald & Graves, 2004; Gersten, Taylor, & Graves, 1999; Graham & Harris, 2005; Graves, Gersten, & Haager, 2004; Vaughn, Wanzek, Murray, Scammacca, Linan-Thompson, & Woodruff, 2009). Those students needing learning-strategies instruction often have content-area, academic, and English-language development issues. They present learning challenges and require language-sensitive instruction (Baca & Cervantes, 2004; Jiménez & Gersten, 1999; McIntosh, Graves, & Gersten, 2007). Language-sensitive instruction focuses simultaneously on developing content-area knowledge, academic proficiency, and English-language proficiency (Gersten, Baker, Haager, & Graves, 2005; Jiménez, 2003).

*T*ypes of Learning Strategies

A learning strategy is a series of steps that can be repeated numerous times to solve a problem or to complete a task. Some students develop learning strategies on their own. Obviously, the teacher would not teach these students strategies explicitly. Instead, he or she should simply encourage them to use the effective strategies that they have developed spontaneously. However, if a student is not spontaneously generating the strategy and is struggling to succeed in a given learning or behavioral situation, strategies must be explicitly taught. The goal for all the students in learning any strategy is to be able to independently use it as soon as possible. The teacher's goal is always to give students a "fishing pole," not a fish, that is, to empower them to be self-sufficient in post-secondary pursuits.

There is a long history of the use of learning strategies instruction, rooted in cognitive behavioral psychological principles (Woolfolk, 2013). Strategy instruction has been implemented as a supplemental strand of instruction when a student is struggling to access fundamental skills either behaviorally or in content areas. The issues around whether a student is labeled with a learning disability are very complex (Figueroa & Newsome, 2006; Rueda & Windmueller, 2006). In any case, the use of learning strategies instruction as a pre-referral intervention can help school personnel avoid unnecessary labeling and is critical for teachers to consider as an instructional option whenever students may be struggling to keep up or to learn new content. The learning strategy methodology can benefit English learners as well (Graves, Duesbery, Pyle, Brandon, & McIntosh, 2011).

Explicitly taught learning strategies can benefit students throughout the stages of language proficiency. Recall that the levels are (see Figure 1.7 in Chapter 1): (1) Entering, (2) Beginning, (3) Developing, (4) Expanding, (5) Bridging, and (6) Reaching. For example, students in Levels 1 and 2 are more likely to need vocabulary development strategies such as the four-square strategy where students divide a card or paper into four squares, writing the word, giving the definition, using the word in a sentence, and drawing a picture. Students in Levels 3, 4, and 5 are likely to need academic language and procedural development strategies such as finding main ideas, learning the steps of an experiment in science, and identifying the parts of an expository paragraph. Students in Levels 4, 5, and 6 are likely to need study, advanced reading comprehension, self-monitoring, and other advanced strategies.

A teacher can formulate and explicitly teach strategies when students do not develop them on their own. To adapt the strategies to language proficiency levels, students in Level 1 and Level 2 have emerging skills, students in Level 3 and Level 4 have expanding skills, and students in Levels 5 and 6 have advanced or bridging skills. With knowledge of student levels gained from assessment, teachers can adapt the instruction accordingly. For example, for the English Language Arts, Common Core State Standard, Reading Level is equivalent to grade level—Reading Level 3.9: "Compare and contrast the most important points and key details presented in two texts on the same topic." In this case the teacher would assess students to determine if this skill is already known. For those who have not mastered the ability to compare and contrast two texts, the teacher would work on differentiated instruction driven first by language proficiency level. If students are emerging, the teacher may recommend the use of native language demonstrations as well as a visual support such as a Venn diagram while he or she provides a model. For those whose skills are expanding in Levels 3 and 4, depending on the individual profiles, the teacher may conclude that explicit strategy instruction with detailed specific steps to follow would benefit the students most. However, this type of scaffolding would be phased out as the students become more self-reliant and independent in the comparing and contrasting tasks. Finally, for more advanced students, applications in the context of text analysis would be appropriate.

Strategies enhancing academic and English proficiency can improve the reading, writing, language, or math work of students (August & Shanahan, 2006; Vaughn et al., 2009). For example, finding main ideas is a reading strategy important to academic proficiency that is useful in many different learning situations (see Figure 6.1). Consider a student who seems lost when reading and writing tasks assigned in a history course. For him and other students like him, reading comprehension strategies can be very helpful for developing academic proficiency. A learning strategy such as one to assist students in "finding main ideas" can benefit a student in all pursuits involving reading.

Your Turn

Think of a student with an "expanding" level of language proficiency who has not been able to spontaneously generate reading comprehension strategies. Design a "compare and contrast" strategy with appropriate adaptations for this student's language level.

FIGURE 6.1 Science Strategy: Steps for an Experiment

Step 1: Write or state the purpose of the experiment and the expected outcome(s).
Step 2: Gather materials.
Step 3: Write a summary of the procedures.
Step 4: Carry out the experiment (observe and take notes).
Step 5: Write exact results.
Step 6: Discuss and summarize expectations versus actual results and what the results mean.

To use learning strategies in thinking, reading, and writing in content-area work, teachers can provide a mini-lesson (about 15 minutes daily) on the strategy (Ellis & Graves, 1990). Mini-lessons allow students to learn the strategy in a controlled practice situation during a designated period of time. Teachers can provide opportunities to memorize and use the strategy during a practice session before requiring strategy use in a content-area application. Learning strategies can be developed not only for academics but also for language acquisition and many other areas, such as social skills and vocational skills. Learning strategies are not a curriculum. Instead, strategies are used as a part of the curriculum to enhance access to content, academic, or life skills proficiency. Strategies enhancing access to content are used in literature, science, social studies, and math classes and facilitate gaining knowledge. For example, knowing the steps for writing about an experiment is a science strategy taught at the beginning of the school year. It should increase the knowledge a student gains from science lessons (see Figure 6.2). The science strategy can be reused for future science work and can be employed as a general problem-solving method if students are instructed on how to use it systematically (Lee & Buxton, 2013).

Strategies can enhance language acquisition and second-language listening and thinking skills. Such learning strategies provide a series of steps to integrate language knowledge and content knowledge (Brown & Doolittle, 2008; Cloud, Genessee, & Hamayan, 2009; Fitzgerald & Graves, 2004; Gersten, Taylor, & Graves, 1999; Herrell, 2000; Jiménez, 2003; Jiménez, García, & Pearson, 1996). For example, the use-of-cognates strategy has five steps (see Figure 6.3). Other language-acquisition strategies can be used to think back and forth between languages and to help focus thinking while listening (Fitzgerald, 2003; Klinger, Artilles, & Barletta, 2006). These mini-lessons with a skills focus could also work well in the context of the Response-to-Intervention or tiered model where this fits for Tier 2 or Tier 3 instruction (see Chapter 1 for more details on this).

In addition, for students who are struggling with behavior problems or other issues related to conduct in school, social skills strategies and interpersonal strategies can be taught as early as preschool to assist these students in learning how to get along with peers and teachers. For example, in social situations, students can be taught the series of steps necessary to solve a social problem (see Figure 6.4). As students mature, the life skills strategies they are taught could relate more to community- or work-related

FIGURE 6.2 Use-of-Cognates Strategy
....

Step 1: Read the unfamiliar word in English.
Step 2: Note the spelling of the word.
Step 3: Think of a word that looks or sounds like the English word, a cognate, in your primary language.
Step 4: Think of what that cognate means in your primary language.
Step 5: Guess at the meaning of the unfamiliar word in English.

FIGURE 6.3 Finding Main Ideas
....

Step 1: Read the paragraph.
Step 2: Decide what the whole paragraph is about.
Step 3: Note a few details as well.
Step 4: Check to make sure you have the best answer (the answer that tells what the whole paragraph is about).
Step 5: Reread and start over if you are not sure.
Step 6: If you are sure, write the main idea of the paragraph.

Step 1: Say the problem.
Step 2: Keep a calm body (count to 10).
Step 3: Think of three possible solutions.
Step 4: Decide which is the best solution and do it.
Step 5: Use positive self-talk afterward, telling yourself you did the best you could.

situations. Learning social skills is very important for all students as they progress through school and pursue adult activities. Life skills strategies enhance proficiency in social, vocational, and transition skills. Enhanced proficiency in these areas improves the interpersonal skills and job-related abilities of students and prepares them for the future.

Examples of Specific Strategies in the Content Areas

In a study in the San Diego schools, nine multiple-language, first-grade classroom teachers were observed and rated (Gersten et al., 2005). Their students were assessed on oral reading fluency as part of a small battery of assessments (Graves, Gersten, & Haager, 2004; Graves, Plasencia-Peinado, Deno, & Johnson, 2005). The classrooms were very diverse; for example, in one room, there were five Spanish speakers, seven Somali speakers, three Cambodian speakers, two Hmong speakers, and three Vietnamese speakers. Teachers in these classrooms were compelled to teach in English because it provided common ground for all of the students. Native-language instruction was a logistical impossibility. Results of this study indicated extremely positive ratings for two teachers, and predictably, those teachers' students earned the highest outcome scores on oral reading fluency. Moderately strong correlations ($r = .65$) were found between student outcomes in oral reading fluency at the end of first grade and teacher ratings. Similar patterns were found between English learners and non-English learners in rate and mastery of English reading. These results are similar to those found by others (Chiappe, Siegel, & Wade-Wolley, 2002; Geva, Yaghoub-Zadeh, & Schuster, 2000; Haager & Windmueller, 2001).

Both teachers demonstrated a skill for maximizing time on task, amount of work produced, time spent reading, appropriate length for teaching segments, specialized small-group instruction, structured daily routines, consistent homework assignments, daily writing tasks, assessment of reading and writing progress, and English-as-a-second language development. Written work was corrected on a daily basis, and students were often required to self-correct errors. Both teachers had amassed multiple sets of decodable texts and used them regularly to enhance student reading. Students had their own boxes of books at their desks, including books of different genres and reading levels, but at least 50 percent of the books in each student's box were at his or her own level of decoding.

Your Turn

Imagine that you are teaching students who are non-readers. What are the kinds of steps you could take to create a learning environment that is appropriate for the literacy development of English learners?

Mara, the teacher who received the highest score (3.75), used a structured reading instruction program that included a comprehensive curriculum with special emphasis on phonological awareness and phonics. She appeared to enjoy the challenge of following the linear scope and sequence that the reading series provided along with structured lesson plans. She tended to be quite systematic in her approach to teaching language arts, including consistent assessment and remediation for low performers. Dana, who also received a very high score (3.5), tended to teach reading by pulling materials from many sources of many eclectic origins. She used leveled readers and assigned students to homogeneous small groups that met on a regular basis, and she was diligent about assessment of reading and writing progress. The scope and sequence she used was part of an oral tradition that she can talk about when interviewed but for which she does not have an exact written source. Because she does not use a specific reading series, her activities and segments of instruction are often unique and draw from a range of sources. She was observed delivering instruction in critical domains for reading instruction, such as phonological awareness, phonics, concepts about print, spelling, writing, comprehension, and critical thinking. She is particularly skilled at comprehension questions related to reading material and critical thinking. Videotaped interviews and observations of the two teachers indicated that both teachers use sheltered techniques and considered affective issues, as outlined in Chapters 4 and 5 of this book.

Teaching Reading Strategies in Content-Area Classes

This section contains a series of classroom observations of teachers providing instruction to English language learners (Graves, 1998). To illustrate good reading strategy instruction, three classroom observations are presented. First, in the context of teaching a unit on coastal Native American tribes, a sixth-grade teacher with a number of English learners in the class taught the concept of finding main ideas. Similarly, a seventh-grade science teacher taught the compare-and-contrast technique as part of a unit on ecosystems. Finally, an eighth-grade history teacher taught about using a timeline for note taking while beginning a unit on the colonial period. Notice that in each case, the teacher is blending the implementation of the strategies into a cognitively and motivationally appropriate unit or content area. The strategies become one part of the unit and are often a strand of instruction that continues from one unit to another. That is, if students are learning a strategy to facilitate finding main ideas, they may need continued practice into the next content unit in the subject area.

 Watch this video of content area strategy instruction. Apply its use to something you are teaching.

The sixth-grade teacher started the Native American tribes unit in social studies by showing pictures of coastal tribes and recovered artifacts. The teacher also read some information about various tribes. As part of the effort to teach reading comprehension explicitly while covering content, the teacher established a small group for about a 15-minute segment of instruction based on informal student assessments. The teacher occasionally works with various small groups of students to develop reading or writing skills for short, targeted segments of time. An example of the way this instruction might proceed is for the teacher to display a simple paragraph about a Native American tribe that has a definite main idea and give each student a copy of the paragraph (see Figure 6.5). Visual modeling of finding main ideas is critical to ensure student success. On the first lesson with the small group, the teacher taught main ideas explicitly. He said, "A main

FIGURE 6.5 Finding the Main Idea

109

CHAPTER 6

Learning Strategies

The Chumash once flourished on the southern coast of California. They traveled back and forth between the mainland and the Channel Islands, which are just off the coast. They fished and grew crops for food. The artifacts that they left behind let us know that the most important animal to the Chumash was the dolphin. They made many picture stories in caves and on rocks that include dolphins. War with the Spanish conquistadors and others caused the decline of this great people.

idea tells what the whole paragraph is about. It does not tell what part of the paragraph is about, but it tells what the whole paragraph is about. Watch me as I read this paragraph and decide what the whole paragraph is about." He continued, "Ask yourself if you know the main idea. If you do, make a check at the bottom. If not, go back and reread."

The series of steps used by the teacher was based on research demonstrating the effectiveness of the explicit strategy instruction when teaching reading and writing (Graves, 1986; Graves & Levin, 1989). On subsequent days, the teacher and the students found main ideas together following a series of explicit steps, with the teacher engaging in modeling and prompting to promote student success. The students then worked alone and started to develop confidence and competence. Each day, the students looked pleased with their success. The teacher learned that students who were taught explicitly and then given a range of practice opportunities learned faster and were able to use the skills mastered longer. Later in the year, the students used their strategy for finding the main idea to write reports about what they were reading.

A seventh-grade science teacher had students construct freshwater and saltwater aquariums for a unit on ecosystems. The students wrote reports about the aquariums before constructing them and were integrally involved in the planning and building of each aquarium. After the aquariums were completed, the students wrote about their observations and formulated hypotheses about observed changes in the aquariums.

▶ Watch this video of a science teacher setting up the learning environment to promote vocabulary knowledge, discussions among the students, and a hands-on experiment; later the students will write about their experiences. What strengths do you see for English learners in this type of approach to teaching compared to traditional didactic teaching?

The teacher combined the activities with daily mini-lessons in reading to provide strategies for increasing reading comprehension. For example, she developed a series of 15- to 20-minute segments of instruction on appropriate strategies to use when students were asked to compare. On the first day of the series of lessons, the teacher said, "Watch while I show you a way to compare two items." She drew a Venn diagram (two overlapping circles) on the board. The students were then asked to compare a seahorse to an octopus. The teacher held up a picture of each animal and taped one picture in the outside portion of each circle. She asked the students to describe each animal and made notes under the pictures in each circle. One student said a seahorse is a fish and has a head like a horse. The teacher then asked, "How are they alike?" and wrote the students' comments in the overlapping part of the circles. Students said that both animals live in the ocean, and the teacher added that females of both animals lay eggs. After this initial example, the teacher

Your Turn

Think about the types of teaching styles and describe ones that you think are most effective when students are learning English at the emerging or expanding proficiency levels.

said, "Now, in your groups, compare the freshwater ecosystem to the saltwater ecosystem." Each student group was given a large Venn diagram drawn on poster board. Each diagram had a picture of the saltwater ecosystem taped above the left circle and a picture of the freshwater ecosystem taped above the right circle. The students appeared to transfer the knowledge rapidly and learned a strategy for comparing.

An eleventh-grade history teacher used many demonstrations and visual images, such as maps, globes, graphs, charts, and timelines. To teach the students how to maximize comprehensible input while reading, the teacher demonstrated making a timeline. To provide students explicit instruction, the teacher started the unit by making a timeline of his own life from birth to that day. A personal timeline was drawn on the board with major life events entered in order. The teacher then assisted the students in constructing their own personal timelines and posted the timelines on the bulletin board. In the last 20 minutes of class, the teacher had the students read through the assigned chapter. The teacher made a historical timeline beginning with discussions of early settlements in Africa followed by northern migration of people in concert with climate changes. Students filled in a blank timeline along with the teacher as the discussion ensued. With each new chapter, the students were asked to fill in a blank timeline with the information from the chapter and to keep all the timelines together in one section of their notebooks.

Teaching Writing Strategies in Content-Area Classes

Research has yielded valuable information about teaching writing to students who are struggling in school (Englert, 2009; Graham & Harris, 2005, 2009; Graham, MacAuthur, & Fitzgerald, 2013; Graves & Montague, 1991; Ruiz, 1995a, 1995b). Good writers often use a recursive or circular process during composing (Graves, Semmel, & Gerber, 1995). Students should learn five basic writing steps:

1. Prewriting or planning
2. Composing
3. Revising
4. Editing
5. Final draft or publishing

The circle in Figure 6.6 represents writing-as-a-process, and the arrows pointing each way indicate that a writer can take any number of paths in composing. The writer could start with planning or composing, go back to revising, start composing again, and then go back to revising and editing before completing the final draft.

Writer's Workshop, developed largely by Donald Graves (1983), consists of journal writing, prewriting activities for narrative or expository compositions, the five stages described as writing-as-a-process, and sharing and publishing final drafts. Writer's Workshop is a viable approach up through sixth grade for students learning English (Graham & Harris, 2009; Graves & Rueda, 2008; Graves, Valles, & Rueda, 2000; Ruiz, 1995a, 1995b), although it can also be effective with older students who have had uneven school experiences and are poor writers. Writer's Workshop has been used extensively for students in general education as well as for students who are having problems in school (Englert, 2009; Graham & Harris, 2009; Graves, Valles, & Rueda, 2000; Ruiz, 1995a, 1995b).

Based on observations in upper elementary and secondary schools, two descriptions of classroom practices for teaching writing are presented here. A fourth-grade and a

FIGURE 6.6 Writing-as-a-Process

||||

CHAPTER 6

Learning Strategies

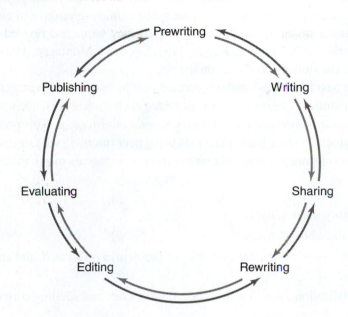

ninth-grade classroom are described. In each classroom teachers used Writer's Workshop while teaching writing to students learning English. In each of these classrooms, teachers often taught strategies and skills explicitly as a supplement to adapted versions of Writer's Workshop.

In a fourth-grade class, the teacher used explicit strategy instruction in writing. After teaching the students each step of the writing process overtly, the teacher used different colors of paper to represent the stages of writing (Englert, 2009). Planning was completed on yellow paper, the first draft was written on orange paper, and the final draft was completed on the computer or on white paper. Revising was accomplished on the orange paper by marking through and correcting spelling and punctuation. Students engaged in the process at least once a week. The students learned to start the writing process by expressing ideas. The writing process occurred in predictable stages.

The teacher consistently used about one-third of the time for writing; one-third for sharing, presenting, revising, or editing; and one-third for mini-lessons or teacher-directed learning (see Figure 6.11 on page 119). The teacher did not accomplish all three aspects each day but spent more than 1 hour each week on writing; this amount of time spent writing is supported by research (Lewis, Graves, Ashton, & Kieley, 1997). The teacher asked the students to pretend they lived at the time of the California gold rush and to write stories about their adventures. The students had 20 minutes each day during the week to complete the assignment. The teacher chose the narrative genre because students are usually comfortable with story structure. When writing in a new language, students must be comfortable with the genre. Story writing often makes history come alive for students. The teacher led a student brainstorming activity to help them get started. The students created their own story webs or outlines, drew illustrations, and wrote first drafts.

> ### Your Turn
>
> What are the critical features of writing instruction that maximize student learning?

For students floundering on the narrative story structure, the teacher used the story grammar cueing system (Graves, Montague, & Wong, 1990). The cueing system is a list of the story grammar parts (setting, characters, problem, resolution, and ending). The students were instructed to think about the parts as they wrote and revised their stories (Graham & Harris, 2009; Graves & Hauge, 1993; Graves & Montague, 1991). The cueing system required the students to reflect on the steps.

During the next lesson, the students formed peer pairs and made corrections and changes to their stories. The peer revision provided each student with abundant feedback. The teacher provided a revision format during several mini-lessons. This process could be expanded to include more formal sessions using peer tutoring (see Greenwood et al., 2001). The revision strategy included four questions for students to ask themselves about their stories:

1. Does the story make sense?
2. What do I like about the story?
3. Does the story have characters, a setting, a problem, a resolution, and an ending?
4. Is the capitalization, overall appearance, punctuation, and spelling correct?

The students needed a significant amount of time to complete the assignment. Teacher intervention was necessary to ensure accomplishment. At the end of the week, the students wrote final drafts on the computer and created a class book. The book was shared with the other fourth-grade classes and was given to the school library as a gift.

A ninth-grade English teacher noted that her students were struggling with writing expository material. She decided to use a think-aloud modeling procedure to teach report writing. As the teacher read to the students about the colonial tradition of Thanksgiving, she modeled the note-taking process. After the reading and note-taking lesson, the teacher taught the five-paragraph essay strategy and gave the students a handout with the format of that strategy specified (see Figure 6.7). The format called for an introductory paragraph, three supporting paragraphs, and a concluding paragraph. The teacher then modeled essay writing by using the format to think aloud about a topic. The students were encouraged to make comments and suggestions during the construction of the outline by the group. If students were each assigned a role, this could be set up as cooperative learning (Chambers, Cheung, Madden, Stavin, & Gifford, 2006). Finally, the teacher talked with students about the accuracy and logic of the outline.

After demonstrating the outlining process on the topic of Thanksgiving, the teacher once again modeled report writing by actually composing a paragraph based on the notes. Welcoming student participation, the teacher made sure to follow the steps designated for an expository paragraph. As the students needed a great deal of the practice, the teacher also had them work together in table groups and to write reports. Much writing practice involves the teacher actively implementing assignments on a weekly basis to elicit writing. One fun writing assignment was for students to work in a group to write about famous people in colonial history, such as Pocahontas, John Smith, and Miles Standish. For 20 minutes each day over the course of a week, each group completed five tasks: reading together while taking notes on orange paper, preparing an outline on pink paper, preparing a first draft on yellow paper, editing the first draft, and entering a final draft into the computer at the end of the week. During the next week, the groups shared their reports with the rest of the class. The students'

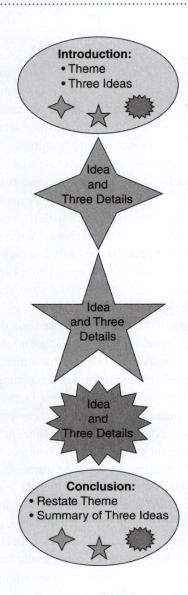

writing quality was good compared to work done before they had been exposed to the essay strategy and the writing-as-a-process strategy.

Guidelines for Selecting a Learning Strategy

Students can learn strategies that provide maximum benefits and that can be used in a multiplicity of settings. The following guidelines can assist teachers in determining the strategies most beneficial to students. First, determine the exact knowledge or proficiency level of the student. Second, determine the strategies the student would be likely to use the most. Third, consider teaching the simplest and most useful strategies first, and introduce them in an order that reflects the content curriculum and proficiency goals for the year. Finally, use simple wording and the fewest number of steps when teaching each strategy.

Determine Levels of Knowledge and Language Proficiency

Teachers are concerned about students' levels of content knowledge and academic and language proficiency (Espin, Scierka, Skare, & Halverson, 1999). A teacher must determine the level of knowledge students possess in literature, math, science, or social studies and then mold instruction to fit what the students do or do not know. The teacher can use information assessment to determine the current reading, studying, and computational skills of students and then teach accordingly. Based on the informal assessment phase, the teacher can construct new materials or use existing materials to test students. The tests may be traditional or nontraditional. For example, a nontraditional test might ask students to choose a book and read a few pages out loud. From the test, the teacher can gather baseline information on reading skills, reading level, and reading comprehension. Examples of tests that provide valuable performance information on basic skills include the Diagnostic Indicators of Basic Early Literacy Skills (Good & Kaminski, 1996) and Curriculum-Based Measurement (Deno, 1985; Espin et al., 1999; Graves, Plasencia-Peinado, Deno, & Johnson, 2005). The tests allow the teacher to determine what students know and to figure out what to teach. Strategies may be part of the curriculum. For example, if at the beginning of the year the teacher finds that history students do not know the steps needed for making an outline, the teacher might teach everyone a strategy for outlining. If the teacher determines that students have difficulty writing an expository paragraph, he or she might explain the steps for writing a paragraph and provide a useful strategy for improving academic proficiency. For example, the teacher might explain how to use an introductory sentence describing the intended content, three detail sentences elaborating on the content, and a conclusion sentence summarizing the content.

Regarding language proficiency, as outlined in Chapter 1, it is essential to use a variety of data to determine the proficiency levels of learners. This will assist the teacher in adapting a learning strategy to better meet student needs. For example, if a student is at Level 1 or Level 2, trying to teach a strategy in English is not likely to help the student. Teaching a strategy in the native language, on the other hand, could benefit the student greatly in that it could help a student understand new vocabulary to search for cognates or to define new words. As the student progresses to Levels 3 and 4, the teacher should still consider the individual language proficiencies of the learners when planning to teach a strategy. The strategy should be one they have not spontaneously generated and it should be taught in simple steps with language that is absolutely comprehensible to the learners. Finally, in Levels 5 and 6, strategies should be targeted focusing on advanced study, note taking, writing, and reading progress.

Determine Which Strategies Will Be Most Useful

A lesson on the paragraph-writing strategy fulfills the second guideline for choosing a strategy, because the learning strategy is useful in other subjects and many life tasks. Grade, performance level, and life goals are important considerations when determining

Your Turn

How do you decide which learning strategies to teach?

the strategies most useful to students. For example, in middle school math, for students who are struggling with English and who have very weak math skills, a teacher would be more likely to teach a check-writing strategy than a scientific notation strategy. Teachers should teach strategies that students can use repeatedly. For example, strategies for finding the main idea in reading or regrouping in math obviously have significant applications. On the other hand, teachers may need to teach scientific notation as part of math instruction, but they would be wise not to create a formal strategy for this because it may not have broad enough application. If teachers create strategies for everything students are learning, students will be less likely to remember the key strategies and their long-term applications.

Decide Order of Instruction

Once the most beneficial strategies are determined, the teacher must determine the teaching order. He or she should analyze the strategies and decide if they are embedded in one another or if one strategy is a prerequisite of another. For example, when students need to learn note taking from chapters in a book, finding main ideas is a prerequisite. The teacher can focus on the steps for finding main ideas until the use of those steps is automatic and part of the student's permanent repertoire. The note-taking strategy will be easier to teach once students can successfully find the main ideas in a section or chapter and then write notes about them.

Use Simple Wording and the Fewest Number of Steps

For students to understand a strategy, each step must be as simple as possible. Students are more likely to remember a strategy if it is stated in clear, concise words. Teachers should highlight or underline keywords within steps and encourage the students to memorize the keywords. Unnecessary words and steps should be eliminated to simplify the strategy. The teacher must think: Is the strategy as simple as possible? Are all the words clear and necessary? Many times, students will start to memorize strategy steps and reword what teachers have specified. The teacher can facilitate learning by changing the strategy to conform to the student-created version if it improves the efficiency of the strategy or the economy of words. Some teachers use acronyms when teaching strategies by taking the first letter of each of the steps to form a new word. This mnemonic device often facilitates the memorization of a strategy. For example, for the editing strategy capitalization, overall appearance, punctuation, spelling, COPS is a great acronym (see Figure 6.8). The teacher can reinforce the strategy with the visual image of a "cop" looking over the paper to make sure everything is correct. However, an acronym should not be used as a mnemonic device if it must be forced in place. Teachers should not try to create an acronym by using sophisticated wording or stretching the strategy to accommodate it. Students focus on memorizing the keywords of a simple strategy quickly and often do not need an acronym to remember the strategy. If a strategy becomes more complex in order to create an acronym that works, the teacher can defeat the purpose of the learning strategy (that is, to enhance the academic and language proficiency of the learner).

FIGURE 6.8 The COPS Strategy
....

- Capitalization
- Overall appearance of paper
- Punctuation
- Spelling

*T*eaching Learning Strategies

Research indicates explicit instruction in learning strategies facilitates and improves proficiency for students with learning and behavioral challenges and for language (Abedi & Lord, 2001; Graham & Harris, 2005; Graves & Rueda, 2008; Linan-Thompson, Cirino, & Vaughn, 2007). Explicit instruction requires sound lesson structure, lesson preparation, and extensive teacher–student interaction to enhance learning.

Optimal learning strategy instruction requires a teacher to (1) determine the preskills students need to learn the strategy and to teach them; (2) arrange lessons with an opening, a body (including modeling and guided practice), and a closing; (3) plan a series of lessons over time to allow the mastery and generalized use of the strategy; (4) add a self-monitoring component requiring students to check off steps when they use the strategy; and (5) constantly consider the language proficiency level of the students and pull examples from the content-area studies to embed the strategy work in the subject matter being studied.

Determine Preskills and Preteach Them

The teacher can analyze the strategy and list all of the preskills a student must know before the strategy will be easy for the student to learn. A strategy involves a multiplicity of actions. Students will learn the strategy more easily if the difficult steps are taught before the complete strategy is introduced. If students are unable to perform the difficult steps, the entire strategy will be more difficult to accomplish.

Embedded in the steps of a strategy are preskills, concepts, and rules. For example, if a teacher decides to teach an editing strategy to students, such as the COPS strategy (see Figure 6.8), necessary preskills are the ability to write a paragraph, the ability to use correct sentence structure, and handwriting proficiency. Some concepts for the successful use of this strategy are capitalization, neatness, punctuation, and spelling. Some rules for the successful use of this strategy are:

1. Capitalize the first word in each sentence.
2. Capitalize proper nouns.
3. Write on the line.
4. Use the one-finger rule between words.
5. Use the two-finger rule between sentences.
6. Indent paragraphs.
7. Use an end punctuation mark.
8. Try to spell words correctly but check to determine correctness.

Students may need significant instruction in these underlying concepts and rules before they can successfully learn the editing strategy. Rules are taught by focusing on critical attributes, which are the defining elements of each rule. Defining elements are used to create examples to illustrate a rule. Defining elements are also used to create non-examples to sharpen understanding of the application of the rule. The non-examples serve as distracters in an example set and hone the discrimination skills necessary for correct rule applications. For example, in teaching students to indent paragraphs, the teacher will give examples of proper indentation and incorrect indentation in order to clarify exactly how to follow the rule. Lessons that focus on the rules are important precursors to strategy instruction. Once the identified concepts and rules are mastered, students are better prepared to learn a strategy. Learning a strategy requires automatic knowledge of all preskills. This allows the student to focus on the application of the strategy and helps him or her avoid a struggle with the semantic or procedural knowledge that is inevitably embedded in the strategy.

Include an Opening, a Body, and a Closing

Opening. At the beginning of each strategy instruction mini-lesson, the teacher should review relevant preskills. For example, in the COPS strategy lesson, the teacher might review rules for capitalization, neatness, and punctuation before introducing the strategy. The teacher should also describe the strategy and explain how it can be used. For example, to introduce a strategy on good listening, the teacher tells the students about the importance of listening and talks to them about when not listening could adversely affect them (for example, if the teacher tells them to raise their hands if they like ice cream, because Juan's mother is bringing ice cream for everyone who raises a hand). The teacher might also ask students to think of times when good listening is important. After the students understand why the strategy is important, the teacher should state the goal of the lesson. The teacher might tell them that for the next few weeks, they are going to work very hard on becoming good listeners and that today they are to learn some steps to follow to become good listeners. Teachers must use language the students understand to emphasize what is being taught and to explain why the students will benefit from learning the strategy.

Body. The body of the strategy instruction mini-lesson contains three basic steps.

1. The teacher demonstrates or models.
2. The teacher and students practice together.
3. Students practice using the strategy independently.

The demonstration and modeling by the teacher is the most critical part of the lesson. A strategy should be taught using a two-stage model. The first stage is verbal rehearsal. The steps of the strategy are explicitly stated, and the students practice the words of the steps repeatedly. If the students are readers, they should be given a list of the steps, and the steps should be written on a wall chart or shown on the overhead projector. The teacher can underline or highlight the key words for each step and illustrate any action involved in the step. For example, if students are learning a good-listening strategy, the teacher might draw a set of eyes beside the step "Look at the person" (see Figure 6.9). In

FIGURE 6.9 Good Listener Strategy (including use of visuals)

Step 1: Look at the person

Step 2: Keep your hands and body still

Step 3: Keep a pleasant face

FIGURE 6.10 Capitalization in the COPS Strategy*

Step 1: Check for Capitalization
    (Capitalization Rules)
    ☐ Each sentence must begin with a capital letter.
    ☐ Each proper noun must begin with a capital letter.

*See Figure 6.8 for the complete COPS strategy.

a more elaborate strategy such as COPS, for the step "Capitalization," the teacher might write capital letters beside the step and write the two rules for capitalization in smaller print underneath or beside it (see Figure 6.10).

The second stage of modeling is the physical model. During this stage, the teacher actually demonstrates the strategy step by step for students. As part of the demonstration, the teacher might think aloud through each step. In teaching the COPS strategy, the teacher might say, "Step 1: Check for capitalization. Hmmm, I'd better think about each rule for capitalization. The first one is: Each sentence must begin with a capital letter. Hmmm, does each sentence begin with a capital letter? Yes, but here's one that doesn't; I'd better fix it." The teacher can continue to demonstrate each step by correcting a writing sample shown on an overhead transparency. After the teacher has demonstrated the steps of the strategy sufficiently, students can be asked to practice the process with the teacher. The teacher uses new examples of sentences that need to be corrected and continues to apply the steps of the strategy, working together with the students. For the COPS strategy, the teacher and the students go through each step talking about it and answering together. Students are encouraged to ask questions and to continue practicing the steps of the strategy until no errors occur. If errors do occur, the teacher can repeat the demonstration, modeling in a manner similar to the original. Hearing the same words from the teacher and seeing the same behaviors reinforces the steps for the students and helps clear up any misunderstandings. In the final part of the body of the lesson, the teacher gives feedback while the students practice the strategy on their own. The students may work in small groups, in pairs, or on their own when practicing the steps and completing the strategy. The first practice examples should be short and simple. The subsequent samples should progress to grade-appropriate and perhaps to more difficult examples. After enough varied practice, students should be able to apply the strategy to different situations. The examples show how the strategy is applied to other subjects and to real-life situations such as letter writing.

Closing. At the end of each lesson, the teacher may focus the students on homework or on the lessons to follow. During the closing, the teacher typically assigns independent practice for a later time during class or as homework. The teacher can also preview the next lesson or review the strategy either by repeating the steps or by asking the students to reflect on uses for the strategy.

Plan a Series of Lessons

A lesson plan for most days should include work on the strategy preskills, concepts, or rules. Over time, given enough instruction and practice, students can master the strategy. A 10- to 15-minute mini-lesson on the strategy works best as part of the instructional period (see Figure 6.11). For example, in elementary school, typically an hour-and-a-half is designated for language arts. During that time, the students may engage in various

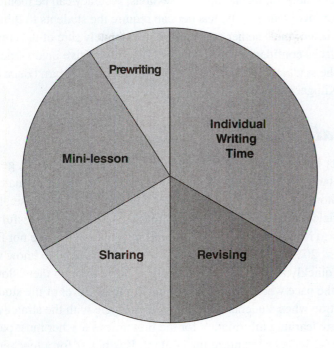

15- to 20-minute activities. Focusing on an important learning strategy could be just one of the segments of the language arts or content-area instructional period. If the strategy is taught, be sure to post it on the wall, on the student's desk, or in the notebook to enhance memory and use. Strategy instruction is not intended to be a one-time lesson; instead, the instruction becomes a strand, stretching across several weeks. A series of lessons provides the students ample time to practice, apply, and master the strategy.

Presentation Methods Used to Teach Learning Strategies

The type of interaction a teacher chooses to maximize student learning is based on many of the aspects of sheltered instruction. For strategy instruction, teachers can focus on (1) active student involvement with maximum student participation; (2) the appropriate pace that helps students to move neither too rapidly nor too slowly through the material; (3) careful monitoring so error correction occurs immediately; or (4) independent practice, controlled practice, and grade-appropriate practice.

Active Student Involvement

Active student involvement is a recurrent theme throughout this book, as it is in the literature on instruction for English learners. In the context of learning-strategy instruction, teachers may ask students to tell them about why a strategy will be useful. Teachers can ask students to talk more about when a strategy could be used and what has happened when they have used the strategy. They can ask what made the strategy work and what could be done to make it work better the next time. The teacher can also ask students to engage in verbal rehearsal of the steps of the strategy. During practice the teacher can ask, "Did we use the strategy properly? How do you know?" When the teacher poses questions like this often throughout demonstration and practice sessions, accuracy can be monitored to ensure maximum learner involvement. The teacher can require the students to think about the strategy and can determine whether each student is absolutely sure of the correct application of a strategy or lacks confidence or knowledge. The more active involvement the teacher can elicit from the students, the more likely the students are to learn (Baca & Cervantes, 2004; Harry & Klingner, 2006).

Appropriate Pacing

Effective teacher interaction is characterized by precise, slow speech, gestures, and controlled vocabulary. Controlled vocabulary involves the use of cognates and the limited use of idiomatic expressions. Consistent wording without the use of synonyms is critical for efficient language development. Teachers are most successful when they avoid references to reading materials and cultural information that are not familiar to the learners (Jiménez, 2003). Pacing is also important. Teachers need to know when to move through lessons quickly and when it is necessary to move through them slowly. A teacher should quicken the pace when the confidence and accuracy level of the students increases. The opposite is true when students make errors or struggle with the strategy application. When students are learning information for the first time, a teacher must pace the lesson carefully so the students can capture the content. It is better for a teacher to proceed slowly during the modeling and prompting than to go back and correct errors or to repeat lessons. Of course, at times the latter is necessary and can be the appropriate choice.

Monitor and Correct Errors

The teacher can monitor each phase of a lesson to decide how to pace the lesson, which lesson parts to repeat, and which examples will maximize learning. This monitoring provides teachers with information on when to mediate learning and when to provide student feedback. During strategy instruction, error correction is determined by the type of response the student gives. If the error is careless, the teacher may ask the student to repeat the answer. If the error is due to a lack of knowledge, the teacher should return to the model, repeat the steps, and involve the student in additional practice. The teacher should work with the student to practice the strategy. One point of contention between researchers and practitioners is when to provide corrective feedback. Whole language and writing-as-a-process approaches often prohibit error correction, particularly at the beginning of reading and writing development. It is commonly believed that as students progress, they will start to notice correct forms and begin to use them spontaneously. Reyes (1992) claims that this practice is not always best for learners. Her research indicates that students who were not corrected did not progress and were often left further and further behind. These conclusions lend support to the "perfect final copy" requirement of the Writer's Workshop approach. Many teachers insist that students continually rewrite their work until everything is perfect, hence insisting on self-correction.

To minimize anxiety, teachers can approach error correction cautiously when students are learning content material (Graves & Rueda, 2008). Students who have experienced school failure or who are learning to speak English as a second language often need to be praised when they have responded correctly. Teachers can approach error correction indirectly (Baca & Cervantes, 2004). For example, in a sixth-grade sheltered instruction class, a student described a close-up picture by saying, "It looks more big." The teacher responded indirectly and said, "Yes, it looks bigger." The student understood the correction and repeated, "Yes, it looks bigger." The student seemed to appreciate the information. Reyes (1992) and Short (1994) report positive results from explicit teaching of vocabulary, academic language, academic strategies, and English language, followed by teacher monitoring and nonthreatening error correction. The direct feedback approach requires the teacher to model the correct response and ask the student to repeat or copy it. The teacher then asks a related question that requires the student to use the correct information. If an English learner writes "bruder" in his journal instead of the word "brother," the teacher can write the correct word above the misspelling and ask the student to spell the word correctly the next time. At the same time, the teacher should compliment the student's work, respond in writing to its content, and point out correctly spelled words.

Controlled, Grade-Appropriate Practice and Independent Practice

Practice is necessary when students are learning strategies. Once they have memorized the steps of a strategy, they must practice with clear examples. Suggestions on how to design learning strategies have been very clearly articulated in the work of Deshler and colleagues at the University of Kansas (Deshler & Schumaker, 1994) and Graham and his colleagues for teaching writing strategies (Graham, MacArthur, & Fitzgerald, 2012). Both researchers have emphasized the self-regulation aspects of strategy instruction, that is, the generalization and transfer of these strategies to become a permanent part of the repertoire of the learner. This work is an extension of a long tradition in educational research with a focus on the importance of generalization and transfer (Woolfolk, 2013).

The first practice phase for learning a strategy is controlled practice. For example, a student has learned to sound out a word by looking at the word, saying all the letter sounds without stopping between sounds, and saying the word the "fast way." The controlled practice examples are words that are absolutely decodable, such as *on, cat,* or *mast.* The examples provide practice of the sounds the student knows.

After students master controlled practice, grade-appropriate practice should follow (Ellis & Graves, 1990). This will include grade-level reading words that might be found in content-area reading assignments. Grade-appropriate practice shows students the range of a strategy's application and teaches them how to generalize and transfer the knowledge they have gained. In this process, students learn that the strategy works better with some words than with others. They learn the limitations and the value of the strategy as it applies to their own life experiences.

Independent practice is appropriate only after students have mastered a strategy. A student can practice a strategy without supervision when it can be performed without frustration and error. If students practice applying the strategy to grade-appropriate words for homework too soon, errors may go uncorrected and cause confusion. The strategy is likely to be more valuable to students when the teacher avoids assigning homework or independent practice before they are quite familiar and comfortable with it. An alternate homework assignment when students are learning a strategy is practicing one of the early example sets that have already been mastered. The assignment would then be relevant but would not require the students to perform the strategy prematurely in a frustrating situation.

Summary

Explicit teaching of learning strategies can assist students in overcoming challenges they face in school. The teacher should provide explicit instruction to help a student that has difficulty understanding a concept or rule. Additionally, concepts and strategies should be adapted to be accessible to English learning with varying English proficiency. The teacher should provide specific lesson descriptions and classroom examples that demonstrate various types of learning strategies, including guidelines for selecting learning strategies and planning lesson segments. Ensure that various methods are used to teach specific learning strategies to promote learning skills and remember that strategies are essential for developing academic proficiency, but are only a part of a quality instruction program for English learners.

Specifically, as a reader you

- defined the term *learning strategy* and delineated types of learning strategies.
- presented examples of specific strategies for reading, writing, and content areas that you think would be useful when teaching and stated why they might be useful.
- restated the guidelines for selecting learning strategies.
  - explained why these guidelines are important.
- described five implementation considerations when teaching learning strategies.

Activities

1. Seven students in your tenth-grade history class are struggling with reading and writing tasks. What type of information needs to be gathered about these students (see Chapter 1)? If the teacher is currently involving students in role-plays and utilizing video and other concrete examples of historical events, what other options does the teacher have to improve reading and writing performances?
2. If you are teaching a learning strategy to students with intermediate fluency in English, what specific guidelines are critical for you to consider when you are planning your mini-lesson?
3. Outline the parts of a mini-lesson intended to teach the COPS strategy explicitly. What preskills must be mastered before the strategy is taught? When you teach the strategy, what parts will you include in your mini-lessons?
4. Create a schedule of one hour in your teaching day. Plan to teach a mini-lesson for about 15 minutes of the time. Plan that segment of instruction. Then describe what the other segments need to reflect in order to provide the best instruction to students.

CHAPTER 7

Differentiated Instruction

LEARNING OBJECTIVES:

- Provide at least five examples of cultural and linguistic differentiation of instruction.
- Identify examples of instructional differentiation for students with emerging English skills, expanding English skills, and advanced or bridging English skills.
- List examples of accommodations for academic content.
- Discuss the types of adaptations made for advanced learning and studying, as well as the level of language proficiency required for effective implementation.

Previous chapters provide numerous examples of accommodations, adaptations, and modifications that teachers can make to provide differentiated instruction, as this book is entirely about how to differentiate instruction for English learners with diverse abilities. One of the most challenging aspects of differentiation is providing appropriate accommodations, adaptations, and modifications of textbooks, materials, and assignments because they can be difficult semantically and syntactically for all students, including those learning English (Carlo et al., 2004; Lucas & Katz, 1994; Moran, Stobbe, Baron, Miller, & Moir, 2000; Short, 1989, 1992). The new California Teachers of English Learners (CTEL) guidelines specify a domain on the importance of differentiated instruction.

Michaeljung/Fotolia

This chapter provides more information on how to differentiate instruction, with emphasis on appropriate texts, materials, and assignments (Fuchs & Fuchs, 2001; Jiménez, 2003; Meskill & Mossop, 2001). A major focus of the chapter is to address the great challenge that teachers have to make curriculum accessible to all students (Artiles & Bal, 2009; Bell, 2000; Chang, 1992; Cheng, 1995; Genesee, Lindholm-Leary, Saunders, & Christian, 2005; Graves & Rueda, 2008; Lucas & Katz, 1994; Short, 1994). Examples of accommodations, adaptations, and modifications for students in elementary and secondary classrooms are provided (Graves, Duesbery, Pyle, Brandon, & McIntosh, 2011; Graves & Rueda, 2008) so that teachers might be better prepared to differentiate instruction.

Demonstrating Sensitivity to Cultural and Linguistic Diversity

One very important differentiation of instruction is to have culturally and linguistically appropriate curriculum (Gay, 2000). The CTEL includes a domain devoted specifically to culturally sensitive instruction. When culturally relevant literature is used in the classroom, students perform better. (For full review, see Baca and Cervantes, 2004.)

 Watch this video and describe ways that a teacher can increase cultural sensitivity.

 Watch this video and describe the importance of valuing cultures.

 Watch this video and define *intercultural competence.*

Modifying and adapting lessons to include culturally relevant information and examples enhances student motivation (Klingner, Artiles, & Barletta, 2006). Making lessons culturally relevant is described as culturally and linguistically responsive teaching (Lindholm-Leary & Genessee, 2012). An example of how culturally and linguistically appropriate material can be motivating took place in a social studies class that we observed. The social studies unit was adapted to include a significant amount of information on cultural diversity in America at the time of the Revolution (Short, 1994). This unit illustrated to recent immigrant students how culturally diverse the United States has been since its inception. Books emphasizing the historical contributions of African Americans, Asian Americans, Latinos, and Native Americans throughout history are recommended. When teachers use familiar current events as examples when defining historical terms such as *protest,* they are using responsive teaching. For example, newspaper clippings and pictures about the marches for immigration rights might be shown as a modern example of protest. Respecting and using students' native languages is integral to responsive teaching (Cummins, 1999). Native-language instruction has linguistic,

Your Turn

Think about culturally and linguistically appropriate curricula you have seen. What are the features that might promote a sense of belonging and motivation for students?

cultural, cognitive-academic, and affective psychological benefits for individuals who are learning a new language (Baca & Cervantes, 2004). Snow and Katz (2010) discuss the potential benefits of the biliterate approach to transferring background knowledge to the topic at hand. In one example, the teacher presents key vocabulary in social studies classes in both English and Spanish. In a lesson on the Pilgrims and Thanksgiving, the teacher discusses vocabulary words and uses the whiteboard or Promethean Board to diagram his thoughts in both English and Spanish.

 Watch this video and list 5 ways that the classroom setting can affect language learning.

 Watch this video and discuss how learning cultural knowledge can benefit instruction.

In addition, linguistic accommodations are critical using language proficiency levels as guide (see Figure 1.7 in Chapter 1). The importance of native-language support was discussed in Chapter 5 from a psychological and self-esteem-building perspective, and in addition, there are instructional and learning benefits. Lessons can be modified and adapted to include short segments of native language to clarify meaning for students. Tapping into students' ability to retrieve words in a known language facilitates their progress in a new language (Carlo et al., 2004). For example, when learning about the solar system, many of the words in English are similar to those in Spanish: *Mercurio* is Mercury, *Marte* is Mars, and *planetas* are planets. These are good examples of words that can be used in implementing the cognate strategy presented in Chapter 6.

The Common Core State Standards and career and readiness standards are the basis for the first consideration of whether differentiated instruction is needed. With the advent of fewer, clearer, and higher standards, teachers can begin to determine the type of instruction that is best suited to their students, keeping language proficiency levels in mind: (1) Entering, (2) Beginning, (3) Developing, (4) Expanding, (5) Bridging, and (6) Reaching. For example, students in Levels 1 and 2 are likely to need significant vocabulary support including native-language clarifications and connections. Students in Levels 3, 4, and 5 are likely to need strategic and advanced learning approaches such as finding important information, studying text, and improving written expression. Students in Levels 4, 5, and 6 are likely to need study, advanced reading comprehension, self-monitoring, note-taking, and other advanced strategies.

To adapt the strategies to language proficiency levels, students in Level 1 and Level 2 have emerging skills, students in Level 3 and Level 4 have expanding skills, and students in Levels 5 and 6 have advanced or bridging skills. With knowledge of student levels gained from assessment, teachers can adapt the instruction accordingly. For example, the Mathematics Grade 4 Geometry, Common Core State Standard states, "Recognize a line of symmetry for a two-dimensional figure as a line across the figure such that the figure can be folded along the line into matching parts. Identify line-symmetric figures and draw lines of symmetry." In this case the teacher should assess students to determine existing knowledge. Consideration of language proficiency would then lead the teacher to provide differentiated instruction to facilitate student learning. If students are emerging in their language proficiency, the teacher may recommend the use of native-language demonstrations as well as visual supports such as graphs with lines of symmetry drawn so that students could do their own folding to gain two equal parts. For those whose skills are expanding in language proficiency in Levels 3 and 4, depending on the individual profiles, the teacher may conclude that explicit strategy instruction with detailed specific steps to follow would benefit the students most.

However, this type of scaffolding would be phased out as the students become more self-reliant and independent in the finding lines of symmetry and the checking for equal parts. Finally, for more advanced students, applications in lines of symmetry examples might extend to word problems and more sophisticated graphing examples.

With regard to science, the National Center for Educational Statistics (2011) released "A Framework for K–12 Science Education" that is guiding the development of the Next Generation Science Standards. Lee, Quinn, and Valdéz (2013) join many others in the field in asserting that language opportunities are embedded in content-area studies. The intersection with language proficiency level is critical to support students appropriately while students are empowered to "do" specific things with language, so that content-area work and language can be supported and promoted simultaneously. The Common Core State Standards and "next generation" standards provide numerous opportunities for students to learn language while learning content.

*P*roviding Adequate Background Knowledge

Helping learners retrieve relevant background knowledge facilitates understanding of the lesson content and increases the likelihood of learning and retention. In addition to native-language support, other ways of providing and using background knowledge are listed in Figure 7.1. Depending on the level of language proficiency of the students, teachers may have students brainstorm at the beginning of a lesson to encourage them to share what they already know about a topic and use language, which facilitates learning (Linan-Thompson, Cirino, & Vaughn, 2007). Another way a teacher can enhance background knowledge is to provide students with direct experience through videotapes, Internet information, and field trips (Gorski, 2001). Once students have a personal store of knowledge in a content area, the teacher can assist them in connecting new knowledge to what is already known (Beck, McKeown, & Kucan, 2007). In one lesson, a science teacher presented a month-long unit on marine biology in phases. In the first phase of the unit, the teacher focused on oceans by asking students to brainstorm about their own relevant experiences. Students who had lived near an ocean were asked to talk about what they had observed. Their comments were written down by the teacher and then copied and distributed.

In the second phase of the unit, the teacher provided opportunities for students to develop knowledge of and experiences with the ocean by planning a field trip to a marine biology center near the ocean. When students returned to school after the trip, they were again asked to talk and write about what they had observed. Their comments and observations were written down by the teacher on acetate and copied for all to study. The students also watched videotapes, the teacher read a few books aloud, and the students found library books and websites about ocean life.

FIGURE 7.1 Phases for Providing Adequate Background Knowledge

Phase 1: Brainstorm with the whole group.

Phase 2: Provide direct experiences, read sources, watch videos, and provide information-gathering opportunities.

Phase 3: Provide a forum for using background knowledge and for adding knowledge gained (choosing a topic and preparing a report).

In the final phase of the unit, each student chose an ocean animal to study; students were then assigned to take notes on cards, write a report, draw a picture, and make a map about their animal. One student chose the sea turtle. He found a few books on sea turtles in the library, wrote notes on cards, transferred the information to a final draft on the computer, drew a picture of a sea turtle, and made a map of places in the world where sea turtles are most prevalent. On one of the final days of the marine biology unit, the students were putting the finishing touches on their projects and presenting them. The students, who were largely English learners, seemed to particularly enjoy drawing and coloring their animals and making the maps. Each presented his or her animal report to the class and chose a spot for it to be displayed in the class.

Building Academic Proficiency

In each subject area, teachers should be concerned with at least two important curricular strands: determining the content knowledge the students must master in subject areas (e.g., information about the solar system, the American Revolution, the chemical composition of colors, or the names of the characters in a given literary work) and determining the background academic skills necessary for students to learn and study content knowledge effectively.

Content Knowledge

Teachers can develop an annual plan by reviewing textbooks, curriculum guides, and teacher manuals to determine the essential content for the specific grade level and course. Planning involves linking critical concepts and ideas into meaningful, connected units that build upon each other. When the most important concepts have been determined, the nonessential details can be eliminated (Hoover & Patton, 2005).

Interdisciplinary curricula and thematic units provide students with helpful links between subjects and are considered highly valuable for students. For example, in a fifth-grade American history course, the teacher might first analyze the content by constructing a timeline to span the entire year of study and then determine the relevant information to be covered. The teacher might focus on how pieces of history fit together and how patterns in history repeat. To include interdisciplinary curricula, the teacher can rely on information shared by students in cooperative groups or in classroom exchanges. Hence, grade-level teams of teachers plan thematic interdisciplinary content and draw up examples that can be included across subjects to enhance learning. For example, a team of teachers in a coastal Southern California community developed a thematic unit on coastal Native Americans. In this unit, students simultaneously studied tribal life and history in their social studies class, oceanography in science class, whale and dolphin counting and recordkeeping in math class, and *The Island of the Blue Dolphins* (O'Dell, 1970) in English class.

After essential content knowledge is determined and unit lesson planning is complete, teachers should focus on determining the prerequisite or background knowledge the students need to understand the course content (Klingner, Artilles, & Bartella, 2006). For example, when faced with a science unit on energy, teachers must first determine the experience level the students have with the concepts and content to be taught (such as heat and friction). Next, the teacher must determine the experiences that need to be provided in order to equip students for understanding the content of the course. A teacher could use class experiments or projects, videotapes, or library visits (see Figure 7.1) to provide this information. During the unit, field trips to electrical power plants or to a solar heat pump company might help students with background knowledge. The teacher can adapt the curriculum to provide students with experiences to enhance and formulate background knowledge. Students should also be encouraged to discuss and write about their own thoughts and reactions to experiences provided in the class. Class journals can provide a forum for students to express their ideas.

Academic Proficiency Skills

Talking, listening, reading, writing, thinking, and studying are academic proficiency skills necessary for success in school (Genessee et al., 2005; Graves, 1987). In combination with the Common Core State Standards by grade level, this focus on critical school skills is the basis by which a teacher will differentiate instruction, often by adapting the approach and the intensity of instruction.

Currently, the "tiered model" as discussed in Chapter 1 (Fuchs, Fuchs, & Vaughn, 2008; McIntosh, Graves, & Gersten, 2007; Vaughn et al., 2009) is an effective way to monitor students' learning and adjust instruction to increase academic proficiency skills for students who are behind in academic proficiency skills or basic, grade-level skills. The three-tier approach suggests that teachers in general education provide effective instruction and conduct benchmark assessments for all. Students who are significantly behind may receive intensive small-group instruction (Tier 2). This type of additional support may bring them to grade-level proficiency. Teachers can determine the type of academic background skills necessary by analyzing the tasks required of the students and studying scope and sequence of academic proficiency skills (Gersten, Woodward, & Darch, 1986). They can determine that certain skills are necessary for studying, reading, and understanding the aspects of the content area to be covered throughout the year. They can then conduct an informal assessment of students' skills in the content areas (Gattullo, 2000). After the initial informal assessment, teachers can determine which skills the students already have and identify those they need to acquire. When determinations are made, the teacher designs a plan to teach and practice the skills gradually throughout the year (Graves, 2012; Graves, Duesbery, Pyle, Brandon, & McIntosh, 2011).

To best support students in learning academic background skills, Vaughn et al. (2009) and Reyes (1992) contend that teachers are most effective when they follow through by insisting that students demonstrate correct use of what has been taught. For example, after a strategy for recognizing main ideas is taught and practiced, students should be able to identify a main idea in a social studies text. If the main idea is misidentified, the student must be corrected. Focusing on form tends to build superior skill use while building self-esteem because the teacher uses a nonthreatening manner (Gonzales, Moll, & Amanti, 2005; Reyes, 1992).

Some practitioners contend that accommodations do little for the overall outcomes of English learners (Destefano, Shriner, & Lloyd, 2001; Fuchs et al., 2008). If a student is not responding to Tier 1 and Tier 2 interventions, teachers and parents may determine that he or she would benefit from a more individually designed Tier 3 intervention that may or may not involve referral to special education. Other team problem solving can also be implemented with the notion in mind that all children can learn and benefit from instructional assistance. This is consistent with the belief that teachers should be part of professional learning communities embracing the attitude that all students have the ability to succeed (see Chapter 8).

Providing Language Development Opportunities

Language and vocabulary development in content areas is an important part of differentiated instruction for students who are learning English (Beck et al., 2007; Carlo et al., 2004; Cummins, 1989; Graves, August, & Mancilla-Martinez, 2012). Students need adequate preparation to be able to understand the content material. Having the language skills required for participation in lessons and knowing the vocabulary associated with lessons leads to academic success. Therefore, students need opportunities to develop the English skills necessary for academic achievement as well as for use outside the classroom across their life span.

Language Proficiency

English proficiency is the greatest determinate of academic success for English learners, more than all other factors combined (Suarez-Orozco, Suarez-Orozco & Todorova, 2008). So, it is critical that teachers be aware of the importance of language development and provide a language-rich classroom with ample opportunities to talk, read, and write at each student's level of language proficiency. As presented in Chapters 1 and 2, students' level of language development must be assessed and instruction differentiated to meet their language development needs and promote continuous progress.

In their comprehensive discussion of literacy instruction for English learners, Cloud, Genesee and Hamayan (2009) suggest several ways that teachers can promote language learning in the classroom. Suggestions include first, making sure your speech is clear and maintains a good pace. Repeat important details as necessary. Second, ensure that all students have an opportunity to participate. As discussed in chapter 2, their participation should be at their level of proficiency. Third, be active in investigating the kinds of language and high-frequency words that must be learned. Fourth, don't stray from the target language. Stay on point and make the meanings clear. Lastly, integrate language practice into all activities and lessons.

When students are in the early stages of language development, teachers can ask questions that require students to raise their hands or put their thumbs up if they agree. Teachers can ask the class to answer yes or no in unison. Teachers can give each student two pictures, one of mammals and one of birds. The student is asked to hold up the appropriate picture when the teacher mentions a characteristic of a group or a particular animal. Alternatively, a teacher could simply write the words "mammal" and "bird" on the board and ask the students to answer with the correct word when a characteristic or animal is mentioned. Simple answers reinforce and build knowledge with minimal language requirements but allow students a safe environment for language development.

For students at higher levels of language development, the teacher provides many opportunities for language use while simultaneously developing content knowledge. Language development activities can include student pairs or small student groups talking about issues or content, reading aloud or silently, writing group reports, or solving group problems. In the social studies lesson about coastal Native Americans, each cooperative group chose a coastal tribe. Each group then wrote and illustrated a report and presented the report to the class. The group worked out the plan for accomplishing all the tasks and assignments within the group. The negotiations, discussions, and actions taken by each group were socially relevant opportunities for language use and development. Similarly,

Lee and Buxton (2013) found that English language learners improved both English skills and content knowledge when they were taught science with "sheltered" adaptations for varying levels of language proficiency (see Chapter 3).

A teacher can speed language development by providing a connection to native-language vocabulary (Howard, Sugarman, Christian, Lindholm-Leary, & Rogers, 2007). A seventh-grade English teacher helped students develop language knowledge by writing a keyword or words in English on the board accompanied by pictures or examples. Each day the teacher said, "¿Qué es esto?" or "¿Cómo se dice en Español?" These simple phrases elicited the Spanish words and allowed the students to determine if the new English vocabulary was related to Spanish or if cognates existed. This method also allowed students to continue language development in both languages.

Academic Language

Academic language—those words and ways of expressing and understanding the language of the classroom—is essential for success in school. Educators and researchers in the field of second-language acquisition and literacy have offered several definitions of academic language or academic literacy. A report on adolescent English learner literacy (Short & Fitzsimmons, 2007, p. 2) concludes that academic literacy uses necessary skills, like reading and writing, to be an active learner in the classroom. It is possible for variations to exist depending on subject area and the knowledge of multiple genres of text, text media, and the purposes of text. Academic literacy is influenced on a students' personal life and cultural experiences.

Another report (Torgesen, et al., 2007, p. 3), defined academic literacy as a type of reading proficiency that constructs meaning and is usually assessed on state-level measures like using context clues to learn vocabulary, infer ideas form text, comparing text, and summarizing material.

The ESL Standards for Pre–K–12 Students (TESOL, 1997) defined academic language as the use of language that strongly associates literacy with academic achievement and is used in a formal learning environment. It is important for learning academic subject matter and is related to each field of study which requires academic terms, technically language, and speech registers.

Bailey (2007) offers a more concise definition. Academic language is "a precise and predictable way of using language that places demands on the user not typically encountered in everyday settings." In the Common Core adaptations for English learners, academic language is a strand for all learners beginning with the emerging skills in English up through the bridging skills.

While there are academic words that are content specific, there are general academic vocabulary words that cross content areas. For example, content-specific vocabulary in math are words such as *add, total, in all, pattern,* and *sort.* Academic words that go across content areas are words such as *conclusion, indent, main ideas, inference, objective,* and *evaluation.*

Often, a student cannot comprehend a lesson without knowing critical vocabulary. One strategy for developing general academic vocabulary is having the teacher use short, explicit class segments for directly teaching key vocabulary (Beck et al., 2007; Carlo et al., 2004; M. F. Graves et al., 2012; Jiménez, García, & Pearson, 1996). This is also the case when teaching vocabulary to students with learning disabilities (Jitendra, Edwards, Sacks, & Jacobson, 2004). Five-minute segments that include both teacher and student activity are recommended. The teacher says the vocabulary word and writes the word on the board. The students then repeat the word and write the word on paper. Finally, the teacher defines the word and uses pictures, demonstrations, and examples relevant to the students. In one situation (Short, Fidelman, & Longuit, 2012), the teacher said the vocabulary word *protest* and wrote it on the board. The students repeated and wrote the word. The teacher then showed pictures of the African Americans who marched with Martin Luther King, Jr., to protest segregation. The teacher also showed pictures of the outdoor mall in Washington, DC, covered with quilts to protest the level of funding for AIDS research. Jiménez et al. (1996) point out that good bilingual readers are focused on increasing vocabulary knowledge. Particularly with new vocabulary, research shows that less is more.

 Watch this video and discuss at least two ways of teaching vocabulary to promote memory and long-term use.

Discipline-Specific Vocabulary Development

Content-area courses in science, social studies, literature, and math are built around relevant vocabulary. Teachers need to explicitly teach those content-specific terms that bring meaning to the lesson (Short et al., 2012).

When a teacher chooses vocabulary sparingly but teaches the vocabulary in depth, the vocabulary will likely be retained. A sixth-grade math teacher taught the vocabulary word *sort* in great depth (Graves & Rueda, 2008). Although this is a word that was part of a math unit on graphing, it is also a general academic word used in word problems and in other content areas. To teach the word *sort,* the teacher used kitchen items, spoons, spatulas, and two buckets. The teacher started the lesson by telling students that today they would "sort" the shoes in the room and graph the number in each group. The teacher then said, "Let's learn what the word *sort* means," and wrote the word on the board. The teacher then said, "Watch. I am going to sort these. Let's see . . . This is a spoon so this goes here in bucket 1. This is a spatula so this goes here in bucket 2. This is a . . ." After a few examples, the teacher became playful and said, "This is a spoon, so it goes in bucket 2 . . . Oops. No, it goes in bucket 1 with the other spoons." The concept of sorting was demonstrated without actually defining the word sort. Thinking aloud made the process overt for the students. The teacher also provided both examples and non-examples of correct sorting to clarify the concept.

Following the demonstration, the students sorted items on their own. Each student was given an envelope containing three 25-cent coupons and three 50-cent coupons. The students sorted the coupons in piles on their desks as the teacher monitored. The teacher spent about 10 minutes on one vocabulary word rather than following the more traditional approach of writing five words on the board and defining each one at the beginning of the lesson. Using demonstrations, modeling, thinking aloud, and visual representations to teach *sort* allowed all the students to comprehend the concept.

In one English lesson on poetry, the teacher wanted to teach the words *alliteration* and *rhyme*. The Spanish words are *aliteración* and *rima*. The teacher wrote *rhyme = rima* on the board first, thinking the students would know the meaning of the word but be unfamiliar with the word in English. The students immediately responded by saying "Ah, *rima*." The looks on their faces and nodding heads indicated they understood the word. The teacher said, "We see *rhyme* in this poem; I'll show you two words that rhyme—*love* and *dove*. Now, find two more words that rhyme." Students were able to talk among themselves and locate more examples of rhyming words. Their discussions and continued reading of the poem facilitated language development.

Your Turn

Think of two vocabulary words that you want to teach students. Using the guidelines presented here, how will you teach each one?

For the word *alliteration,* the teacher knew the students might not know the meaning of either the English word or the Spanish word. When the teacher asked about the word, some of the students looked to each other and shrugged their shoulders. The teacher used a handheld computer to find the word in Spanish and wrote *aliteracíon = alliteration* on the board. Handheld computers can translate up to 20 languages and can be invaluable tools for teachers working with students learning English. The teacher asked one of the Spanish-speaking teachers for some examples of alliteration in Spanish to further prepare for the lesson. The teacher was careful to define *alliteration* in concise and consistent language: "*Alliteration* means words in a row with the same beginning letter sound. Listen to examples in Spanish: '*La luna lumbra la loma y Tito toma té y tamales.*' Now listen in English: '*Slippery slimy slivering snake.*' Now listen again: '*Happy lovable dog.*' This is not alliteration. Why? Yes, because these are not words in a row with the same beginning letter sound." The teacher carefully provided examples and non-examples to clarify the concept. The teacher also used consistent wording. The teacher did not say "same beginning letter sounds" one time and "same beginning letters" another time. The students were encouraged to generate examples in Spanish. The teacher could recognize alliteration in Spanish without understanding all the words in the examples generated by the students. Students shared their examples and the teacher continued providing examples from the poem as students read in English. In the end, the teacher asked students to find more English examples of alliteration and rhyme in the poem.

Modifying Lesson Plans and Text

Often, when differentiating instruction, the teacher modifies lesson plans to meet the needs of those students who are not making adequate progress to meet benchmarks. Web sources can provide teachers with abundant information for transforming curriculum and instructional practices (see Figure 7.2). Teachers can modify difficult sections of text as follows:

- Add graphic depictions.
- Outline the text.
- Rewrite the text.
- Use audiotapes.
- Provide live demonstrations.
- Use alternate books.

Short (1989) used an original text about truck farms in the Middle Atlantic states to make a dense, difficult-to-read section of text comprehensible (see Figure 7.3). The original text is referred to throughout this section.

Add Graphic Depictions of the Text. Graphic depiction of the text improves student performance and appears to benefit English learners, students in general education, and students with learning and behavior challenges. Teachers of English learners can effectively use graphic organizers and visual displays such as charts, graphs, Venn diagrams, maps,

Language Arts
- Study skills and self-help:
  - testtakingtips.com
  - how-to-study.com
- Archer, A. (2001). Rewards. Sopris West:
  - sopriswest.com
  - Green, J. F. (2000). Language! Sopris West:
    - perfectionlearning.com
- Teaching tips:
  - teachingtips.com
- Collection of language arts websites:
  - ginaotto.com
  - free.ed.gov
  - alline.org
  - promisingpractices.net
  - mcgraw-hill.co.uk
  - talkingfingers.com
  - readingnaturally.com
- Writing Instruction
  - literacyleader.com
  - doc.renlearn.com
  - wire.rutgers.edu
- What's the Word? Vocabulary-Building Product—A vocabulary-building product utilizing videos, flashcards, and workbooks to teach over 600 commonly tested words; use for test prep and basic vocabulary building for ages 13 to adult:
  - whats-the-word.com

Math
- Saxon Math:
  - saxonmath.com
- Touchmath:
  - touchmath.com
- Connecting the Concepts:
  - mcgraw-hill.com

Science Adaptations
- lessonplanspage.com
- reachoutmichigan.org

Social Studies Adaptations
- socialstudieslessons.com
- lesson-plans.theteacherscorner.net
- neat-schoolhouse.org

Peer Tutoring
- study-guide-services-review.toptenreviews.com
- ncrel.org

English as a Second Language (ESL) and Sheltered Content Instruction
- siop.pearson.com
- pearsonpd.com
- teachingenglishlearners.com
- eslmonkeys.com

(continued)

FIGURE 7.2 Continued

- Internet TESOL Journal—A monthly web magazine for ESL teachers and students; includes lesson plans, classroom handouts, links of interest, articles, research papers, and other materials of immediate practical use:

    iteslj.org

- EslGames.com—Home page of Edutainment, a photocopy-free book on the subject of teaching with games; provides free samples, as well as an essay on why pop music should be integrated into the English curriculum:

    eslgames.com

- Welcome to ESL Research—Indexes ESL, TESOL, EFL journals, online journals, search engines, and databases for ESL and applied linguistics professionals:

    eslresearch.com

- moramodules.com

- cal.org

FIGURE 7.3 Original Text

Agriculture. Farmers in Middle Atlantic States grow many kinds of crops. In much of the region, the soil is fertile, or rich in the things plants need for growth. There is usually plenty of sunshine and rain. Each state has become famous for certain crops. New York is well-known for apples. New Jersey tomatoes and blueberries, Delaware white sweet corn, Pennsylvania mushrooms, and Maryland grains and other well-known crops. Herds of dairy cattle and livestock for meat are also raised in Atlantic States. The region produces a great deal of food for millions of people who live there.

Truck Farms. New Jersey is famous for its truck farms, which grow large amounts of many different vegetables for sale. Truck farms usually sell their products to businesses in a nearby city. New Jersey truck farms are the best known, but truck farms are found in all the Middle Atlantic States.

  Another way truck farmers sell their crops is at farmers' markets in cities. Sometimes a farmers' market is outside, on the street, or in a city park. A market may be in a railroad station or in the lobby of a skyscraper. At a farmers' market, city people and farmers can meet each other face to face.

Source: D. J. Short, Adapting materials for content-based language instruction, *ERIC/CLL News Bulletin, 13* (no. 1, 1989), 1, 4–8.

timelines, and clusters to modify difficult texts. For example, the segment on agriculture in the Middle Atlantic states can be illustrated by a visual depiction of the states (see Figure 7.4), with pictures of crops grown in each state (see Figure 7.5). Photographs, drawings, videotapes, and the Internet provide a number of visual representations useful for the topics covered.

  Graphic organizers and visualization strategies are useful tools in helping students organize their thoughts in a meaningful way, enabling them to recall information and to recap a theme or topic. (For additional examples, see www.GraphicOrganizers.com, a website created by Ed Ellis and colleagues at the University of Alabama.)

 Watch this video and discuss how graphic organizers are picture representations of strategies.

  One type of graphic organizer is a web or a map. Webs provide simple visualization strategies. In a cluster, the parts of a topic are written in a radiating pattern around the encircled word. When teaching a second-grade class about the parts of a story, the teacher writes the title in a big circle in the center and the story parts in smaller circles radiating

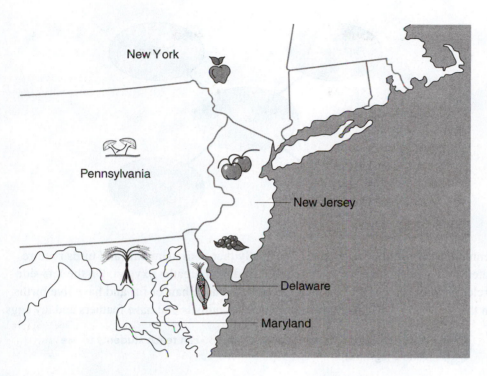

Source: D. J. Short, Adapting materials for content-based language instruction, *ERIC/CLL News Bulletin, 13* (no. 1, 1989), 1, 4–8.

FIGURE 7.5 Pictures of Crops

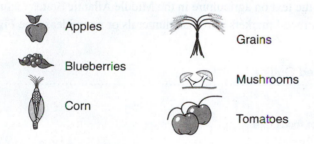

Source: D. J. Short, Adapting materials for content-based language instruction, *ERIC/CLL News Bulletin, 13* (no. 1, 1989), 1, 4–8.

from the center (see Figure 7.6). The teacher uses the graphic organizer after students read each new story. The parts of the story and the graphic organizer thus become ingrained in the students' thinking.

A Venn diagram is also a good example of a graphic organizer that can be used to modify a text and to reduce important points to an easily observed, simple format. The Venn diagram concept, borrowed from set theory in mathematics, can be used to demonstrate differences and similarities among situations, characters, or other selected aspects of a work. The differences are listed in large left and right circle portions, and the similarities are listed in the intersection of the two circles. For example, in a science lesson on a comparison of mammals with birds, the intersection of two circles in a

FIGURE 7.6 Story Mapping

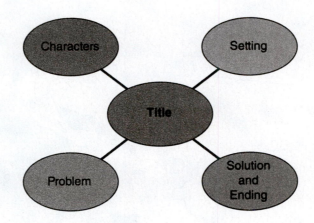

Venn diagram could be used to show visually that both mammals and birds require water, move independently, are warm blooded, and breathe oxygen. On the left-side circle, mammals are represented as animals that have hair or fur and have live births. On the right-side circle, birds are represented as animals that have feathers and lay eggs.

 Watch this video and think about how you can teach students to use Venn Diagrams.

Outline the Text. Several types of outlining can be effective for summarizing and emphasizing important information in a text. The traditional framed outline allows the student to see and prioritize key points, which facilitates understanding and memory. A framed outline has major chapter sections represented by roman numerals, main ideas by capital letters, and important details by numbers under each capital letter. For example, the framed outline for the text on agriculture in the Middle Atlantic States includes agriculture, truck farms, and farmers' markets as roman numerals or main ideas (see Figure 7.7).

FIGURE 7.7 Framed Outline

Middle Atlantic States
I. Agriculture
   A. Many kinds of food crops
   B. State crops
      1. New York: apples
      2. New Jersey: tomatoes, blueberries
      3. Delaware: corn
      4. Pennsylvania: mushrooms
      5. Maryland: grains
   C. Cows for milk and meat
II. Truck Farms
   A. Many truck farms in New Jersey
   B. Sell vegetables to stores in a city
III. Farmers' Markets
   A. Farmers sell crops in the city
      1. On a street
      2. In a park
      3. In a train station
      4. In a building
   B. Farmers and city people meet

Source: D. J. Short, Adapting materials for content-based language instruction, *ERIC/CLL News Bulletin, 13* (no. 1, 1989), 1, 4–8.

Your Turn

> How can you use graphic organizers to represent strategies? Think of a learning strategy you would like to teach and make up a graphic organizer to represent that strategy. How can the use of graphics enhance memory?

Rewrite the Text. Rewriting curriculum is an effective way to differentiate materials. Teachers of English learners agree that most texts are written at or above grade level. As a result, many students do not read at the grade level for which the reading materials are intended. Written materials should be organized in small, sequential steps, avoiding long passages with dense groups of words. Short, simple sentences are preferable to long, complex sentences. Here is an example of a complex sentence from a science text: "Electrons have negative electric charges and orbit around the core, the nucleus, of an atom." The sentence can be improved by forming several new sentences: "Electrons have negative electric charges. They orbit around the atom. The core of the atom is called the nucleus."

If a text is rewritten, paragraphs must include a topic sentence and several supporting detail sentences. The rewritten text should maintain a specific format to promote easy reading. All sentences in the rewritten text should be direct and relevant to the subject. For example, the original text (see Figure 7.3) is a series of sentences, some of which do not relate to the topic. When the paragraph is rewritten (see Figure 7.8), there is a clear topic sentence: "Farmers grow many foods, or crops, in the Middle Atlantic states." The detail sentences follow and support the topic sentence. Key information can be listed with bullets or indented lines. The rewritten paragraphs are shorter and focus only on the central information.

When a text is rewritten, often the academic tasks that accompany the text must be modified as well. For example, when rewriting a section in a text, questions should be written to accompany the section. If the paragraph has been rewritten to reflect a main idea, the students can be asked to identify the main idea of the paragraph. For example, "What types of crops are grown by farmers in the Middle Atlantic states?" is a logical question to accompany the rewritten paragraph. When modifying a text, the number of questions and the number of pages assigned can be modified to structure the activities for maximum success.

FIGURE 7.8 Original Text, Rewritten

Agriculture in the Middle Atlantic States
Farmers grow many foods, or crops, in the Middle Atlantic States. The soil is good for plants. The plants have enough sunshine and rain to grow. Each state has one or two special crops:

    New York: apples
    New Jersey: tomatoes and blueberries
    Delaware: corn
    Pennsylvania: mushrooms
    Maryland: grains

The farmers also raise cows. They get milk from some cows. They get meat from other cows.

New Jersey has many truck farms. The farmers grow a lot of vegetables. They bring the vegetables to the city by truck. They sell the vegetables to stores in the city.

Farmers also sell their crops at farmers' markets. Some markets are outside. They can be on streets or in city parks. Other markets are inside. They can be in train stations or in buildings. City people and farmers can meet each other at the markets.

Source: D. J. Short, Adapting materials for content-based language instruction, *ERIC/CLL News Bulletin, 13* (no. 1, 1989), 1, 4–8.

Questions can be rewritten and presented one at a time, or students can use a reading window to frame one question at a time on the paper. A reading window is made by cutting an inch-high slot the width of a printed page in a sheet of cardboard.

Written directions in text or on handouts should be rewritten to conform to the lowest reading level in the class. If directions are convoluted, they should be rewritten and simplified. For the preceding text on agriculture, the original directions read, "Once you have read the passage below, determine what the author is trying to express. Mark the key words and the most important points." The directions were rewritten to read, "Read this paragraph. Underline one main idea. Circle three key words."

Audiotape Versions of the Text.   Teachers can put sections or entire chapters on audiotape. Students with reading difficulties can listen to the tape and hear the material come alive. Since 2007, the federal government has allocated extensive funding to strengthen and add to the number of books on tape for the blind, visually impaired, and dyslexic. However, these materials are available to the public and could be very beneficial for second-language learners as well (see www.LearningAlly.org for full and detailed information). Students can also listen to tapes over and over again to reinforce learning. Teachers can ensure the information necessary for assignments and testing is recorded for class members to use. Students can be assigned to help with the recording. Each week a group of students can be made responsible for recording the material that will be made available for the class.

Provide Live Demonstrations.   Live demonstrations can bring life to a text. In the agriculture example, if the teacher brings vegetables and fruits to class representing the various crops, the lesson will be more interesting. If the teacher shows a videotape on farming or picking crops like those mentioned in the lesson, the lesson may be more realistic. Of course, video examples are excellent and can often be used to illustrate content (Gersten, Baker, Smith-Johnson, Dimino, & Petersen, 2006).

Use Alternate Books.   Teachers can select alternate books with similar concepts but at an easier reading level as a modification, meaning that the standard may be adapted for the learner. Alternate books are typically called high-interest–low-vocabulary books. For specific examples of available books and series see: childrensbooks.about.com/od/toppicks/tp/hi_lo_books.htm

Alternate books focus on the same required curriculum material but are written to make reading automatic. The focus is on the curriculum rather than on the challenges of decoding the vocabulary and reading the text. Teachers in many different grades find that students with two sets of books progress faster. One set of books kept at school and one set at home aid the student in doing home reading and homework assignments. (See Chapter 5 for information on parent support and involvement.)

Modifying Assignments

If the student understands the information but is unable to express this knowledge in writing, he or she should be provided alternative forms of expression (Bos, 1995; Fitzgerald & Graves, 2004). Language-proficiency level must not be confused with a student's knowledge of the subject matter. Teachers are often quite knowledgeable about a variety of topics, but if they were asked to explain a concept, such as the three branches of the government, in a language other than English, most would be unable to communicate their knowledge. The same is true of English learners. Their language skills may restrict expression of actual understanding of a subject matter. Examples of alternate assignments include the following:

- objectives
- drawing maps or pictorial representations
- oral discussions in pairs or small groups
- changing the length and complexity of assignments

Students' performances improve if they use set formats for note taking, writing activities, practice activities, homework, and progress checks. Examples of each type of modified assignment follow, based on the unit on consumerism described in Chapter 3.

Use Simplified Objectives.   As with the Common Core State Standards, having fewer objectives that are clearer and more focused on higher expectations can be more powerful than the alternatives. A simplified lesson clearly specifies objectives and focuses on products and learning that directly relate to the objective. For example, a third-grade science chapter on the solar system could have the simple objectives of teaching students to say the names of the planets and having them construct a clay-and-wire model of the planets and their relationships to the sun. Information about miles from the sun, moons, gases, makeup of the surface of the planets, and so on will not be included in the objectives. The simplified objectives require fewer chapter questions and less reading in the chapter, while still reflecting grade-level students.

In the lesson from Chapter 3 on consumerism, the teacher simplified objectives recommended in the text. The original objectives were (1) to help students identify what health values to look for in products and services; (2) to learn how product labels can help consumers; (3) to learn how consumers can make informed decisions; and (4) to study how advertising can help consumers. Instead, the teacher offered these objectives each day: (1) "Today we will learn how to buy healthy products." (2) "Today we will learn how to buy wisely." (3) "Today we will learn how to read labels when we buy." and (4) "Today we will learn how to study advertisements before we buy." By focusing on one objective per day, reading loads were reduced and students were able to concentrate on one aspect of being a consumer without complicating their thinking.

Ask Students to Draw.   Requiring students to draw maps or pictures enhances learning and functions as an alternate form of expression for students struggling with English. This type of assessment adaptation is highly recommended when possible and can offer another bit of evidence as to the knowledge and skills of the learner. For example, a high school science teacher asked students to draw a map of the water cycle during a lesson about condensation and evaporation. Drawing a map of the water cycle was an alternate way to find out what the students had learned. In another example, third-grade students were asked to draw a story map of *How the Children Stopped the Wars* (Wahl, 1969). The students drew the series of events and the characters from the story and placed the pictures in the appropriate order on a storyboard. The students were able to draw the pictures conveying their understanding even though oral expression of the story line was still quite difficult for them.

In the unit on consumerism, students were asked to draw a model of the steps to take when making a purchase. In groups, students drew a person looking for cheaper prices, thinking about what healthy products to buy, reading labels, and comparing prices and health values before buying. Students illustrated a story about saving the family money and what the savings could be used to purchase.

Promote Collaborative, Interpretive, and Productive Experiences.   As presented in the language development section of this chapter, the teacher can provide many opportunities for language use while simultaneously developing content knowledge. Language-development activities can include student pairs or small student groups in which students talk about issues or content, read aloud or silently, write group reports, or solve group problems (Arreaga-Mayer, 1998; August & Shanahan, 2006). A middle school social studies teacher paired strong English learners with students weaker in English. When the teacher asked a question that required more than a one-word answer, the students were asked to talk to their partners about the answer. The teacher also created problem-solving activities and projects where students were placed in four-person cooperative groups. In the groups were usually two English learners with strong skills and two who were not fluent. A cooperative group assignment required the students to construct an Old West Boomtown. Each group had access to wooden sticks, glue, colored paper, markers, crayons, and scissors. Students constructed the towns based on their knowledge of the Gold Rush and the types of businesses likely to be present at that time. Alternate group structures and alternate assignments can both be ideal for students struggling to learn English and content material.

In the unit on consumerism, the students who received sheltered instruction participated in hands-on activities with partners and in small groups. Students discussed items at the stations such as shampoo, soap, shoes, and socks. The students were to decide which items were the best buys and why. Students strong in English were sometimes paired with weaker students. Answers were written on workstation sheets cooperatively.

During other assignments in the unit on consumerism, students formed cooperative groups to score advertisements. For this activity the teacher established a 4-minute time limit. This allowed students to talk among themselves but provided structure for the activity. Students were able to complete more activities and have time to share results with each other when the teacher imposed time constraints.

Collaborative Strategic Reading (CSR) (Klingner, Vaughn, Arguelles, Hughes, & Leftwich, 2004) is an example of alternative cooperative grouping designed to teach students to use comprehension strategies such as previewing the text; giving ongoing feedback by deciding "click" (I get it) or "clunk" (I don't get it) at the end of each paragraph; "getting the gist" of the most important parts of the text; and "wrapping up" key ideas. To introduce how the students could use the strategies, the teacher models the use of the strategies by demonstrating and asking students to take turns being the teacher. The concepts are made clear to students before they participate in cooperative group learning in that the teacher typically asks students to make predictions and find important information in other contexts. Once students are in their groups, they are able to work more cooperatively to answer important questions and comprehend text because they already know the concepts. Students are more successful in the groups when they have cue cards or think sheets that remind them of the steps of each strategy, for example:

> Step One: Make a prediction
> Step Two: I get it; OR reread
> Step Three: Summarize
> Step Four: State three or four big ideas

Reduce the Length and Difficulty of Assignments.   Teachers can choose assignments carefully and make them extremely useful to the students. Teachers can also try additional accommodations to reduce the length and complexity of assignments. Here are some examples of ways to modify and adapt assignments.

- Use clear, simple wording.
- Reduce the number of spelling words in spelling tests to include only the most functional.
- Provide an alternative to written assignments, such as clay models, posters, panoramas, or collections (such as posters of the steps to take when buying wisely).
- Focus on mastery of only key concepts. (For example, the glossary in the consumer unit can be modified to five terms.)
- Pare down complex assignments into simpler, more meaningful parts.
- Assign the students only one page of a workbook at a time so they are not overwhelmed.
- Make bright construction paper borders or reading windows (made from the faces of window envelopes) for the students to place around reading material or vocabulary words to keep their attention.
- Allow students to use a highlighter to identify keywords, phrases, or sentences.
- Establish expectations based on students' needs and review expectations frequently (that is, determine how students are responding and decide to move on or to review material already covered).

Preparing for Advanced Academic Engagement

For students at Levels 4, 5, and 6 in their language proficiency, advanced academic engagement is critical. The teacher may differentiate instruction in order to ensure success by making structural and strategic accommodations and adaptations to provide additional support. Important activities for academic success include note taking, study sheets, homework, progress monitoring, using rewriting text, highlighting main points for the class, study resource guides, and encouraging cooperative efforts with other teachers.

Note taking. When teachers demonstrate a form of note taking, students learn how it can be used in other academic and personal areas. For example, all teachers in a middle school were trained in the use of a modified version of the Cornell note taking system invented by Dr. Walter Pauk at Cornell University. The original version involved five simple stages for taking notes: record, reduce, recite, reflect, and review. The school modified the language of the system and made the note-taking strategy less complex by using familiar words. The modified version had four stages: write notes, write keywords, remember, and study. At the beginning of the year, each teacher in the school introduced the four-stage-note-taking strategy. The students were taught to divide each notebook page into two columns by drawing a vertical line down the paper about 2 inches from the left margin. The left column was to remain blank while students wrote notes in the right column. During the next class, the notes in the right column were used to recall key points, and those points were written in the left column adjacent to the notes. After the keywords were written, the students covered the right column with a piece of paper and looked only at the keywords to trigger their memories. The students reviewed the material each night until a test was given. This note-taking strategy can help all students organize their schoolwork. In the unit on consumers, students could use this format first to define terms, placing the words in the left column and the definitions in the right column. Students could then proceed to list key points about wise consumers on the right side, with keywords to remind them about each of the points. For example, in the unit on consumerism presented in Chapter 3, in the right column a student might enter: "Consumers can use ads to get important information but should be wary of false advertising." To the left, the students might write: "Use of advertising." Students could be encouraged to take notes from what the teacher wrote throughout the unit. Students could also work together in pairs to read and make notes about the content.

Study Sheets and Homework.   Teachers of English learners can differentiate assignments by modifying study sheets, worksheets, and homework assignments to reduce their difficulty yet maximize their comprehensibility and applicability. For example, the number of science terms on a study sheet can be reduced or the assignment due date can be extended. Written materials and assignments are most effective if they are simply worded and directly related to the material taught in the class. Short words and simple sentences are best for directions. Study sheets are most appropriate when they reduce the covered material to the basic elements. Redundancy is maximized when students repeat information on the same study sheet. Anxiety can be reduced if students use the same types of study sheets for all units. When teachers clearly state expectations and instructions, student learning and efficiency are maximized. Homework provides students with opportunities to practice skills and learn material. Homework in its best form requires students to complete tasks or use information already mastered in the classroom. Students benefit from the home practice of concepts, vocabulary, or writing activities with which they feel comfortable. Good homework assignments reduce the possibility students will become frustrated with tasks requiring unfamiliar language or concepts. Unfamiliar directions or tasks are inappropriate for any types of written assignments. Students may build an aversion to written assignments of any kind if they do not understand an assignment. In the consumer unit in Chapter 3, the teacher provided study sheets to be used during various activities or done as homework. For example, students had worksheets to fill in as they analyzed advertisements and products. The worksheets were simple and had redundant questions, such as, "Look at this advertisement and write the important information. Also, write the information that is not important." The study sheet for products said, "Look at these two types of shoes. Which ones are the best buy? How do you know?" Students were encouraged to take study sheets home with their notes. A typical homework assignment was, "What kind of toothpaste does your family buy? How much did it cost? Was it the best buy? How do you know?" Students could use study sheets from class to complete homework. All of this information could be used to study for tests.

Assessment and Instruction Cycle.   Teachers need to know the progress of each student in order to modify and change instruction to meet curriculum objectives. Outcome-based accountability is essential in establishing improvements in both English language knowledge and content knowledge. Progress must be checked several times a week. Progress checks can range from informal study sheets and short writing assignments ("quick writes") to formal quizzes or tests and Writer's Workshop-style writing assignments. Interviews with students can also be useful as progress checks. Students' perceptions of their own work and abilities are often quite revealing. Individual portfolios and journals allow teachers to keep a chronological assessment of their students' daily work. Teachers are the best observers of student performance in the classroom. Modifications of assignments are necessary if students are performing below appropriate levels for individual language development and content mastery.

In the consumer unit, all of the papers and assignments a student completed were placed in a folder with his or her name on it. On the inside cover of each folder was a grid that listed all of the assignments and homework. The teacher graded each assignment and placed either a check or a grade beside each completed item on the rubric. Students were also required to include notes taken, tests taken, and reports written in their folders. All of these activities were marked on the grid so students and parents could see what had been completed at a glance. Then, both students and parents could review the students' work in greater depth as they looked through the folder. The teacher gained valuable information about the level of performance of each learner through this progress-monitoring system.

Using Study Resource Guides.   Study resource guides can maximize the use of visual aids and other materials. Teachers often express the need for more materials and visual aids that are appropriate for teaching English learners. Photographs, slides, sketches, and videotapes are effective supplementary materials. Providing concrete, hands-on experiences serves to increase students' understanding of the subject matter. Most districts provide a list of resources for teachers to use in supplementing the curriculum. Options for supplementing the core curriculum are often included in resource guides. Rather than researching topics and spending time looking for materials, a teacher might find supplemental material listed in a district guide. For example, on the topic of the War for Independence, the district resource guide may provide suggestions for activities such as creating a colonial newspaper, a list of relevant movies (such as *Crossing the Delaware* or *A Fireball in the Night*), or a list of reading selections (for example, *Paul Revere's Ride,* by Henry Wadsworth Longfellow, or *I'm Deborah Sampson: A Soldier in the War of the Revolution,* by Patricia Clapp).

Have Students Rewrite.   One way to facilitate differentiated instruction is to have students rewrite texts as part of course assignments. Students can write paragraphs in their own words. For example, cooperative groups of four students could rewrite a certain section of the text using specified guidelines for proper paragraph formation. Or teachers could require students to rewrite sections individually. In still another variation, teachers could use a language experience approach to facilitate curricular adaptation. The whole class or small student groups could decide through discussion how to rewrite sections of the text. The teacher might then write what the students suggest on the board. Over time, if the teacher collects the rewritten texts, it can be reused to support the learning of future students as well.

Highlight Main Points.   A similar method could be used to highlight the main points of a text. The students could use highlighting markers to focus on and mark the most salient aspects of the chapter. Teachers could give the text to the students and have them highlight as they read. Students could focus on and highlight main ideas and two supporting details for each main idea in a section or a chapter. The students could accomplish the task individually, in small groups, or as a whole-class activity. Students could also be asked to compare and contrast individual highlighting and reach a consensus on what should be highlighted before submitting the activity for a grade.

Encourage Cooperative Efforts Among Teachers.   In order to maximize outcomes and minimize effort, a cooperative project is possible in which each teacher is assigned to modify a number of chapters in the textbook using agreed-upon guidelines. The modified chapters are compiled and distributed. The project could be at grade level, or could be a school-wide or district-wide project. Schools improve the performances of students if they encourage similar differentiated instruction in grade-level teams of teachers and among school professionals in a learning community (see Chapter 8 for more information on this). Schools that adopt school-wide plans for differentiated instruction of study strategies, assignment calendars, homework systems, report-writing strategies, and the like are more inclined to increase the overall success of struggling learners. Redundancy in assignments and school policies strengthens the overall consistency and effectiveness of a school.

Summary

It is important to differentiate instruction to make it appropriate for all students—including English learners. Differentiated instruction for students who are learning English requires teachers to accommodate individually, adapt content, analyze content material, teach academic proficiency, rewrite curriculum, modify assignments, and maximize visual aids and resources. Make sure there is a focus on adapting instruction to include opportunities for students to listen, speak, read, and write in English while teaching content knowledge.

Specifically, as a reader you

- provided at least five examples of cultural and linguistic differentiation of instruction.
- identified examples of instructional differentiation for students with emerging English skills, expanding English skills, and advanced or bridging English skills.
- listed examples of accommodations for academic content.
- discussed the types of adaptations made for advanced learning and studying, as well as the level of language proficiency required for effective implementation.

Activities

1. Choose a lesson plan and provide differentiated instruction for it in these two ways:
   a. Demonstrate sensitivity to cultural and linguistic diversity.
   b. Provide background knowledge necessary for better understanding.
2. Use the lesson plan and analyze the material. Write objectives for essential content, content vocabulary, and areas of academic language development.
3. Using the same lesson plan, outline five possible text or assignment modifications to accommodate students who are English learners.
4. List several options teachers may use for obtaining assistance in differentiating instruction.

CHAPTER 8

Becoming a Reflective Practitioner

LEARNING OBJECTIVES:

- Explain the relationship between reflective practice and improved teaching.
- Describe the benefits of each of three types of professional development activities that lead to enhanced teaching.
- Identify the characteristics that distinguish videotape analysis from other types of reflective practice.
- Evaluate your teaching and set goals for improving performance.
- Find a pattern between the student vignettes and your goals for improving performance.

The Importance of Reflective Practice

Ongoing professional development is widely recognized as an important part of professional growth and as a way to improve teaching. While professional development takes on many forms, for it to be effective and take root in practice, teachers need to think about their experience, consider students' reaction to their

Annie Pickert Fuller/Pearson Education

146
....

CHAPTER 8

*Becoming a
Reflective
Practitioner*

teaching, and make adjustments. From the time of Dewey (1938) the relationship between experience and learning has been an integral part of effective teaching. That is, experience leads to learning and learning informs the way we approach new experiences. Teachers should reflect on their teaching and on how well students learned from the lesson based on observation and assessments (experiences), and then consider what changes are called for (learning). Adjustments to teaching reflect what was learned from the experience.

Reflective practitioners ask themselves what worked, what didn't work, and what should be changed in the next lesson. Formative and summative assessments provide valuable information for reflection. Teacher reflection informs planning, which in turn "sculpts their practices and results in increased student achievement" (Taylor & Pillets, 2010, p. 96). Since student learning and achievement is the ultimate goal of teaching, reflective practice ought to be an integral part of the teaching process.

In this chapter, we discuss the importance of professional development and explore three ways that it can be carried out. This discussion is situated in the idea that all professional development should result in teachers becoming more reflective as practitioners. In that vein, we conclude the chapter with a framework for readers' own reflection.

*P*rofessional Development

Although thinking about one's teaching, reflecting on it, and making adjustments are part of effective instruction, having an understanding of what works with English learners is an important first step in the process. Many teachers find themselves unprepared to work effectively with English learners because they did not receive adequate training in their teacher education program. They are not sure what are the most effective techniques and practices to use with students who are learning in and through a new language. Although adequate teacher preparation and support are critical for those teaching English learners, they are typically in short supply. As one study revealed, "One of the most profound challenges that mainstream content-area teachers face in meeting the needs of English learners is the lack of ongoing support for working with such diverse student populations" (Bunch, Abram, Lotan, & Valdes, 2001, p. 24). In reality, teacher preparation is a process—not a set of courses—that lasts throughout one's career.

In this section, we discuss three ways that teachers can engage in professional development: through inservice programs, professional learning communities (PLC), and action research. These professional development activities are not mutually exclusive, and one can support the others.

For any type of professional development to be effective, there needs to be a school "culture" that encourages teacher growth and improvement. To best serve English learners—and all students—we advocate a schoolwide system that allows for planning time, collaboration, discussion, and reflection.

The following conditions are recommended for optimal professional growth (Standards from the National Staff Development Council, 2001). High-quality professional development:

- requires and fosters a norm of continuous improvement.
- entails long-term sustained involvement rather than brief, one-shot sessions.
- aligns with school and district content and performance standards.
- requires adequate time during the work day for staff members to learn and work collaboratively.

These conditions for changing and improving practice are part of a school's commitment to sustained professional development. The content of professional development—that is, what teachers will learn, grapple with, discuss, implement, and reflect on—is based on the needs of the staff and students. One source for professional development topics is the Teaching English to Speakers of Other Languages (TESOL) standards for ESL teachers. These standards address many topics that are also pertinent for any teacher of English learners. The domains include the following: Language (Language as a system; Language acquisition and development), Culture (as it affects students' learning), Planning, Implementing, and Managing Instruction (Standards-based ESL and content instruction), Assessment (Issues of assessment for English learners; language proficiency assessment; classroom-based assessment for ESL), and Professionalism (ESL research and history; professional development, partnerships, and advocacy).

As you can see, there are conditions for professional development as well as content that teachers of English learners should learn and reflect on in their practice. This can be done through a variety of professional development activities. Each of the three types of professional development—inservice sessions, action research, and PLCs—is enhanced when teachers strive to be reflective in their practice.

Inservice Sessions

As the number of English learners continues to increase, more districts offer inservice programs to help teachers work effectively with these students. Often, general education and special education teachers lack either sufficient preparation in second-language teaching methodology or experience in supporting second-language development, while those teachers who are English as a second language (ESL) certified may not have the content background to meet the increasing demands of standards-based content area curricula. Inservice sessions that include all teaching personnel allow for interaction and shared knowledge among staff.

Typically, inservice sessions are conducted by district staff with expertise on a topic or by outside consultants who are experts in an area or who may bring a fresh perspective to a topic. Session content might include supporting second-language development, involving parents as partners in the school, and implementing effective sheltered instruction. The knowledge gained through inservice sessions may be used for discussions in PLC meetings or may stimulate an action research project. For example, if the inservice topic is implementing effective sheltered instruction, a PLC discussion may revolve around ways to make lessons more comprehensible. Teachers may plan lessons together that include comprehensible input techniques. Some teachers may also decide to do action research by collecting student work samples from a lesson where comprehensible input techniques were used and comparing the work to that of previous lessons.

Action Research

The word *research* is sometimes intimidating to teachers and connotes a process involving statistics and formal writing. However, research is simply investigation, exploration, inquiry. In the context of teaching it is the ability to reflect on one's own actions (e.g., lesson planning, interacting with students, explaining a concept) with intention. It is a mindset for teaching that involves being observant, thoughtful, and willing to think about one's own actions with the students' best interest and best teaching practices in mind (Pelton, 2010).

148
....

CHAPTER 8

*Becoming a
Reflective
Practitioner*

Being an action researcher entails more than being a teacher who conducts an action research project. An action researcher continually learns from her teaching throughout her career and thus develops the skills and practices of systematic critical inquiry (Darling-Hammond & Friedlander, 2008). It is asking the basic question: How well are my students learning what I am teaching?

There are a variety of ways to conduct action research, and most include some form of the following stages (Freeman, 1998; Pelton, 2010; Sagor, 2011):

1. Identifying an issue or target. In this stage, you ask yourself: What do I want to accomplish? Develop specific goals and have a clear vision of what the outcome will be.

 Watch the video to see how one teacher identified the issue she wanted to research. What was her question?

2. Action planning. In this stage you ask yourself: What is the best approach for realizing my goals? Create a plan for your action, including the data that you will collect (e.g., work samples, monitoring of oral language production, and check lists).

3. Implementing the plan and collecting data. In this stage you ask yourself: What am I learning about teaching as I teach? Implement the plan, but be open to making adjustments as you proceed in order to create better results for your students. Collect the data that was part of your plan.

4. Reflecting on the outcome. In this stage, you ask yourself: Based on the data, how should I adjust my future actions (teaching)? Analyze the data you collected to determine what impact your actions had on your students. Use the data, your own observations and experience, and reflect on what worked and what didn't work. These reflections will inform your teaching and help you develop the mindset of an action researcher.

 Watch the video to see how the same teacher described one of the challenges she faced in analyzing the data. How does action research differ from quantitative research studies?

Action research also may be supported by other forms of professional development. For example, the issue or target of the investigation (Stage 1) might originate from inservice sessions. If an inservice addressed ways of improving the oral language proficiency of English learners, the target of the action research might be to increase oral language production. The plan would include structured opportunities for students to work in small groups or pairs and discuss the lesson's topic, and then monitor and assess their language production. The content of the inservice provided the impetus for the action research. Further, the results of the action research may be shared in a PLC meeting. Action research can also be conducted collaboratively within a PLC (Sangor, 2010).

Professional Learning Communities (PLC)

The need for sustained and more internally developed professional improvement in the schools is well established (Darling-Hammond & Bransford, 2005; Gallimore, Ermeling, Saunders, & Goldenberg, 2009; Short, 2000). Professional learning communities are developed by the teachers themselves in an effort to improve their own instruction as well as to respond to learners and their families, particularly those students who are not thriving in school. An important feature of any successful learning community is the belief that problems can be solved and that all students can learn (Huffman & Jacobson, 2003). Such a belief helps divert teachers from thinking that struggling students should be labeled with learning disabilities and refocuses them on continual development of responsive instruction when students are having difficulty in school (Rueda & Windmueller, 2006).

To prepare students to be college and career ready and to provide instruction that is responsive to the needs of English learners and struggling learners, teachers in professional learning communities:

- continue to learn more about the subject matter, deeply and flexibly thinking about the content to be taught.
- continue to gain knowledge about learning (teaching strategies, decision-making strategies about the content to cover and the best way to do so, assessment strategies, language acquisition theory).
- use skills in differentiating instruction, curriculum resources, and technologies.
- collaborate with parents, grade-level peers, special education teachers, and other teachers who have direct knowledge about the students.
- analyze and reflect on teaching practices.
- assess the effects of teaching practices through formative and summative assessments.
- continue to refine and improve teaching practices.

As you can see, these recommendations are aligned with the purpose of other professional development activities such as inservice sessions and action research. Professional development activities can be mutually supportive. Inservice sessions from an outside "expert" or a trainer from the district office can be used as the agenda for action research or a PLC.

Professional learning communities are critical for building a school culture that is responsive to students who are not thriving (Brown & Doolittle, 2008; Darling-Hammond & Bransford, 2005; Sangor, 2011). For change to occur at the school level, teachers need time to meet together and opportunities for self-evaluation, goal setting, and discussions of common problems (Capps et al., 2005; Goldenberg, 2004; Saunders et al., 2009). Credential candidates can also benefit from collaboration with peers and can begin the process early in their preparation to think about working together to solve problems in the schools. Four features tend to enhance this process: meeting time with skilled consultants and tapping into existing knowledge and skills on the team, meetings organized around perceived needs or areas of concern, evaluations of lesson delivery and student achievement, and videotaping of lessons to allow for analysis and review.

Mastery of the elements of sheltered instruction presented in this book requires systematic implementation and practice. Although many features of sheltered instruction are not necessarily new, they seem more complex when teachers are striving to achieve consistently effective lessons with a heterogeneous group of students. The collaborative group can share readings on sheltered instruction, garnering ideas to put into practice. Teachers in the group can assist one another in planning specific lessons, designing action research, or developing a comprehensive curriculum plan for the whole year. For more reflection on PLCs, please see the Your Turn feature.

Your Turn

Some of the teachers in your school want to form a professional learning community as a way to collaborate with each other, gain ideas, grapple with improving lessons, and improve their teaching. What might be three considerations for the group to discuss as you plan to get your PLC started?

The Value of Video Reflection and Analysis

The SIOP® Model discussed in Chapter 3 was used for three years to train and coach middle school teachers in implementing effective sheltered lessons in their classes in four urban school districts, two on the East Coast and two on the West Coast (Echevarria, Short, & Powers, 2006). The English learners in the classes ranged in English proficiency levels from beginning to advanced and represented a number of native-language groups. The teachers and researchers met monthly to discuss successes and challenges of implementing the SIOP, and each summer, a three-day summer institute was held. Also, teachers were videotaped three times per year, and the videotaped lessons were often used for reflection, analysis, and discussion at meetings. The project helped teachers expand their knowledge base and refine their practice.

The process of videotaping a lesson, analyzing it, and discussing it with colleagues creates a context for reflection, prompting thought about what goes on in the lesson and toward what end. A group of teachers involved in the process suggested that meetings take place once a week, but if that was not possible, then at least once a month to monitor progress and stay on track. As one put it, "It forces you to think about what you're doing. Teachers tend to zip through the lesson, the week, and the year without really reflecting." Teachers in the group learn from one another by sharing concerns or describing areas in which they are struggling. The group can offer assistance by validating the positive aspects of lessons and constructively pointing out areas that need improvement. Much more can be accomplished by peers viewing videotapes of lessons than by a teacher doing it alone. Most teachers find the work group supportive, offering constructive comments when needed and compliments on positive outcomes. Teachers consistently say that hearing the ideas of others helps: "Sometimes you know something was wrong or didn't work but you couldn't think of how to do it differently."

A forum in which teachers can share areas of need and elicit ideas from one another has proven beneficial in sustaining ongoing movement toward change (Gallimore et al., 2009). The evaluation of classroom lesson delivery should be as much a part of the learning process as is the evaluation of student achievement (Dutro & Kinsella, 2010). The process of meeting together, discussing readings, and analyzing videotaped lessons and student performance assists teachers to better conceptualize and implement sheltered techniques. As group members grapple with implementing specific features of sheltered instruction and share activities that are particularly effective, they become more conscious of what it is they are doing every day in the classroom and become more reflective as practitioners.

Videotaping teachers' lessons and providing opportunities for them to review, reflect on and analyze their efforts is indispensable. It is one thing for teachers to plan to improve a particular aspect of their teaching, but it is quite another to see exactly how the lesson unfolds. Videotape offers a completely objective set of eyes that capture not only the teacher's role in the lesson but also the students' participation levels and reactions to the lesson. A high school teacher commented, "It is more than seeing [the lesson] in your mind; you're a little more removed from the lesson itself and can give it an objective look." That objectivity reveals the parts of the lesson that went well and identifies things that could have been done differently. Visuals that were particularly helpful in illustrating a point or an activity that was fun and instructive will surely warrant being used again. Some parts of the lesson may need to be altered—maybe too much time was spent on a certain part and the students lost interest—while other parts may need to be left out altogether. In the process of teaching, it is nearly impossible to deliver the lesson and at the same time to reflect on the effectiveness of every aspect.

Sheltered lessons are most effective when teachers reflect on their own teaching behaviors and compare them to the components discussed in Chapter 3. Videotape allows teachers to monitor behaviors such as using gestures (frequency and timing), talking too fast, using idioms, and enunciation. One teacher said, "I never realized I said 'um' and 'okay' and 'you guys' too much." Another teacher acknowledged that she used gestures quite effectively, while a colleague noticed that he used idioms, which he had not realized previously. For example, he repeated several times "You've got that down pat" and "Keep your shirt on" in addition to saying "This is a kick-back activity" and "Don't blow this question off."

Videotape can also yield valuable information regarding student behavior. It becomes clear when students are bored with an activity or when there is too much teacher talk—they disengage, talk among themselves, put their heads down, and so forth—as well as when they are particularly stimulated by an activity or discussion. Perhaps the students did not comprehend something, but at the time the teacher was unaware and forged ahead. Later viewing can show what teacher behaviors led to the confusion: Did the teacher use only verbal explanation without any visuals? Was the pace too fast? Was there sufficient guided practice? Such information helps in planning future lessons, reflecting on aspects that need modification. In terms of behavior management, one teacher realized from watching the videotape that every time she turned to write on the blackboard, one student began fooling around, punching the student next to him. Based on this information, she began using an easel on which she could write while facing the group. A fifth-grade teacher commented, "There are so many things you're not aware of because you're focusing on the moment. You need to step back and see what's going on."

While there is little question that videotaping may be the single-most effective way for teachers to reflect, self-analyze, and improve their teaching, it is also difficult for many teachers to be videotaped, particularly if colleagues will be viewing the tape. One teacher commented, "I hated it. I was petrified. I couldn't sleep. But it did really help. I saw my kids in a different way. They loved it." Another said, "It takes a lot of guts to face yourself. I hate hearing myself on tape or seeing myself on video." Frequently, the idea of seeing oneself on videotape is more difficult than actually doing it. Teachers overwhelmingly endorse the value of analyzing videotape and often tape themselves for their own benefit. However, for those teachers who are reticent about videotaping themselves, audiotaping lessons can also be quite informative. It is less intrusive and teachers can analyze many aspects of their teaching by reflecting on the audio version of lessons.

Self-Evaluation and Goal Setting

The purpose of this section is to provide a framework (see Figure 8.1) to assist teachers in self-evaluation and goal setting in order to improve their instruction of English learners. When students struggle due to learning challenges or second-language issues, it is the responsibility of the teacher to adjust the learning environments to meet students' needs (Echevarria, Richards-Tutor & Vogt, 2014; Figueroa & Newsome, 2006). Teachers can rate themselves on a scale of 1 to 5 on each item in the framework (5 = outstanding, 4 = very good, 3 = marginal, 2 = needs improvement, 1 = not being addressed).

FIGURE 8.1 Framework for Self-Assessment and Goal Setting Within the Professional
Learning Community

Steps and Factors to Consider

1. Conduct Assessment of Student Learning on an Individual Basis and Plan Instruction Accordingly
   a. Native-language knowledge and home experience
   b. English-language knowledge for instruction including annual assessment data
   c. Data on successful school experience
   d. Establish monthly goals
   e. Learning and behavior patterns including gifts and talents
   f. Consider using tiered instruction as an approach for teaching

2. Consider Theories Across Disciplines
   a. Reviewing—check previous day's work and reteach if necessary—connect to practices and learning theories reflecting the language background knowledge
   b. Clarify objectives for teaching and for the learner
   c. Verify that content/skills are appropriate to grade level
   d. Present a variety of delivery modes including modeling, demonstration, and visual representations
   e. Provide ample student practice including frequent questions, verbal encouragement, and feedback
   f. Provide ample independent practice including higher-order skills such as problem solving, hypothesizing, organizing, synthesizing, categorizing, evaluating, and self-monitoring
   g. Provide weekly and monthly reviews

3. Use Sheltered Instruction
   a. Clearly defined content and language objectives
   b. Use supplementary materials when appropriate to improve the lessons
   c. Provide concrete examples of content
   d. Adapt content to students' academic levels
   e. Adjust speech appropriate to students' proficiency levels
   f. Link learning to students' experiences
   g. Select and teach key vocabulary

4. Explicitly teach academic language
   a. Develop and teach language objectives
   b. Adjust your language so that it is comprehensible
   c. Use interactive approaches
   d. Activate and use background knowledge
   e. Promote complex language and expression
   f. Require students to support stated positions with sources
   g. Ask many questions for which there are no single right answers
   h. Encourage student elaborations
   i. Encourage student dialogue about topics
   j. Provide a challenging but nonthreatening atmosphere
   k. Encourage equal participation and open forum discussions

5. Promote Affective and Cultural Connections
   a. Provide reading and writing activities that enable success
   b. Provide ample practice and careful corrections
   c. Focus on relevant background knowledge
   d. Actively involve learners
   e. Use alternative grouping
   f. Provide native-language support
   g. Focus on content and activities that are meaningful to students

FIGURE 8.1 Continued

153

CHAPTER 8

Becoming a Reflective Practitioner

     h. Create roles in the classroom for family and community members

     i. Hold high expectations for all learners

     j. Be responsive to cultural and personal diversity

6. Use Learning Strategies

     a. Define a learning strategy and delineate types of learning strategies

     b. Provide guidelines for selecting learning strategies

     c. Describe lesson formats when teaching learning strategies

     d. Identify presentation methods used to teach learning strategies

     e. Embed specific strategies in reading, writing, and content areas

7. Use Differentiated Instruction

     a. Demonstrate sensitivity to cultural and linguistic diversity

     b. Provide relevant background knowledge

     c. Analyze curriculum into domains of content knowledge and academic proficiency and provide accommodations for both

     d. Provide language, vocabulary, and academic language development

     e. Modify text

     f. Modify assignments

     g. Assign note taking, study sheets, homework, and progress monitoring

     h. Use study resource guides

     i. Encourage collaboration

8. Engage in Self-Evaluation and Goal Setting

     a. Score yourself on a scale of 1 to 5 on the previous steps

     b. Set goals by focusing on those areas that have the lowest scores

9. Collaborate with Colleagues

     a. Plan an action research project on your own or with colleagues.

     b. Meet in peer work groups and encourage schoolwide and coordinated change

     c. Exchange lessons and discuss steps 1 to 8

     d. Plan that each teacher will share successes and challenges

     e. Videotape lessons and analyze according to steps 1 to 8

     f. Plan a unit together and brainstorm applications from steps and factors above

Teachers can use these ratings to set personal goals, focusing on areas that need improvement. This process provides teachers with an opportunity for reflective teaching. Teachers are able to continually extend their knowledge, work at perfecting their techniques, and analyze the merits of both older and newer pedagogical approaches.

*R*evisit Student Vignettes and Reflect on Practice

In Chapter 1, we described the four students who represent four types of English learners: Nico, Rahul, Agnessa, and Luisa. Think of them as you use the framework and consider which of your students are similar to the learners described here.

Nico is a tenth-grader who was born in Guatemala. He moved to Southern California in the second grade. He was a good student in Guatemala and learned to read and write in Spanish. When he began school in the United States, he was placed in a bilingual classroom, where he received native-language support before transitioning into English instruction. Now in high school, he is performing at or above grade level in mainstream classes and has communication and literacy skills in his native language as well. Because Nico can speak, read, and write well in both languages, his English teacher is considering referring him to the gifted program at her school.

Rahul is a recent immigrant who attends middle school. He has grade-level academic ability in his native language but speaks very little English. Since he has lived all his 13 years outside the United States, certain kinds of cultural knowledge present difficulties for him. Rahul is quite shy and does not seek help readily. He has excellent social and academic language skills in his primary language and has already studied English for a few years, but his proficiency is limited. His history of learning and behavior at school, at home, and in the community is positive. He is described as a good citizen and a student who demonstrates appropriate behavior in most settings.

When *Agnessa* was six years old, an American family adopted her from an orphanage in Russia. She has an older brother who is the biological child of her parents. Now in third grade, Agnessa has very limited literacy skills. Even her spoken English is quite limited when she interacts with students and the teacher in class. Her family is concerned that Agnessa doesn't seem to be making sufficient academic progress and she has had a number of behavior problems in school. She has been caught stealing twice this year, and she is often uncooperative in class.

Born in an urban U.S. city, *Luisa* is a friendly 15-year-old who sits quietly in class, as if she understands everything. When written assignments are given, she writes them down and begins to work. Her handwriting, however, is illegible and her spelling is extremely poor. Spanish is her first language, although her family speaks a mix of English and Spanish at home. She writes in English in a knowledge-telling mode without recognizable structure in her sentences or in her paragraphs. Luisa can converse quite well in both languages but for some reason has not made academic progress in either language. She has been labeled with a learning disability. Although she is popular at school, she is at risk for dropping out because of consistent underachievement.

These are some of the types of learners who are represented in schools today and who need the instructional practices presented in this book. The framework provided in Figure 8.1 is a series of nine steps that can assist a teacher in reflecting on and evaluating current instructional practices and setting goals that will produce change for both teacher and students.

Step 1 on the framework is taken from Chapter 1. It illustrates areas needing both assessment and instructional planning: native-language knowledge, English-language knowledge, school experience and academic background, and learning and behavior patterns. Instructional planning starts after assessment of the student and can be developed keeping all of the factors we have discussed in Chapters 1 to 7 in mind.

Step 2 on the framework is derived from Chapter 2. We concluded in this chapter that teachers make instructional choices that reflect particular theoretical perspectives. In Step 2, we have listed some factors that are sometimes referred to as effective instruction. Theorists agree that students learn more if a teacher reviews previous work and relevant content before beginning a lesson. This includes assisting students in focusing on relevant background knowledge. After this, the teacher makes a goal statement in language understandable to the learners. As the teacher begins the lesson, new content and skills are at an appropriate grade level for learners and the teacher is careful to use many different approaches, including modeling, presenting concrete objects when possible, setting up group work, and encouraging opportunities for active learning. Practice takes place with the teacher present, and much independent practice in groups, with partners, or by individuals is important for maximum learning. As the students become more independent, the teacher assigns critical-thinking and higher-order applications of the content.

Step 3 on the framework recommends sheltered instruction, which uses specific strategies and techniques for making the content understandable for English learners while developing their English language proficiency. The SIOP® Model of sheltered instruction is scientifically validated and provides concrete examples of the features of sheltered instruction that can enhance and expand a teacher's instructional practice (Echevarria, Vogt, & Short, 2013). Some of the features of the SIOP include clearly defined content and language objectives, adaptation of content to students' levels, use of speech that is appropriate for students' levels, linking new learning to students' background experiences, providing sufficient wait-time for students' responses, consistent use of scaffolding, and assessing students' comprehension and learning of objectives. The SIOP has been shown to significantly improve the literacy skills of students whose teachers implemented the model over time (Echevarria, 2012; Short, Echevarria, Richards-Tutor, 2011).

Step 4 encourages teachers to be conscious of the language demands of lessons. Teachers must explicitly teach the English skills needed to be successful in the lesson through language objectives and with opportunities to use and practice English, the target language. Interactive discussions between teacher and students and among students provides much-needed practice with both content concepts and language. One model of interaction is instructional conversations (ICs). The crux of the instructional conversations approach is the teacher's ability to elicit complex language from students, including the framing of postulates, arguments, elaborations, and dialogue. Teachers provide a nonthreatening atmosphere that challenges all students and often encourages open-forum discussions.

Step 5 encourages teachers to focus on culturally and affectively responsive teaching. Teachers can organize and manage their classrooms in such a way as to enhance the self-concept and self-esteem of each learner. The infrastructure of all units of instruction must have a foundation in which these affective issues are consistently part of the way in which lessons are configured. By allowing students to construct their own meaning through reading and writing and to practice whatever they are learning so they become successful, the teacher focuses on factors that enhance the self-concept and self-esteem of the learner. This is a focus on affective issues. Other ways to facilitate high self-esteem and self-concept as they relate to school are to focus on relevant background knowledge, actively involve learners, use alternative grouping, focus on content and activities that are meaningful to students, provide native-language support, create roles in the classroom for family and community members, hold high expectations for all learners, and be responsive to cultural and personal diversity. Students who receive these opportunities are likely to perform at a higher level in school and may like school better than students who do not have these opportunities.

Step 6 calls on teachers to use learning-strategy instruction when students do not appear to generate necessary learning strategies on their own. This instruction should always be a supplementary segment during a class or period. Such instruction might continue across many days until students understand and can apply the strategy, but the instruction should not continue longer than 15 or 20 minutes on any one day. Teachers carefully select learning strategies to teach students based on the individual or group needs of those students. The teachers present the strategy in a concise format so that students are sure to learn it. Teachers are careful to embed the strategy into a meaningful lesson. Teachers move from a segment on teaching a learning strategy into an instructional segment in which students participate actively in problem solving, conversations, or learning-centered work. In this way, the segment is sandwiched in between meaningful content instruction.

Step 7 calls for the teacher to use instruction that benefits all students with an emphasis on differentiated instruction using accommodations, adaptations, and modifications. When adapting instruction for English learners and struggling learners, the use of curriculum that is sensitive to cultural and linguistic diversity is critical. In addition, curriculum must be adapted to include relevant background knowledge and relevant academic proficiency skills instruction. Language development as well as content vocabulary development should be part of most lessons including instruction in academic language. Texts and assignments can be modified. Resource guides can provide adaptations that have already been prepared to save teachers effort. Teachers are advised to delegate tasks because adaptations can be very time consuming.

Step 8 encourages teachers to be reflective practitioners. Teachers rate each of the factors in the previous steps and decide which areas are strongest and which need improvement. Teachers select a lesson, think about which types of learners are in the class, and then rate each of the factors. Priority should be given to setting goals in the areas that received scores of 1, 2, or 3. Teachers can plan which goals to address and how those goals will be met. They should then make a list of the areas that need additional work in a prioritized fashion. This provides teachers with a plan of action for change.

This type of self-evaluation and reflection is much more powerful and effective when teachers share in the process and work together to bring about change. In addition, students benefit when teachers at a school engage in similar approaches and provide a common "culture" for learning.

The framework presented may be used as a guide in teacher preparation courses (Gravois & Rosenfeld, 2006) or as a tool for continued teacher reflection and professional development (Kane, Rockoff, & Staiger, 2007). In the previous seven chapters, we have presented information based on research in the areas of second-language instruction, general education, and special education. Also, we have provided examples from classroom observations and our own research on teaching English learners. In implementing the practices about which we have written, we encourage readers to engage in action research and become more reflective in practice, both individually and in collaboration with other school personnel. To underscore the importance of these efforts, research suggests that well-prepared teachers have a greater impact on student achievement than do the influences of student background factors such as poverty, language, and minority status (Artiles, Trent, & Palmer, 2004; August & Shanahan, 2006; Genessee, Lindholm-Leary, Saunders, & Christian, 2006; Klingner, Artiles, & Bartella, 2006; Linan-Thompson, Cirino, & Vaughn, 2007; McIntosh, Graves, & Gersten, 2007; Saunders & O'Brien, 2006; Snow & Katz, 2010; Vaughn et al., 2009).

SUMMARY

Being a reflective practitioner contributes to one's own ongoing professional development. This chapter focused on ways that teachers can continually improve their practice, which in turn improves student achievement.

Specifically, as a reader you

- explained the relationship between reflective practice and improved teaching.
- described the benefits of each of three types of professional development activities that lead to enhanced teaching.
- identified the characteristics that distinguish videotape analysis from other types of reflective practice.
- evaluated your own teaching and set goals for improving performance.

- revisited student vignettes in Chapter 1 and identified a pattern between the student vignettes and your goals for improving performance.

ACTIVITIES

1. With a teacher or on your own, select any English learner who has been placed in special education and write a summary of the available information according to Step 1 (Assessment) of the Framework for Self-Assessment and Goal Setting (Figure 8.1). Next, write recommendations regarding the assessment process. Were all the factors considered in the assessment?

2. Based on what you have learned about good instruction, plan a lesson that you will teach and videotape. Use the SIOP protocol in Chapter 3 to rate your lesson. Reflect on the aspects of best practices for English learners that were present and absent in your lesson.

3. Meet with a group of three to six colleagues or your professional learning community and plan a sheltered lesson. Teach the lesson, assess student performance, and then meet again to discuss the successes and challenges of the lesson. Provide a self-assessment and goal-setting description of your teaching. Include the key factors for best assessment and instructional practices.

4. Choose a lesson plan from a curriculum guide or a teacher-made plan and revise it. Adapt the plan using the information from Steps 3, 4, 5, 6, and 7 of the Framework for Self-Assessment and Goal Setting (Figure 8.1). Be sure to describe how you imagine the lesson being adapted and implemented.

5. Using a lesson you have taught, reflect on what worked and what didn't work, and think about what you would do differently. Write and conduct an action research plan based on your experience. Be sure to include the four stages described in the chapter.

GLOSSARY

Academic language Language used in formal contexts for academic subjects. The type of language connected with literacy and academic achievement. This includes technical and academic terms, and reading, writing, listening and speaking skills as used in school to acquire new knowledge and accomplish academic tasks.

Accommodations Adjustments to the instructional program that take into consideration or "accommodate" a student's learning needs and provide the support required to improve academic performance. An example is allowing a student to use assistive technology for test taking. Standards are not changed but adjustments are made to support student performance.

Assessment The orderly process of gathering, analyzing, interpreting, and reporting student performance, ideally from multiple sources over a period of time.

Assessment-driven instruction Using data from formative and summative assessment to adjust teaching and provide optimal learning outcomes for students.

Bilingual instruction School instruction using two languages, generally the native language of a student and a second language. The amount of time that each language is used depends on the type of bilingual program, its specific objectives, and students' levels of language proficiency.

Common Core State Standards (CCSS) A common set of Grades K–12 English language arts and mathematics standards, adopted by most states in the U.S.

Content objectives Statements that identify what students should know and be able to do in a particular content area for a given lesson. They support school district and state content standards and learning outcomes, and they guide teaching and learning in the classroom.

Content standards Definitions of what students are expected to know and be capable of doing for a given content area; the knowledge and skills that need to be taught in order for students to reach competency; what students are expected to learn and what schools are expected to teach. These may be national, state, or district standards.

Core curriculum The planned instruction in a content area, which is central and usually mandatory for all students of a school (e.g., reading, math, science).

Culture The customs, lifestyle, traditions, behavior, attitudes, and artifacts of a given people. Culture also encompasses the ways people organize and interpret the world, and the way events are perceived based on established social norms. It is a system of standards for understanding the world.

Data-based decision making The use of students' data to guide the design, implementation, and adjustment of instruction. It is considered by some to be synonymous with progress monitoring because both require the collection and use of data.

Dialect The form of a language distinctive to a specific region. Dialects feature a variation in vocabulary, grammar, and pronunciation.

Differentiated instruction Instruction that matches the specific strengths and needs of each learner; examples include providing alterations to curriculum, instruction, and assessment that recognize students' varying background knowledge, language proficiency, and academic abilities.

Early intervention services A set of coordinated services for students in kindergarten through grade 12 (with particular emphasis on students in kindergarten through grade 3) who are not currently identified as needing special education or related services, but who need additional academic and behavioral support to succeed in general education.

Elementary and Secondary Education Act (ESEA) Title I The nation's major federal law related to education from pre-kindergarten through high school, with the most recent version known as No Child Left Behind. Title I of ESEA provides funding for high-poverty schools to help students who are behind academically or at risk of falling behind.

Engagement When students are fully taking part in a lesson, they are said to be *engaged*. This is a holistic term that encompasses active listening, reading, writing, responding, and discussing. The level of students' engagement during a lesson may be assessed to a greater or lesser degree. A low SIOP® score for engagement would imply frequent chatting, daydreaming, nonattention, and other off-task behaviors.

English language development (ELD) A term used in some regions to refer to programs and classes to teach students English as a second (additional) language. (*See* ESL.)

English language proficiency (ELP) standards Definitions of what students are expected to know and be capable of doing in English; the knowledge and skills that need to be taught in order for students to reach competency; what students are expected to learn and what schools are expected to teach. These may be national, state, or district standards. Each state is required by the federal government to have ELP standards and related assessments.

English learners (ELs) Children and adults who are learning English as a second or additional language. This term may apply to learners across various levels of proficiency in English. English learners may also be referred to as English language learners (ELLs), non-English speaking (NES) students, limited English proficient (LEP), and non-native speaker (NNSs).

EO Used in some regions, English-only or EO refers to students whose native language is English.

ESL English as a second language. Used to refer to programs and classes to teach students English as a second (additional) language. It may also refer to the language teaching specialists and their teaching certifications or endorsements.

ESOL English speakers of other languages. Students whose first language is not English and who do not write, speak, and understand the language as well as their classmates. In some regions, this term also refers to the programs and classes for English learners.

Evaluation Judgments about students' learning made by interpreting and analyzing assessment data; the process of judging achievement, growth, products, processes, or changes in these; judgments of education programs. The processes of assessment and evaluation can be viewed as progressive: first, assessment; then, evaluation.

Evidence-based instruction Instructional approaches that have been shown through research to improve the academic performance of most students. (*See* Research-based instruction)

Explicit instruction Instruction that is clear, deliberate, and visible.

Fidelity of implementation Using instruction or materials in the way they were designed to be used with accuracy and consistency. With RTI, the process itself must be implemented with fidelity as well as the methods used for instruction and interventions.

Five "Big Ideas" or pillars of reading Critical aspects of reading for all RTI tiers: phonemic awareness, phonics, fluency, vocabulary, and comprehension; many reading experts believe the "big ideas" represent a narrow view of the process of reading. Allington (2008) recommends an additional five "big ideas" that are particularly relevant to RTI: (1) classroom organization; (2) matching pupils to texts; (3) access to interesting texts, choice, and collaboration; (4) writing and reading as natural, reciprocal processes; and (5) expert tutoring.

Formative assessment   Ongoing collection, analysis, and reporting of information about student performance for purposes of instruction and learning.

Grouping   The assignment of students into groups or classes for instruction, such as by age, ability, or achievement; or within classes, such as by reading ability, proficiency, language background, or interests. Flexible grouping enables students to move among different groups based on their performance and instructional strengths and needs.

Home language   The language, or languages, spoken in the student's home by people who live there. Also referred to as first language (L1), primary language, or native language.

Individuals with Disabilities Education Act (IDEA)   The federal law dealing with the education of children with disabilities. IDEA requires all states that accept IDEA federal funds to provide a free appropriate public education to all children with disabilities in the state.

Informal assessment   Appraisal of student performance through unstructured observation; characterized as frequent, ongoing, continuous, and involving simple but important techniques such as verbal checks for understanding, teacher-created assessments, and other nonstandardized procedures. This type of assessment provides teachers with immediate feedback.

Instructional conversations (IC)   An approach to teaching that is an interactive dialogue with an instructional intent. An IC approach encourages thoughtful discussion around a concept or idea with balanced participation between teacher and students.

Instructional intervention   Clear, deliberate, and carefully planned instruction used by trained personnel to teach a student in an area of learning or behavioral difficulty to try to improve performance and achieve adequate progress.

Intensive intervention   Explicit and systematic instruction delivered by highly skilled teacher specialists that provides students with increased opportunities for guided practice and teacher feedback. This instruction is targeted and tailored to meet the needs of struggling learners in small groups.

Language minority   In the United States, a student whose native language is not English. The individual students' ability to speak English will vary.

Language objectives   Statements that identify what students should know and be able to do while learning English (or another language) in a given lesson. They support students' language development, often focusing on vocabulary, functional language, language skills in reading, writing, listening and speaking, grammatical knowledge, and language learning strategies.

Language proficiency   An individual's competence in using a language for basic communication and for academic purposes. May be categorized as stages of language acquisition (*see* Levels of language proficiency).

Levels of language proficiency   Students learning language progress through stages. The stages or levels may be labeled differently across states. In their seminal work in this area, Krashen and Terrell (1983, 1984) described the stages as the following: Preproduction, Early production, Speech emergence, Intermediate fluency, and Advanced fluency. At present, many states have levels similar to those in the

WIDA (World-class Instructional Design and Assessment) English language proficiency standards (WIDA, 2007):

Entering (Level 1): Lowest level, essentially no English proficiency. Students are often newcomers and need extensive pictorial and nonlinguistic support. They need to learn basic oral language and literacy skills in English.

Beginning (Level 2): Second lowest level. Students use phrases and short sentences and are introduced to general content vocabulary and lesson tasks.

Developing (Level 3): Next level of proficiency. Students can use general and specific language related to the content areas; they can speak and write sentences and paragraphs although with some errors, and they can read with instructional supports.

Expanding (Level 4): Akin to an intermediate level of proficiency. Students use general, academic and specific language related to content areas. They have improved speaking and writing skills and stronger reading comprehension skills (compared to the Developing level).

Bridging (Level 5): Akin to advanced intermediate or advanced level of proficiency. Students use general academic and technical language of the content areas. They can read and write with linguistic complexity. Students at this level have often exited the ESL or ELD program but their language and academic performance is still monitored.

Reaching (Level 6): At or close to grade-level proficiency. Students' oral and written communication skills are comparable to native English speakers at their grade level. Students at this level have exited the ESL or ELD program but their language and academic performance is still monitored.

Limited English Proficient (LEP)   A term used to refer to a student with restricted understanding or use of written and spoken English; a learner who is still developing competence in using English. The federal government continues to use the term *LEP*, while *EL* or *ELL* is more commonly used in schools.

Modifications   Changes a teacher makes during instruction or supports he or she offers that help students to be successful academically. An example is slowing the pace of instruction or providing sentence frames during oral language activities.

Native English speaker   An individual whose first language is English.
Native language   An individual's primary, home, or first language (L1).
No Child Left Behind (NCLB) Act of 2001   A major school reform initiative developed and regulated by the federal government. It holds schools accountable for the success of all of their students and requires highly qualified teachers in core content areas. Each state has standards for mathematics, reading/language arts, English language development, and science, and all implement high-stakes tests based on these standards.

Non-English speaking (NES)   Individuals who are in an English-speaking environment (such as U.S. schools) but who have not acquired any English proficiency.

Outcome assessment   The measurement of how students perform academically at the end of planned instruction or at the end of the year.

Primary language   An individual's home, native, or first language (L1).
Problem-solving team   *See* School-based team.
Progress monitoring   A scientifically validated way of assessing students' academic performance and evaluating the effectiveness of instruction. Progress monitoring can be implemented with individual students or an entire class.

Pull-out instruction   Students are "pulled out" from their regular classes for special classes of ESL instruction, remediation, or acceleration. These classes are more commonly found in elementary programs.

Register In linguistics, a register is a variety of a language used for a particular purpose or in a particular social setting. For example, when speaking in a formal setting, an English speaker may be more likely to use standard English grammar and choose more formal words (e.g. *provide* vs. *give*, *student* vs. *kid*.).

Reliability Statistical consistency in measurements and tests, such as the extent to which two assessments measure student performance in the same way.

Research-based instruction Curriculum, instruction, and/or interventions that have been proven through research to be effective for most students. Also called *evidence-based instruction* and *research-validated instruction*.

Research-validated instruction *See* Research-based instruction.

Response to Intervention (RTI) The intent of RTI is to identify at-risk learners early and, using a tiered system, provide effective instruction in general education first (typically called Tier I) followed by targeted intervention (Tier 2 and Tier 3) as needed. This process is designed to reduce the number of students eligible for and in need of special education services (typically Tier 3 or Tier 4). The focus is on finding ways to change instruction (or student behaviors) so the learner can be successful. RTI involves documenting a change in behavior or performance as a result of intervention and assessments.

Rubrics Statements that describe indicators of performance, which include scoring criteria, on a continuum; may be described as "developmental" (e.g., emergent, beginning, developing, proficient) or "evaluative" (e.g., exceptional, thorough, adequate, inadequate).

Scaffolding Adult (e.g., teacher) support for learning and student performance of the tasks through instruction, modeling, verbal prompts (e.g., questioning), feedback, graphic organizers, and more, across successive engagements. These supports are gradually withdrawn, thus transferring more and more autonomy to the child. Scaffolding activities provide support for learning that can be removed as learners are able to demonstrate strategic behaviors in their own learning activities.

School-based team A group of school personnel who work collaboratively to address the needs of struggling students. Schools use a variety of terms for school-based teams such as *instructional intervention team, RTI team, multidisciplinary team, student assistance team,* or *student progress monitoring team*.

Scientific, research-based instruction (*See* Research-based instruction.)

SDAIE (Specially Designed Academic Instruction in English) A term for sheltered instruction used mostly in California and Nevada. It features strategies and techniques for making content understandable for English learners. Although some SDAIE techniques are research based, SDAIE itself has not been scientifically validated. (*See* Sheltered instruction.)

Sheltered instruction (SI) A means for making content comprehensible for English learners while they are developing English proficiency. The SIOP® is a research-validated model of sheltered instruction. Sheltered classrooms, which may include a mix of native English speakers and English learners or only English learners, integrate language and content while infusing sociocultural awareness. (*See* SDAIE and SIOP®.)

SIOP® (Sheltered Instruction Observation Protocol) A scientifically validated model of sheltered instruction designed to make grade-level academic content understandable for English learners while at the same time developing their English language ability. The protocol and lesson-planning guide ensure that teachers are consistently implementing practices known to be effective for English learners.

Social language Basic language proficiency associated with fluency in day-to-day situations, including the classroom.

Special education Instruction that is specifically designed to meet the individual needs of a child with a disability, according to the federal special education law, the Individuals with Disabilities Education Act (IDEA 2004).

Standard *See* Content standards.

Standard American English "That variety of American English in which most educational texts, government, and media publications are written in the United States; English as it is spoken and written by those groups with social, economic, and political power in the United States. Standard American English is a relative concept, varying widely in pronunciation and in idiomatic use but maintaining a fairly uniform grammatical structure" (Harris & Hodges, 1995, p. 241).

Standardized assessment A test that is administered and scored in a consistent, or "standard" manner. Standardized assessments are designed in such a way that the questions, conditions for administering, scoring procedures, and interpretations are consistent and are administered and scored in a standard manner.

Standards-based assessment Assessment involving the planning, gathering, analyzing, and reporting of a student's performance according to ESL and/or content standards.

Strategies Mental processes and plans that people use to help them comprehend, learn, and retain new information. There are three types of strategies—cognitive, metacognitive, and social/affective—and these are consciously adapted and monitored during reading, writing, and learning.

Summative assessment The final collection, analysis, and reporting of information about student achievement or program effectiveness at the end of a given time frame.

Task An activity that calls for a response to a question, issue, or problem; an instructional activity.

Universal screening A process used early in the school year to identify or predict students who may be at risk for poor learning outcomes. Universal screening tests are typically brief, conducted with all students at a grade level, and followed by additional testing as required.

Validity A statistical measure of an assessment's match between the information collected and its stated purpose; evidence that inferences from evaluation are trustworthy.

REFERENCES

Abedi, J., & Lord, C. (2001). The language factor in mathematics tests. *Applied Measurement in Education, 14*(3), 219–234.

Agirdag, O. (2009). All languages welcome here. *Educational Leadership, 66*(7), 8–13.

Aguila, V. (2009). Schooling English learners: Contexts and challenges. In California Department of Education (Ed.), *Improving education for English learners: Research-based approaches.* Sacramento, CA: CDE Press.

Arreaga-Mayer, C. (1998). Language-sensitive peer-mediated instruction for language minority studies in the intermediate elementary grades. In R. Gersten & R. Jiménez (Eds.), *Promoting learning for culturally and linguistically diverse students: Classroom applications from contemporary research.* Belmont, CA: Wadsworth.

Artiles, A. J., & Bal, A. (2008). The next generation of disproportionality. *Journal of Special Education, 42*(1), 4–14.

Artiles, A. J., Harry, B., Reschly, D. J., & Chinn, P. C. (1999, November). *Placement of students of color in special education classes, an overview.* Nashville, TN: The Alliance Project, Vanderbilt University.

Artiles, A. J., Rueda, R., Salazar, J., & Nigareda, I. (2002). English language learner representation in special education in California urban school districts. In D. Losen & G. Orfield (Eds.), *Racial inequity in special education* (pp. 117–136). Cambridge, MA: Harvard Education Press.

Artiles, A. J., Trent, S. C., & Palmer, J. D. (2004). Culturally diverse students in special education: Legacies and prospects. In J. Banks & C. A. McGee Banks (Eds.), *Handbook of research on multicultural education* (pp. 716–735). San Francisco, CA: Jossey-Bass.

Au, K., & Blake, K. (2003). Cultural identity and learning to teach in a diverse community: Findings from a collective case study. *Journal of Teacher Education, 54*(3), 192–205.

August, D., & Shanahan, T. (Eds.). (2006). *Developing literacy in second-language learners: A report of the National Literacy Panel on Language-Minority Children and Youth.* Mahwah, NJ: Erlbaum.

August, D., & Shanahan, T. (2010). Effective English literacy instruction for English learners. In California Department of Education (Ed.), *Improving education for English learners: Research-based approaches* (pp. 209–250). Sacramento, CA: CDE Press.

Baca, L., & Almanza, E. (1996). *Language minority students with disabilities.* Reston, VA: Council for Exceptional Children.

Baca, L., & Cervantes, H. (2004). *The bilingual special education interface* (4th ed.). Columbus, OH: Merrill.

Bailey, A. (Ed.). (2007). *The language demands of school: Putting academic English to the test.* New Haven, CT: Yale University Press.

Baker, C. (1992). *Attitudes and language.* Clevedon, England: Multilingual Matters.

Baker, C. (1993). *Foundations of bilingual education and bilingualism.* Philadelphia, PA: Multilingual Matters.

Banks, J. S., & McGee Banks, C. A. (2001). *Multicultural education: Issues and perspectives* (4th ed.). New York, NY: Wiley.

Barnes, C., Mercer, G., & Shakespeare, T. (1999). *Exploring disability: A sociological introduction.* Cambridge, UK: Policy Press.

Barratt-Pugh, C., & Rohl, M. (2001). Learning in two languages: A bilingual program in Western Australia. *The Reading Teacher, 54,* 664–676.

Batsche, G., Elliott, J., Graden, J., Grimes, J., Kovaleski, J., Prasse, D., Reschly, D., Schrag, J., & Tilly, W. D. (2005). *Response to intervention: Policy considerations and implementation.* Alexandria, VA: National Association of State Directors of Special Education.

Beaumont, C. J. (1999). Dilemmas of peer assistance in a bilingual full inclusion classroom. *Elementary School Journal, 99,* 233–254.

Beck, I., McKeown, M. G., & Kucan, L. (2007). *Bringing words to life: Robust vocabulary instruction.* New York, NY: The Guilford Press.

Bell, J. S. (2000). Literacy challenges for language learners in job-training programs. *The Canadian Modern Language Review, 57,* 173–200.

Bialystok, E. (2001). *Bilingualism in development: Language, literacy and cognition.* London, England: Cambridge University Press.

Bialystok, E., & Hakuta, K. (1994). *In other words: The science of psychology of 2nd language acquisition.* New York, NY: Basic Books.

Brice, A. E., & Brice, R. (2004). Identifying Hispanic gifted children: A screening. *Rural Special Education Quarterly, 23*(1), 8–14.

Bickel, W. E., & Bickel, D. D. (1986). Effective schools, classrooms, and instruction. *Exceptional Children, 52*(6), 489–500.

Blackorby, J., & Wagner, M. (1996). Longitudinal post school outcomes of youth with disabilities: Findings from the National Longitudinal Transition Study. *Exceptional Children, 62*(5), 399–414.

Bos, C. (1995). *Accommodations for students with special needs who are learning English.* Paper presented at the First Congress on Disabilities, Mexico City, Mexico.

Brown, J. E., & Doolittle, J. (2008). *A cultural, linguistic, and ecological framework for response to intervention with English language learners.* The National Center for Culturally Responsive Educational Systems (NCCRESt). Retrieved from www.nccrest.org

Bunch, G., Abram, P., Lotan, R., & Valdes, G. (2001). Beyond sheltered instruction: Rethinking conditions for academic language development. *TESOL Journal, 10*(2/3), 28–33.

California Department of Education. (2004). Statewide Stanford 9 test results for reading: Number of students tested and percent scoring at or above the 50th percentile ranking. Retrieved from http://www.cde.ca.gov/dataquest/

California Department of Education. (2012). *Teachers of English Learners (CTEL): Overview of domains and competencies.* Retrieved from http://www.ctel.nesinc.com

Capps, R., Fix, J., Murray, J., Ost, J., Passel, J. & Herwantoro, S. (2005). *The new demography of America's schools: Immigration and the No Child Left Behind Act.* Washington, DC: Urban Institute.

Carhill, A., Suarez-Orozco, C., & Paez, M. (2008). Explaining English language proficiency among adolescent immigrant students. *American Educational Research Journal, 45*(4), 1155–1179.

Carlo, M. S., August, D., McLaughlin, B., Snow, C. E., Dressler, C., Lippman, D. N., Lively, T. J., & White, C. E. (2004). Closing the gap: Addressing the vocabulary needs of English-language learners in bilingual and mainstream classrooms. *Reading Research Quarterly, 39*(2), 188–215.

Cazden, C. B. (2001). *Classroom discourse: The language of teaching and learning.* (2nd ed.) Portsmouth, NH: Heinemann.

Cazden, C. B. (1992). *Language minority education in the United States: Implications of the Ramirez report* (Educational Practice Report: 3). Santa Cruz, CA: National Center for Research on Cultural Diversity and Second Language Learning.

CELDT Assistance Packet—California English Development Test. (2008). http://www.cde.ca.gov/ta/tg/el/documents/celdt08astpkt1.pdf

Center for the Improvement of Early Reading Achievement (CIERA). (1998). *Improving the reading achievement of America's children: 10 Research-based principles.* Ann Arbor, MI: Author.

Chambers, B., Cheung, A. C. K., Madden, N. A., Slavin, R. E., & Gifford, R. (2006). Achievement effects of embedded multimedia in success for all reading programs. *Journal of Educational Psychology, 98*(1), 232–237.

Chang, J. M. (1992). Current programs serving Chinese-American students in learning disabilities resource issues. In *Proceedings of the Third National Research Symposium on Limited English Proficient Issues: Focus on Middle and High School Issues* (pp. 713–736). Washington, DC: U.S. Department of Education, Office of Bilingual Education and Minority Language Affairs.

Chang, J. M. (2001). *A scaffold for school–home collaboration for reading and language development* (Research Brief No. 9). Santa Cruz, CA and Washington, DC: Center for Research on Education, Diversity & Excellence. Retrieved from www.cal.org/crede/pubs/ResBrief.htm

Chang, J. M. (2004). *Family literacy nights: Building the circle of supporters within and beyond school for middle school English language learners* (Educational Practice Report No.11). Santa Cruz, CA and Washington, DC: Center for Research on Education, Diversity & Excellence.

Cheng, L. L. (1995). ESL strategies for API population. In L. L. Cheng (Ed.), *Integrating language and learning for inclusion: An Asian-Pacific focus.* San Diego, CA: Singular.

Chiappe, P., Siegel, L., & Wade-Wolley, L. (2002). Linguistic diversity and the development of reading skills: A longitudinal study. *Scientific Studies of Reading, 6,* 369–400.

Cline, T., & Frederickson, N. (1999). Identification and assessment of dyslexia in bi/multilingual children. *International Journal of Bilingual Education and Bilingualism, 2,* 81–93.

Cloud, N. (1994). Special education needs of second language students. In F. Genesee (Ed.), *Educating second language children: The whole child, the whole curriculum, the whole community.* New York, NY: Cambridge University Press.

Cloud, N., Genesee, F., & Hamayan, E. (2009). *Literacy instruction for English language learners: A teacher's guide to research based practices.* New York, NY: Heinemann.

Collier, V. (1987). Age and rate of acquisition of second language for academic purposes. *TESOL Quarterly, 21,* 617–641.

Collier, V. (1989). How long? A synthesis of research on academic achievement in a second language. *TESOL Quarterly, 23,* 509–531.

Collier, V. (1995). Acquiring a second language for school. *Directions in Language and Education, 1*(4), 1–12.

Common Core State Standards. (2013). Retrieved from www.doe.in.gov/commoncore

Crandall, J. (1995). *Developing content-centered language learning: Strategies for classroom instruction and teacher development.* Thailand: Chulalongkorn University.

Crawford, J. (1991). *Bilingual education: History, politics, theory and practice* (2nd ed.). Los Angeles, CA: Bilingual Educational Services.

Cummins, J. (1980). The cross-lingual dimensions of language proficiency: Implications for bilingual education and the optimal age issue. *TESOL Quarterly, 14*(2), 175–187.

Cummins, J. (1981a). Age on arrival and immigrant second language learning in Canada: A reassessment. *Applied Linguistics, 2,* 131–149.

Cummins, J. (1981b). The role of primary language development in promoting educational success for language minority students. In *Schooling and language minority students: A theoretical framework.* Los Angeles, CA: California State University, National Evaluation, Dissemination and Assessment Center.

Cummins, J. (1984). *Bilingualism and special education: Issues in assessment and pedagogy.* Clevedon, England: Multilingual Matters.

Cummins, J. (1989). A theoretical framework for bilingual special education. *Exceptional Children, 56,* 111–128.

Cummins, J. (1992). Bilingual education and English immersion: The Ramirez report in theoretical perspective. *Bilingual Research Journal, 16,* 91–104.

Cummins, J. (1994). Primary language instruction and the education of language minority students. In *Schooling and language minority students: A theoretical framework* (2nd ed.). Los Angeles, CA: California State University, National Evaluation, Dissemination and Assessment Center.

Cummins, J. (1996). *Negotiating identities: Education for empowerment in a diverse society.* Los Angeles, CA: California Association for Bilingual Education.

Cummins, J. (1999, Autumn). The ethics of doublethink: Language rights and the bilingual education debate. *TESOL Quarterly,* 13–17.

Cummins, J. (2000). *Language, power and pedagogy: Bilingual children in the crossfire.* Clevedon, England: Multilingual Matters.

Cummins, J. (2003). Reading and the bilingual student: Fact and fiction. In G. Garcia (Ed.), *English learners: Reaching the highest level of English literacy* (pp. 2–33). Newark, DE: International Reading Association.

Darling-Hammond, L. (2000). Teacher quality and student achievement: A review of state policy evidence. *Education Policy Analysis Archives, 9,* 1.

Darling-Hammond, L., & Bransford, J. (2005). *Preparing teachers for a changing world: What teachers should learn and be able to do.* San Francisco, CA: John Wiley and Sons.

Darling-Hammond, L., & Friedlander, D. (2008). Creating excellent and equitable schools. *Educational Leadership, 65*(8), 14–21.

Deno, S. L. (1985). Curriculum-based measurement: The emerging alternative. *Exceptional Children, 52,* 219–232.

Deshler, D., & Schumaker, J. (1994). Strategy mastery by at-risk students: Not a simple matter. *The Elementary School Journal, 94,* 153–167.

Destefano, L., Shriner, J. G., & Lloyd, C. A. (2001). Teacher decision making in participation of students with disabilities in large-scale assessment. *Exceptional Children, 68,* 7–22.

Dewey, J. (1938). *Experience and education.* New York, NY: Touchstone.

Dolson, D., & Burnham-Massey, L. (2010). *Improving education for English learners: Research-based approaches.* Sacramento, CA: CDE Press.

Dong, Y .R. (2009). Linking to prior learning. *Educational Leadership, 66*(7), 26–31.

Doughty, C., & Long, M. (2003). *The handbook of second language acquisition.* Oxford, England: Blackwell Publishing Ltd.

Dutro, S., & Kinsella, K. (2010). English language development: Issues and implementation at grades six through twelve. In *Improving education for English learners: Research-based approaches.* Sacramento, CA: CDE Press.

Dweck, C. (2007). *Mindset: The new psychology of success.* New York, NY: Ballantine.

Echevarria, J. (1995a). *Instructional conversations: Understanding through discussion. Facilitator's guide.* Santa Cruz, CA: National Center for Research on Cultural Diversity and Second Language Learning.

Echevarria, J. (1995b). Interactive reading instruction: A comparison of proximal and distal effects of instructional conversations. *Exceptional Children 61*(6), 536–552.

Echevarria, J. (2001). *Improving content literacy for English language learners.* Paper presented at the California Reading Association Conference, Ontario, CA.

Echevarría, J. (2012). *Effective practices for increasing the achievement of English learners.* Washington, DC: Center for Research on the

Educational Achievement and Teaching of English Language Learners. Retrieved from http://www.cal.org/create/resources/pubs/

Echevarria, J. (Producer & Writer), & Silver, J. (Producer & Director). (1995). [Videotape]. *Instructional conversations: Understanding through discussion.* Santa Cruz, CA: National Center for Research on Cultural Diversity and Second Language Learning.

Echevarria, J. & Graves, A. (2010). *Sheltered content instruction: Teaching students with diverse needs* (4th ed.). Boston, MA: Allyn & Bacon.

Echevarria, J., Greene, G., & Goldenberg, C. (1996). *A comparison of sheltered content instruction and effective instruction.* Unpublished pilot study.

Echevarria, J., & Hasbrouck, J. (2009). Response to Intervention and English learners (CREATE BRIEF). Washington, DC: Center for Research on the Educational Achievement and Teaching of English language learners.

Echevarria, J., Powers, K., & Elliott, J. (2004). Promising practices for curbing disproportionate representation of minority students in special education. *Issues in Teacher Education, 13*(1), 19–33.

Echevarria, J., Richards-Tutor, C., Canges, R., & Francis, D. (2011). Using the SIOP® Model to promote the acquisition of language and science concepts with English learners. *Bilingual Research Journal, 34*(3), 334–351.

Echevarria, J., Richards-Tutor, C., Chinn, V., & Ratleff, P. (2011). Did they get it? The role of fidelity in teaching English learners. *Journal of Adolescent and Adult Literacy, 54*(6) 425–434.

Echevarria, J., Richards-Tutor, C., & Vogt, M.E. (2014). *Response to intervention and English learners: Using the SIOP Model.* Boston, MA: Allyn & Bacon.

Echevarría, J., & Short, D. (2011). *The SIOP® Model: A professional development framework for comprehensive schoolwide intervention.* Washington, DC: Center for Research on the Educational Achievement and Teaching of English Language Learners. Retrieved from http://www.cal.org/create/resources/pubs/professional-development-framework.html

Echevarria, J., Short, D., & Powers, K. (2006). School reform and standards-based education: An instructional model for English-language learners. *Journal of Educational Research, 99*(4), 195–210.

Echevarria, J., Short, D., & Vogt, M. (2008). *Implementing the SIOP® Model through effective professional development and coaching.* Boston, MA: Allyn & Bacon.

Echevarria, J., Vogt, M.E., & Short, D. (2000). *Making content comprehensible for English language learners: The SIOP® model.* Boston, MA: Allyn & Bacon.

Echevarria, J., Vogt, M.E., & Short, D. (2004). *Making content comprehensible for English learners: The SIOP® Model* (2nd ed.). Boston, MA: Allyn & Bacon.

Echevarria, J., Vogt, M.E., & Short, D. (2008). *Making content comprehensible for English learners: The SIOP® Model* (3rd ed.). Boston, MA: Pearson Allyn & Bacon.

Echevarria, J., Vogt, M.E., & Short, D. (2011). *The SIOP® Model for Teaching Mathematics to English Learners.* Boston, MA: Allyn & Bacon.

Echevarria, J., Vogt, M.E., & Short, D. (2013). *Making content comprehensible for English learners: The SIOP® model* (4th ed.). Boston, MA: Allyn & Bacon.

Edelsky, C. (1991). *With literacy and justice for all: Rethinking the social in language and education.* London, England: Falmer Press.

Elkind, D. (1970). *Children and adolescents: Interpretive essays on Jean Piaget.* New York, NY: Oxford University Press.

Ellis, E. S., & Graves, A. (1990). Teaching rural students with learning disabilities: A paraphrasing strategy to increase comprehension of main ideas. *Rural Special Education Quarterly, 10*(2), 2–10.

Englert, C. S. (2009). Connecting the dots in a research program to develop, implement, and evaluate strategic literacy interventions

for struggling readers and writers. *Learning Disabilities Research and Practice, 24*(2), 104–120.

Espin, C. A., Scierka, B. J., Skare, S., & Halverson, N. (1999). Criterion-related validity of curriculum-based measures in writing for secondary students. *Reading and Writing Quarterly, 14,* 5–27.

Figueroa, R. A. (1989). Psychological testing of linguistic-minority students: Knowledge gaps and regulations. *Exceptional Children, 56*(2), 111–119.

Figueroa, R. A., & Newsome, P. (2006). The diagnosis of learning disabilities in English learners: Is it nondiscriminatory? *Journal of Learning Disabilities, 39*(3), 206–214.

Fillmore, L. W. (1985). *Second language learning in children: A proposed model.* Proceedings of a conference on Issues in English Language Development for Minority Language Education, Arlington, VA. (ERIC Document Reproduction Service No. ED 273 149).

Fitzgerald, J. (2003). New directions in multilingual literacy research: Multilingual reading theory. *Reading Research Quarterly, 38,* 118–122.

Fitzgerald, J., & Graves, M. F. (2004). *Scaffolding reading experiences for English-language learners.* Norwood, MA: Christopher-Gordon.

Franklin, E., & Thompson, J. (1994). Describing students' collected works: Understanding American Indian children. *TESOL Quarterly, 28,* 489–506.

Fuchs, D., Fuchs, L. S., & Vaughn, S. (2008). *Response to intervention: A framework for reading educators.* Newark, DE: International Reading Association.

Fuchs, L. S., & Fuchs, D. (2001). Helping teachers formulate sound test accommodation decisions for students with learning disabilities. *Learning Disabilities Practice, 16,* 174–181.

Fultz, M., Lara-Alecio, R., Irby, B. J., & Tong, F. (2013). The Hispanic Bilingual Gifted Screening Instrument: A validation study. *National Forum of Multicultural Issues, 10*(1), 1–12.

Gallimore, R., Ermeling, B., Saunders, W., & Goldenberg, C. (2009). Moving the learning of teaching closer to practice: Teacher education implications of school-based inquiry teams. *The Elementary School Journal, 109*(5).

Gandara, P., Moran, R., & Garcia, E. (2004). Legacy of Brown: Lau and language policy in the United States. *Review of Research in Education, 28,* 27–46.

Garcia, E., Jensen, B., & Scribner, K. (2009). The demographic imperative. *Educational Leadership, 66*(7), 8–13.

Garcia, G. N. (2000). *Lessons from research: What is the length of time it takes limited English proficient students to acquire English and succeed in an all-English classroom?* Issue Brief No. 5 (Report No. FL 026 601). Washington, DC: National Clearinghouse for Bilingual Education. (ERIC Document Reproduction Service No. ED450585).

Gass, S. M., & Selinker, L. (2001). *Second language acquisition: An introductory text* (2nd ed.). Mahwah, NJ: Erlbaum.

Gattullo, F. (2000). Formative assessment in ELT primary (elementary) classrooms: An Italian case study. *Language Testing, 17,* 278–288.

Gay, G. (2000). *Culturally responsive teaching: Theory, research, & practice.* New York, NY: Teacher's College Press.

Genesee, F. (Ed.). (1999). *Program alternatives for linguistically diverse students.* Educational Practice Report 1. Santa Cruz, CA: Center for Research on Education, Diversity & Excellence.

Genesee, F., Lindholm-Leary, K., Saunders, W., & Christian, D. (2005). English language learners in U.S. schools: An overview of research findings. *Journal of Education for Students Placed At-Risk, 10*(4), 363–385.

Genesee, F., Lindholm-Leary, K., Saunders, W., & Christian, D. (2006). *Educating English language learners: A synthesis of research evidence.* New York, NY: Cambridge University Press.

Genesee, F., & Riches, C. (2006). Literacy: Crosslinguistic and crossmodal issues. In F. Genesee, K. Lindholm-Leary,

W. Saunders, & D. Christian (Eds.), *Educating English language learners: A synthesis of research evidence* (pp. 109–175). New York, NY: Cambridge University Press.

Gersten, R. M., & Baker, S. (2000). What we know about effective instructional practices for English-language learners. *Exceptional Children, 66*, 456–470.

Gersten, R. M., Baker, S., Haager, D., & Graves, A. W. (2005). Exploring the role of teacher quality in predicting reading outcomes for first-grade English learners: An observational study. *Remedial & Special Education, 26*(4), 197–206.

Gersten, R. M., Baker, S., Smith-Johnson, J., Dimino, J., & Peterson, A. (2006). Eyes on the prize: Teaching complex historical content to middle school students with learning disabilities. *Exceptional Children, 72*(3), 264–279.

Gersten, R. M., Brengelman, S., & Jiménez, R. (1994). Effective instruction for culturally and linguistically diverse students: A reconceptualization. *Focus on Exceptional Children, 27*, 1–16.

Gersten, R. M., Taylor, R., & Graves, A. W. (1999). Direct instruction and diversity. In R. Stevens (Ed.), *Teaching in American schools: A tribute to Barak Rosenshine.* Upper Saddle River, NJ: Merrill/Prentice Hall.

Gersten, R. M., Woodward, J., & Darch, C. (1986). Direct instruction: A research-based approach for curriculum design and teaching. *Exceptional Children, 53*(1), 17–36.

Geva, E., Yaghoub-Zadeh, Z., & Schuster, B. (2000). Understanding individual differences in word recognition skills of ESL children. *Annals of Dyslexia, 50*, 123–154.

Goldenberg, C. (1992–93). Instructional conversations: Promoting comprehension through discussion, *The Reading Teacher, 46*(4), 316–326.

Goldenberg, C. (2004). *Successful school change: Creating settings to improve teaching and learning.* New York, NY: Teachers College Press.

Goldenberg, C., Gallimore, R., Reese, L., & Garnier, H. (2001). Cause or effect? A longitudinal study of immigrant Latino parents' aspirations and expectation, and their children's school performance. *American Educational Research Journal, 38*, 547–582.

Goldenberg, C., Rueda, R., & August, D. (2006). Sociocultural influences on the literacy attainment of language-minority children and youth. In D. August & T. Shanahan (Eds.), *Developing literacy in second-language learners: A report of the National Literacy Panel on Language-Minority Children and Youth.* Mahwah, NJ: Erlbaum.

Goldenberg, S., & Gallimore, R. (1991). Changing teaching takes more than a one-shot workshop. *Educational Leadership, 49*(3), 69–72.

Gonzalez, N., Moll, L. C., & Amanti, C. (2005). *Funds of knowledge: Theorizing practices in households, communities, and classrooms.* Mahwah, NJ: Erlbaum.

Gonzalez, N., Moll, L. C., Floyd-Tenery, M., Rivera, A., Rendon, P., Gonzales, R., & Amonti, C. (1993). *Teacher research on funds of knowledge: Learning from households* (Educational Practice Report: 6). Santa Cruz, CA: National Center for Research on Cultural Diversity and Second Language Learning.

Good, R. H., & Kaminski, R. A. (1996). Assessment for instructional decisions: Toward a proactive/prevention model of decision-making for early literacy skills. *School Psychology Quarterly, 11*(4), 326–336.

Goodlad, J. (1984). *A place called school: Prospects for the future.* New York, NY: McGraw-Hill.

Gorski, P. C. (2001). *Multicultural education and the Internet: Intersections and integrations.* Boston, MA: McGraw-Hill.

Graham S., & Harris, K. R. (2005). Self-regulated strategy development: Helping students with learning problems develop as writers. *Elementary School Journal, 105*, 169–181.

Graham, S., & Harris, K. R. (2009). Almost 30 years of writing research: Making sense of it all with *The Wrath of Khan. Learning Disabilities Research and Practice, 24*(2), 58–68.

Grant, C. A., & Gomez, M. L. (2001). *Campus and classroom: Making schooling multicultural* (2nd ed.). Columbus, OH: Merrill.

Graves, A. W. (1986). The effects of direct instruction and metacomprehension training on finding main ideas. *Learning Disabilities Research, 1*(2), 90–100.

Graves, A. W. (1987). Improving comprehension skills. *Teaching Exceptional Children, 19*(2), 58–67.

Graves, A. W. (1995). Teaching students who are culturally and linguistically diverse. *Teacher Educator's Journal, 15*(3), 32–40.

Graves, A. W. (1998). Instructional strategies and techniques for students who are learning English. In R. Gersten & R. Jiménez (Eds.), *Promoting learning for culturally and linguistically diverse students: Classroom applications from contemporary research.* Belmont, CA: Wadsworth.

Graves, A. W. (1998). Teaching English language learners in middle school. In R. Gersten & R. Jiménez (Eds.), *Promoting learning for culturally and linguistically diverse students: Classroom applications from contemporary research.* Belmont, CA: Wadsworth.

Graves, A. W. (2006). Writing instruction for English learners. In J. Hooker, J. Klingner, L. Baca, & J. Patton (Eds.), *Methods for teaching culturally and linguistically diverse exceptional learners.* New York, NY: Merrill/Pearson.

Graves, A. W. (2010). The longitudinal study of the impact of effective beginning reading instruction for English learners: Literacy, language, and learning disabilities. In T. Scruggs & M. Mastropieri (Eds.), *Advances in learning and behavioral disabilities, 23.* London, England: Emerald.

Graves, A. W. (2012). Curriculum-based measurement for English learners in first grade. In C. Espin, K. McMaster, & M. Wayman (Eds.), *A Measure of success: The influence of curriculum-based measurement on education.* Minneapolis, Minn: Regents of the University of Minnesota.

Graves, A. W., Brandon, R., Duesbery, L., McIntosh, A., & Block, N. (2011). The effects of tier II literacy instruction in sixth grade: Toward the development of a response to intervention model in middle school. *Learning Disability Quarterly, 31*(1), 1 – 14.

Graves, A. W., Duesbery, L., Pyle, N. B., Brandon, R., & McIntosh, A. (2011). Two studies of Tier II literacy development: Throwing sixth graders a lifeline. *The Elementary School Journal, 111*(4), 641–661.

Graves, A. W., Gersten, R., & Haager, D. (2004). Literacy instruction in multiple-language first-grade classrooms: Linking student outcomes to observed instructional practice. *Learning Disabilities Research & Practice, 19*(4), 262–272.

Graves, A. W., & Hauge, R. (1993). Using cues and prompts to improve story writing. *Teaching Exceptional Children, 25*(4), 38–40.

Graves, A. W., & Levin, J. R. (1989). Comparison of monitoring and mnemonic text-processing strategies in learning disabled students. *Learning Disability Quarterly, 12*, 232–236.

Graves, A. W., & Montague, M. (1991). Using story grammar cueing to improve the writing of students with learning disabilities. *Learning Disabilities Research and Practice, 6*, 246–251.

Graves, A. W., Montague, M., & Wong, Y. (1990). The effects of procedural facilitation on story composition of learning disabled students. *Learning Disabilities Research, 5*(4), 88–93.

Graves, A. W., Plasencia-Peinado, J., Deno, S., & Johnson, J. (2005). Formatively evaluating the reading progress of first-grade English learners in multiple language classrooms. *Remedial & Special Education, 26*(4), 215–225.

Graves, A. W., & Rueda, R. (2008). Teaching written expression to culturally and linguistically diverse learners. In G. Troia (Ed.), *Instruction and assessment for struggling writers: Evidence based practices.* New York, NY: The Guilford Press.

Graves, A. W., Semmel, M., & Gerber, M. (1994). The effects of story prompts on the narrative production of students with and without learning disabilities. *Learning Disability Quarterly, 17*, 154–164.

Graves, A. W., Valles, E., & Rueda, R. (2000). Variations in interactive writing instruction: A study of four bilingual special education settings. *Learning Disabilities Research and Practice, 15,* 1–10.

Graves, D. (1983). *Writing: Teachers and children at work.* Portsmouth, NH: Heinemann.

Graves, M. F., August, D., & Mancilla-Martinez, J. (2013). *Teaching vocabulary to English learners.* New York, NY: Teacher's College Press.

Graves, M. F., & Liang, L. A. (2005). *Online resources for fostering understanding and higher-level thinking in senior high school students.* Fifty-first National Reading Conference Yearbook. Chicago, IL: National Reading Conference.

Gravois, T. A., & Rosenfield, S. (2006). Impact of instructional consultation teams on the disproportionate referral and placement of minority students in special education. *Remedial and Special Education, 27,* 42–52.

Greenwood, C. R., Arreaga-Mayer, C., Utley, C. A., Gavin, K. M., & Terry, B. J. (2001). Class-wide peer tutoring management system: Applications with elementary-level English language learners. *Remedial and Special Education, 22,* 34–47.

Guarino, A. J., Echevarria, J., Short, D., Schick, J. E., Forbes, S., & Rueda, R. (2001). The Sheltered Instruction Observation Protocol. *Journal of Research in Education, 11*(1), 138–140.

Guthrie, J. T., & Wigfield, A. (2000). Engagement and motivation in reading. In M. Kimil, P. Mosenthal, P. D. Person, & R. Barr (Eds.), *Handbook of reading research* (Vol. 3, pp. 403–422). Mahwah, NJ: Erlbaum.

Gutierrez, C. (2001). What's new in the English language arts: Challenging policies and practices ¿y que? *Language Arts, 78,* 6.

Haager, D., Klinger, J., & Vaughn, S. (2007). *Evidence-based reading practices for response to intervention.* Baltimore, MD: Paul H. Brookes.

Haager, D. & Windmueller, M. (2001). Early literacy intervention for English language learners at-risk for learning disabilities: Student outcomes in an urban school. *Learning Disability Quarterly, 24,* 235–250.

Hallahan, D., & Kauffman, J. (2004). *Exceptional learners* (8th ed.). Boston, MA: Allyn & Bacon.

Harper, C., & de Jong, E. (2004). Misconceptions about teaching English language learners. *Journal of Adolescent & Adult Literacy, 48*(2) 152–162.

Harry, B., & Klingner, J. (2005). *Why are so many minority students in special education? Understanding race and disability in schools.* New York, NY: Teachers College Press.

Harry, B., Torguson, C., Katkavich, J., & Guerrero, M. (1993). Crossing social class and cultural barriers in working with families: Implications for teacher training. *Teaching Exceptional Children, 26*(1), 48–51.

Hartman, W. T., & Fay, T. A. (1996). Cost-effectiveness of instructional support teams in Pennsylvania. *Journal of Education Finance, 21*(4) 555–580.

Helman, L., & Burns, M. (2008). What does oral language have to do with it? Helping young English-language learners acquire a sight word vocabulary. *The Reading Teacher, 62*(1), 14–19.

Henderson, R. W., & Landesman, E. M. (1992). *Mathematics and middle school students of Mexican descent: The effects of thematically integrated instruction* (Research Report: 5). Santa Cruz, CA: National Center for Research on Cultural Diversity and Second Language Learning.

Henze, R., & Lucas, T. (1993). Shaping instruction to promote success of language minority students: An analysis of four high school classes. *Peabody Journal of Education, 69*(1), 6–29.

Herrell, A. L. (2000). *Fifty strategies for teaching English-language learners.* Upper Saddle River, NJ: Prentice-Hall.

Hildebrand, V., Phenice, L. A., Gray, M. M., & Hines, R. P. (2000). *Knowing and serving diverse families* (2nd ed.). Columbus, OH: Merrill.

Hoover, J., & Patton, J. (2005). Differentiating curriculum and instruction for English-language learners with special needs. *Intervention in School and Clinic, 40*(4), 231–235.

Hoover-Dempsey, K., Battiato, A., Walker, J. M. T., Reed, R. P., DeJong, J., & Jones, K. P. (2001) Parental involvement in homework. *Educational Psychologist, 36*(3), 195–209.

Hornberger, N., & Michaeu, C. (1993). Getting far enough to like it: Biliteracy in the middle school. *Peabody Journal of Education: Trends in Bilingual Education at the Secondary School Level, 69,* 54–81.

Howard, E. R., Christian, D., & Genesee, F. (2003). *The development of bilingualism and biliteracy from grades 3 to 5: A summary of findings from the Cal/CREDE study of two-way immersion education.* Washington, DC: Center for Research on Education, Diversity, & Excellence.

Howard, E. R., Sugarman, J., Christian, D., Lindholm-Leary, K. J., & Rogers, D. (2007). *Guiding principles for dual language education* (2nd ed.). Washington, DC: U.S. Department of Education and National Clearinghouse for English Language Acquisition. www.cal.org/twi/guidingprinciples.htm

Huffman, J. B., & Jacobson, A. L. (2003). Perceptions of professional learning communities. *International Journal of Leadership in Education: Theory and Practice, 6*(3), 239–250.

Hutchinson, M. (2013). Bridging the gap: Preservice teachers and their knowledge of working with English language learners. *TESOL Journal, 4*(1), 25–54.

Jiménez, R. T. (2000). Literacy and the identity development of Latina/o students. *American Educational Research Journal, 37,* 971–1000.

Jiménez, R. T. (2003). Literacy and Latino students in the United States: Some considerations, questions, and new directions. *Reading Research Quarterly, 38*(1), 122–128.

Jiménez, R. T., García, G. E., & Pearson, E. P. (1996). The reading strategies of bilingual Latina/o students who are successful English readers: Opportunities and obstacles. *Reading Research Quarterly, 31,* 90–112.

Jiménez, R. T., & Gersten, R. (1999). Lessons and dilemmas derived from the literacy instruction of two Latina/o teachers. *American Educational Research Journal, 36,* 111–123.

Jitendra, A., Edwards, L. L., Sacks, G., & Jacobson, L. A. (2004). What research says about vocabulary instruction for students with learning disabilities. *Exceptional Children, 70*(3), 220–235.

Johnson J., & Nieto, J. (2007). Truly inclusive? Disability and Deaf experience in multicultural education. *Perspectives on Urban Education, 5*(1), 235–242.

Jong, E. D., Harper, C. A., & Coady, M. R. (2013). Enhanced knowledge and skills for elementary mainstream teachers of English language learners. *Theory into Practice, 52*(2), 89–97.

Kane, T. J., Rockoff, J., & Staiger, D. D. (2007). Photo finish: Certification does not guarantee a winner. *Education Next, 7*(1), 60–67.

Kim, D. H., Lambert, R. G., & Burts, D. C. (2013). Evidence of the validity of *Teaching Strategies GOLD®* assessment tool for English language learners and children with disabilities. *Early Education and Development, 24*(4), 574–595.

Kitano, M. (2003). Gifted potential and poverty: A call for extraordinary action. *Journal for the Education of the Gifted, 26*(4), 292–303.

Klingner, J., Artiles, A., & Barletta, I. M. (2006). English language learners who struggle with reading: Language acquisition or learning disability? *Journal of Learning Disabilities, 39*(2), 108–128.

Klingner, J. K., & Vaughn, S. (1996). Reciprocal teaching of reading comprehension strategies for students with learning disabilities who use English as a second language. *Elementary School Journal, 96,* 275–293.

Klingner, J. K., Vaughn, S., Arguelles, M. E., Hughes, M. T., & Leftwich, S. A. (2004). Collaborative strategic reading: Real world lessons for classroom teachers. *Remedial and Special Education, 25*(5), 291–302.

Krashen, S. D. (1981). *Second language acquisition and second language learning.* London, England: Pergamon Press.

Krashen, S. D. (1982). Accounting for child-adult differences in second language rate and attainment. In S. Krashen, R. Scarcella, & M. Long (Eds.), *Child-adult differences in second language acquisition.* Rowley, MA: Newbury House.

Krashen, S. D. (1985). *The input hypothesis: Issues and implications.* New York, NY: Longman.

Krashen, S. D., & Terrell, T. (1983). *The natural approach: Language acquisition in the classroom.* Englewood Cliffs, NJ: Alemany/Prentice-Hall.

Lee, J. F. (1986). Background knowledge and L2 reading. *Modern Language Journal, 70,* 350–354.

Lee, O., & Buxton, C. A. (2013). Integrating science and English proficiency for English language learners. *Theory Into Practice, 52*(1), 36–42.

Lee, O., Quinn, H., & Valdéz, G. (2013). Science and language for English language learners in relation to next generation science standards and with implications for Common Core State Standards for English language arts and mathematics. *Educational Researcher, 42*(4), 223–233.

Lewis, R. B., Graves, A., Ashton, T., & Kieley, C. (1997). Text entry strategies for improving writing fluency of students with learning disabilities. *Learning Disabilities Research and Practice, 13,* 95–108.

Linan-Thompson, S., Cirino, P., & Vaughn, S. (2007). Determining English language learners' responses to intervention: Questions and some answers. *Learning Disability Quarterly, 30*(2), 186–195.

Lindholm-Leary, K. & Genesee, F. (2010). Alternative educational programs for English learners. In California Department of Education, *Improving education for English learners: Research-based approaches.* Sacramento, CA: CDE Press.

Lipson, M., & Wixson, K. (2002). *Assessment and instruction of reading and writing disability* (3rd ed.). New York, NY: Longman.

Lozano-Rodriguez, J. R., & Castellano, J. A. (1999). *Assessing LEP migrant students for special education services* (Report No. EDO-RC-98-10). Washington, DC: ERIC Clearinghouse on Rural Education and Small Schools. (ERIC Document Reproduction Service No. ED425892).

Lucas, T., & Katz, A. (1994). Reframing the debate: The roles of native languages in English-only programs for language minority students. *TESOL Quarterly, 28,* 537–562.

MacSwan, J. (2000). The threshold hypothesis, semilingualism, and other contributions to a deficit view of linguistic minorities. *Hispanic Journal of Behavioral Science, 22,* 3–45.

Maik, M. (1999). *Reducing class size in America's urban schools* (Report No. UD 033-182). Washington, DC: Council of the Great City Schools. (ERIC Document Reproduction Service No. ED435778).

Marinova-Todd, S., Marshall, B., & Snow, C. (2000). Three misconceptions about age and L2 learning. *TESOL Quarterly, 34*(1), 9–34.

Markham, P., & Gordon, K. (2007). Challenges and instructional approaches impacting the literacy performance of English language learners. *Multiple Voices 10*(1–2), 73–81.

McKeon, R. (1994). *On knowing—teaching and learning the natural sciences.* Chicago, IL: University of Chicago Press.

McIntosh, A., Graves, A., & Gersten, R. (2007). The effects of response to intervention on literacy development in middle school settings. *Learning Disability Quarterly, 30*(2), 197–211.

McIntyre, E., Kyle, D., & Moore, G. (2006). A primary-grade teacher's guidance toward small-group dialogue. *Reading Research Quarterly, 41*(1).

McKay, P. (2000). On ESL standards for school-age learners. *Language Testing 17,* 185–214.

McLaughlin, B. (1987). *Theories of second-language learning.* London, England: Arnold.

McLaughlin, B. (1992). *Myths and misconceptions about second language learning.* Washington DC: Center for Applied Lingusitics.

McLaughlin, B. (2000). Second language learning revisited: The psycholinguistic perspective. In A. Healy & L. Bourne (Eds.), *Foreign language learning.* Mahwah, NJ: Erlbaum.

Mercer, N., & Hodgkinson, S. (2008). *Exploring talk in schools.* Los Angeles, CA: Sage.

Myhill, D., Jones, S., & Hopper, R. (2006). *Talking, listening, learning.* Berkshire, England: Open University Press.

Meskill, C., & Mossop, J. (2001). Electronic texts in ESOL classrooms. *TESOL Quarterly,* 585–592.

Mora, J. K. (2009). From the ballot box to the classroom. *Educational Leadership, 66*(7), 14–19.

Moran, C., Stobbe, J., Baron, W., Miller, J., & Moir, E. (2000). *Keys to the classroom.* Thousand Oaks, CA: Corwin Press.

Myhill, D., Jones, S., & Hopper, R. (2006). *Talking, listening and learning: Effective talk in the primary classroom.* New York, NY: Open University Press.

National Center for Education Statistics. (2011). *The condition of education: Participation in education.* Washington, DC: U.S. Department of Education, Institute of Education Sciences, National Center for Education Statistics. Retrieved from http://nces.ed.gov/programs/coe/indicator_lsm.asp

National Center for Education Statistics. (2012a). *The nation's report card: Mathematics 2011* (NCES 2012–455). Washington, DC: National Center for Education Statistics, Institute of Education Sciences, U.S. Department of Education.

National Center for Education Statistics. (2012b). *The nation's report card: Reading 2011* (NCES 2012–458). Washington, DC: Institute of Education Sciences, U.S. Department of Education.

National Center for Learning Disabilities. (2006). *Taking about LD.* Retrieved from http://www.neld.org/content/view/256/296/

National Clearinghouse for English Language Acquisition (NCELA). (2005). *The growing numbers of limited English proficient students: 1992/93–2002/03.* Retrieved from www.ncela.gwu.edu/policy/states/reports/statedata/2002LEP/Growing_LEP0203.pdf

National Clearinghouse for English Language Acquisition. (2006). *The growing numbers of limited English proficient students 1993/4-2003/4.* Washington, DC: Office of English Language Acquisition, U.S. Department of Education.

National Clearinghouse for English Language Acquisition. (2011). *The growing numbers of English learner students.* Retrieved from www.ncela.gwu.edu/files/uploads/9/growingLEP_0809.pdf

National Clearinghouse for English Language Acquisition. (2013). *Improving Education for English Learners with Special Needs: Promising Practices and Current Challenges.* http://www.ncela.us/featuredtopic/elsn/

National Coalition of Advocates for Children. (1988). *New voices: Immigrant students in U.S. public schools.* Boston, MA: National Coalition of Advocates for Children.

National Staff Development Council. (2001). *NSDC standards for staff development.* Oxford, OH: National Staff Development Council.

New York City Department of Education. (2011). *New York City Department of Education graduation results: 6-year outcome cohorts of 2001–2004 New York State calculation method by English language proficiency.* New York, NY: Author. Retrieved from http://schools.nyc.gov/Accountability/data/GraduationDropoutReports/default.htmhttp://schools.nyc.gov/Accountability/data/GraduationDropoutReports/default.htm

Norris, J., & Ortega, L. (2000, September). Effectiveness of L2 instruction: A research synthesis and quantitative meta-analysis. *Language Learning 50,* 417–528.

Norton, B., & Toohey, K (2011). Identity, language learning, and social change. *Language Teaching, 44,* 412–446.

Norton-Peirce, B. (1995). Social identity, investment, and language learning *TESOL Quarterly, 29*(1), 9–31.

Obi, S. O., Obiakor, F. E., & Algozzine, B. (1999). *Empowering culturally diverse exceptional learners in the 21st century: Imperatives for U.S. educators* (Report No. EC307730). Washington, DC: National Institute of Education. (ERIC Document Reproduction Service No. ED439551).

Ortiz, A., & Graves, A. W. (2001). English language learners with literacy-related learning disabilities. *International Dyslexia Association Commemorative Booklet Series, 52,* 34–39.

O'Dell, S. (1970). *Island of the blue dolphins.* New York, NY: Bantam/Doubleday.

Palincsar, A. S. (1986). The role of dialogue in providing scaffolded instruction. *Educational Psychologist, 21* (Special issue on learning strategies), 73–98.

Pang, V. O. (2001). *Multicultural education: A caring-centered, reflective approach.* Boston, MA: McGraw-Hill.

Parrish, T. B., Linquanti, R., Merikel, A., Quick, H., Laird, J., & Esra, P. (2006). *Effects of the implementation of Proposition 227 on the education of English learners, K-12: Findings from a five-year evaluation.* Submitted to the California Department of Education, Sacramento, CA. San Francisco, CA: American Institutes for Research and WestEd.

Pavri, S., & Monda-Amaya, L. (2001). Social support in inclusive schools: Student and teacher perspectives. *Exceptional Children, 63,* 391–411.

Pease-Alvarez, L., & Winsler, A. (1994). Cuando el maestro no habla Espanol: Children's bilingual language practices in the classroom. *TESOL Quarterly, 28*(3), 507–536.

Pelton, R. (2010). An introduction to action research. In R. Pelton (Ed.), *Action research for teacher candidates.* New York, NY: Rowman & Littlefield Education.

Perez, B. (1993). Biliteracy practices and issues in secondary schools. *Peabody Journal of Education: Trends in Bilingual Education at the Secondary School Level, 69,* 117–135.

Philbrick, R. (1993). *Freak the Mighty.* Chicago, IL: Scholastic.

Philbrick, R. (1998). *Max the Mighty.* Chicago, IL: Scholastic.

Potter, W. J. (2006). Does television viewing hinder academic achievement among adolescents? *Human Communication Research, 14*(1), 27–46. DOI: 10.1111/j.1468-2958.1987.tb00120.x

Pritzos, S. (1992). *Teacher communication in regular and sheltered science classes.* Unpublished Master's Thesis.

Ramirez, J., Yuen, S., Ramey, D., & Pasta, D. (1991). *Executive summary: Final report: Longitudinal study of structured English immersion strategy, early-exit and late-exit transitional bilingual education programs for language-minority children.* (Contract No. 300-87-0156). Submitted to the U.S. Department of Education. San Mateo: Aguirre International.

Reyes, M. de la Luz. (1992). Challenging venerable assumptions: Literacy instruction for linguistically different students. *Harvard Educational Review, 62*(4), 427–446.

Richard-Amato, P. (1996). *Making it happen* (2nd ed.). White Plains, NY: Longman.

Richard-Amato, P. (2010). *Making it happen: From interactive to participatory language teaching—Evolving theory and practice* (4th ed.). Boston, MA: Pearson.

Richards, C., & Leafstedt, J. (2010). *Early reading interventions: Strategies and methods for struggling readers.* Boston, MA: Pearson Allyn & Bacon.

Rivera, C. (Ed.). (1984). *Language proficiency and academic achievement.* Avon, England: Multilingual Matters.

Romaine, S. (1989). *Bilingualism.* Oxford, England: Blackwell.

Rueda, R., & Windmueller, M. P. (2006). English language learners, LD and overrepresentation. *Journal of Learning Disabilities, 39*(2), 99–107.

Ruiz, N. T. (1995a). The social construction of ability and disability I: Profile types of Latino children identified as language learning disabled. *Journal of Learning Disabilities, 28,* 476–490.

Ruiz, N. T. (1995b). The social construction of ability and disability II: Optimal and at-risk lessons in a bilingual special education classroom. *Journal of Learning Disabilities, 28,* 491–502.

Ruiz-de-Velasco, J., & Fix, M. (2000). *Overlooked and underserved: Immigrant students in U.S. secondary schools.* Washington, DC: Urban Institute.

Rumberger, R. (2011). *Dropping out: Why students drop out of high school and what can be done about it.* Cambridge, MA: Harvard University Press.

Sangor, R. (2010). *Collaborative action research for professional learning communities.* Bloomington, IN: Solution Tree.

Sangor, R. (2011). *The action research guidebook* (2nd ed.). Thousand Oaks, CA: Corwin.

Santos, M., Darling Hammond, L., & Cheuk, T. (2012). *Teacher development to support English language learners in the context of the Common Core Standards.* Palo Alto, CA: Stanford Press.

Saunders, W., & Goldenberg, C. (1996). Four primary teachers work to define constructivism and teacher-directed learning: Implications for teacher assessment. *The Elementary School Journal, 97*(2), 139–161.

Saunders, W, & Goldenberg, C. (1999). Effects of instructional conversations and literature logs on limited- and fluent-English-proficient students' story comprehension and thematic understanding. *The Elementary School Journal 99*(4), 277–301.

Saunders, W., & Goldenberg, C. (2010). *Research to guide English language development instruction.* In California Department of Education (Ed.), *Improving education for English learners: Research-based approaches.* Sacramento, CA: CDE Press.

Saunders, W., & O'Brien, G. (2006). Oral language. In F. Genesee et al. (Eds.), *Educating English language learners: A synthesis of research evidence* (pp. 14–63). Cambridge, England: Cambridge University Press.

Saunders, W. M., Foorman, B. R. & Carlson., C. D.. (2006). Is a separate block of time for oral English development in program for English learners needed? *Elementary School Journal 107*(2), 181–198.

Scarcella, R., & Higa, C. (1982). Input and age differences in second language acquisition. In S. Krashen, R. Scarcella, & M. Long (Eds.), *Child–adult differences in second language acquisition.* Rowley, MA: Newbury House.

Schiff-Myers, N. B., Djukic, J., Lawler-McGovern, J., & Perez, D. (1994). Assessment consideration in the evaluation of second-language learners: A case study. *Exceptional Children, 60,* 237–244.

Schumm, J., Vaughn, S., & Leavell, A. (1994). Planning pyramid: A framework of planning for diverse student needs during content area instruction. *The Reading Teacher, 47*(8), 608–615.

Scruggs, T., & Mastropieri, M. (1990). Mnemonic instruction for students with learning disabilities: What it is and what is does. *Learning Disability Quarterly, 13*(3), 271–283.

Short, D. (1989). Adapting material for content-based language instruction. *ERIC/Clearinghouse on Languages and Linguistics News Bulletin, 13*(1): 1, 4–8.

Short, D. (1991). *How to integrate language and content instruction.* Washington, DC: Center for Applied Linguistics.

Short, D. (1992). Adapting material and developing lesson plans. In P. Richard-Amato & M. Snow (Eds.), *The multicultural classroom.* New York, NY: Longman.

Short, D. (1994). Expanding middle school horizons: Integrating language, culture, and social studies. *TESOL Quarterly, 28*(3), 581–608.

Short, D. (1999). Integrating language and content for effective sheltered instruction programs. In C. Faltis & P. Wolfe (Eds.), *So much to say: Adolescents, bilingualism and ESL in the secondary school* (pp. 105–137). New York, NY: Teachers College Press.

Short, D. (2000). What principals should know about sheltered instruction for English language learners. *NASSP Bulletin, 84,* 17–27.

Short, D., & Boyson, B. (2004). *Creating access: Language and academic programs for secondary school newcomers.* McHenry, IL: Delta Systems.

Short, D., & Echevarria, J. (2004–05). Teacher skills to support English language learners. *Educational Leadership, 62*(4) 8–13.

Short, D., Echevarria, J., & Richards-Tutor, C. (2011). Research on academic literacy development in sheltered instruction classrooms. *Language Teaching Research, 15*(3), 363–380.

Short, D., Fidelman, C., & Louguit, M. (2012). Developing academic language in English language learners through sheltered instruction. *TESOL Quarterly 46*(2), 333–360.

Short, D., & Fitzsimmons, S. (2007). *Double the work: Challenges and solutions to acquiring language and academic literacy for adolescent English language learners.* Report to Carnegie Corporation of New York. Washington, DC: Alliance for Excellent Education.

Short, D., Vogt, M.E., & Echevarria, J. (2011). *The SIOP® model for teaching history-social studies to English learners.* Boston, MA: Allyn & Bacon.

Short, D., Vogt, M.E., & Echevarria, J. (2011). *The SIOP® model for teaching science to English learners.* Boston, MA: Allyn & Bacon.

Sirotnik, K. (1983). What you see is what you get—consistency, persistency and mediocrity in classrooms. *Harvard Educational Review, 53,* 16–31.

Slavin, R. E. (1995). *Cooperative learning* (2nd ed.). Boston, MA: Allyn & Bacon.

Slavin, R. E. (2004). Education research can and must address "what works" questions. *Educational Researcher, 33*(1), 27–28.

Slowinski, J. (1999). *Using the web to access online education periodicals* (Report No. EDO-IR-1999-08). Syracuse, NY: ERIC Clearinghouse on Information and Technology. (ERIC Document Reproduction Service No. ED40584).

Snow, C. (1992). Perspectives on second-language development: Implications for bilingual education. *Educational Researcher, 21*(2), 16–24.

Snow, C., & Biancarosa, G. (2003). *Adolescent literacy development among English-language learners.* New York, NY: The Carnegie Corporation of New York.

Snow, M. A., & Katz, A. (2010). English language development: Foundations and implementation in kindergarten through grade five. In *Improving education for English learners: Research-based approaches.* Sacramento, CA: CDE Press.

Sternberg, R., & Williams, W. (2009). *Educational psychology* (2nd ed.). Boston, MA: Allyn & Bacon.

Strong, M. (1983). Social styles and the second language acquisition of Spanish-speaking kindergartners. *TESOL Quarterly, 17*(2), 241–258.

Suarez-Orozco, C., Suarez-Orozco, M., & Todorova, I. (2008) *Learning a new land: Immigrant students in American society.* Cambridge, MA: Harvard University Press.

Taylor, L., & Pillets, S. (2010). Action research and the early childhood educator. In R. Pelton (Ed.), *Action research for teacher candidates.* New York, NY: Rowman & Littlefield Education.

Taylor, R., Smiley, L., & Richards, S. (2009). *Exceptional students: Preparing teachers for the 21st century.* Boston, MA: McGraw-Hill Higher Education.

Teachers of English to Speakers of Other Languages. (1997). *ESL standards for preK–12 students.* Alexandria, VA: Author.

TESOL International Association. (2010). *Standards for the recognition of initial TESOL programs in P–12 ESL teacher education.* Retrieved from http://www.tesol.org/docs/books/the-revised-tesol-ncate-standards-for-the-recognition-of-initial-tesol-programs-in-p-12-esl-teacher-education-(2010-pdf).pdf?sfvrsn=2

Tharp, R., & Gallimore, R. (1988). *Rousing minds to life.* Cambridge, England: Cambridge University Press.

Torgesen, J., Houston, D., Rissman, L., Decker, S., Roberts, G., Vaughn, S., Wexler, J., Francis, D., Rivera, M., & Lesaux, N. (2007). *Academic literacy instruction for adolescents: A guidance document from the Center on Instruction.* Portsmouth, NH: RMC Research Corporation, Center on Instruction.

Torres, C. C. (2000). *Emerging Latino communities: A new challenge for the rural south* (Report No. RC 022 605). Chicago, IL: ERIC Clearinghouse on Rural Education and Small Schools. (ERIC Document Reproduction Service No. ED444806).

Torres, M. N. (2001). Teacher-researchers entering into the world of limited- English-proficiency (LEP) students: Three case studies. *Urban Education, 36,* 256–289.

Torres-Burgo, N., Reyes-Wasson, P., & Brusca-Vega, R. (1999). Perceptions and needs of Hispanic and non-Hispanic parents of children receiving learning disabilities services. *Bilingual Research Journal, 23,* 319–333.

Treuba, H., Jacobs, L., & Kirton, E. (1990). *Cultural conflict and adaptation.* New York, NY: Falmer.

Troike, R. C. (1984). SCALP: Social and cultural aspects of language proficiency. In C. Rivera (Ed.), *Language proficiency and academic achievement.* Avon, England: Multilingual Matters.

Valdes, G., Bunch, G., Snow, C., Lee, C., & Matos, L. (2005). Enhancing the development of students' language(s). In L. Darling-Hammond & J. Bransford (Eds.), *Preparing teachers for a changing world: What teachers should learn and be able to do.* San Francisco, CA: Jossey-Bass.

Vaughn, S., Wanzek, J., Murray, C. S., Scammaca, N., Linan-Thompson, S., & Woodruff, A. (2009). Response to early reading intervention: Examining higher and lower responders. *Exceptional Children, 75*(2), 165–183.

Villegas, A. M., & Lucas, T. (2007). The culturally responsive teacher. *Educational Leadership, 64*(6), 28–53.

Vogt, M.E., Echevarria, J. & Washam, M.A. (2015). *99 MORE Ideas and activities for teaching English learners with the SIOP® Model.* Boston, MA: Allyn & Bacon.

Vogt, M.E., Echevarria, J., & Short, D. (2011). *The SIOP® model for teaching English- language arts to English learners.* Boston, MA: Allyn & Bacon.

Vygotsky, L. S. (1962). *Thought and language* (E. Hanfmann & G. Vaker, Trans.). Cambridge, MA: Massachusetts Institute of Technology Press.

Vygotsky, L. S. (1978). *Mind in society: The development of higher psychological processes.* (M. Cole, V. John-Steiner, & E. Souberman, Eds. & Trans.). Cambridge, MA: Harvard University Press.

Wahl, J. (1969). *How the children stopped the wars.* Berkeley, CA: Tricycle Press.

Waldschmidt, E. D., Kim, Y. M., Kim, J., Martinez, C., & Hale, A. (1999). *Teacher stories: Bilingual playwriting and puppetry with English language learners and students with special needs* (Report No. FL026293). Montreal, Quebec, Canada: ERIC Clearinghouse on Languages and Linguistics. (ERIC Document Reproduction Service No. ED442288).

Wiley, T. (2008). *Language policy in teacher education. In Encyclopedia of language and education* (2nd ed.). New York, NY: Springer.

Wiley, T. G. (1996). *Literacy and language diversity in the U.S.* Washington, DC: Center for Applied Linguistics and Delta Systems.

Wong-Fillmore, L., & Valadez, C. (1986). Teaching bilingual learners. In M. C. Wittrock (Ed.), *Handbook of research on teaching* (pp. 648–685). New York, NY: Macmillan.

Woolfolk, A. (2013). *Educational psychology* (12th ed.). Boston, MA: Allyn & Bacon.

World Class Instructional Design. (2013). http://wida.us/standards/eld.aspx

Yang, N. D. (1999). *The relationship between English as a foreign language learners' beliefs and learning strategy use.* System, 27, 515–535. Available from www.elsevier.com/locate/system

Zehr, M. (2008, May 30). NAEP scores in states that cut bilingual education fuel concern on English language learners. *Education Week,* 10.

INDEX

Note: Page numbers with "f" indicate figures; those with "t" indicate tables.

A

academic background, 19, 21
academic engagement, preparing for, 141–144
  assessment and instruction cycle, 142–143
  cooperative efforts among teachers, encouraging, 143–144
  main points, highlighting, 143
  note taking, 141–142
  rewriting by students, 143
  study resource guides, 143
  study sheets and homework, 142
academic language
  adjusting, with sheltered instruction, 76–80
  defined, 130
  objectives, 74–75
  opportunities for developing, providing, 130–131
  proficiency in, 9, 12, 13, 14f, 36
  understanding, 73–74
  vocabulary as, 74
academic proficiency, 127–128
  background assessment and, 21
  content knowledge for building, 127–128
  skills for building, 128
access to language, in second-language acquisition, 42
accountability, 11, 27
action research, for professional development, 147–148
active learning, 97
activity worksheet, in comparative case study, 63–64, 63f
adaptation of text, in SIOP® model, 56
advanced level, language acquisition, 17f, 18
advertisement activity, in comparative case study, 65–66, 66f
affective issues
  actively involving learners, 93–94
  background knowledge, focusing on, 92–93
  cross-cultural understanding promoted by teacher, 100–101
  cultural connections, focusing on, 92–93
  expectations for learners, 99–100
  family/community classroom involvement, 97–99
  grouping strategies, alternate, 94–95
  meaningful content and activities, 97
  native-language support, providing, 95–96
  practice and corrections, 91–92
  reading and writing activities, 89–91
age, in second-language acquisition, 39–40
alternate books, for modifying lesson plans and text, 138
assessment and instruction cycle, 142–143

assessment instruments, 14, 15f, 16. *see also individually named instruments*
assignments, modifying, 138–141
  length and complexity of assignments, 140–141
  maps or pictorial representations, 139
  objectives, 139
  oral discussions in pairs or small groups, 140
attention, in cognitive learning theory, 45
audio taping text versions, 138

B

background knowledge
  affective issues and, 92–93
  differentiated instruction and, 126–127, 126f
  in instructional conversations, 81
  phases for providing, 126f
basic interpersonal communication skills (BICS), 12, 13, 36
  iceberg analogy, 13, 14f
beginning (level 2) in ELD, 17f, 18
behavioral learning theories, 46–47
behavior problems
  characteristics of students with, 23, 24
  interventions for, 23f, 24–25
  learning strategies for, 106–107, 106f
  minority students and, 22
bias, in assessment instruments, 16
BICS (basic interpersonal communication skills), 12, 13, 36
  iceberg analogy, 13, 14f
bilingual education
  developmental, 7t, 8
  programs, 32–33, 41
  steps for instruction in, 10
  teachers of, 34
bilingual instructional aides (IAs), 8
body, in strategy instruction, 117
brainstorming
  for background knowledge, 93, 126
  in strategy instruction in writing, 111
  vocabulary words, 57
bridging (level 3) in ELD, 17f, 18
Building Background component, in SIOP® Model, 52f
bulletin boards, in SIOP® model, 60

C

California English Language Development Test (CELDT), 14
California Teachers of English Learners (CTEL), 11–12, 11f, 123, 124
CALP (cognitive/academic language proficiency), 12, 13, 36
  iceberg analogy, 13, 14f

capitalization, in COPS strategy, 115, 115f, 116, 117, 118, 118f
capitalization, overall appearance, punctuation, spelling (COPS) strategy, 115, 115f, 116, 117, 118, 118f
career readiness standards, 9, 99, 125
CCSS. *see* Common Core State Standards (CCSS)
CELDT (California English Language Development Test), 14
Center for Research on Education, Diversity & Excellence, 98–99
"chunking" of text, in instructional conversations, 83
Civil Rights Act, 33
classroom discourse, in instructional conversations, 84–86
closing, in strategy instruction, 118
clues
  contextual, 37, 37f, 42
  contextual, in sheltered instruction compared to effective instruction, 68
  visual, offered through technology, 59
cognitive ability, in second-language acquisition, 41
cognitive/academic language proficiency (CALP), 12, 13, 36
  iceberg analogy, 13, 14f
cognitive behavioral psychological principles in learning strategies, 104
cognitive learning theory, 45–46
Collaborative Strategic Reading (CSR), 140
Colorín Colorado website, 99
Common Core State Standards (CCSS)
  academic proficiency skills, 128
  challenges of, 50
  differentiated instruction, 125–126
  expectations, 99
  implementation of, 35
  in instructional conversations, 83
  in planning for instruction, 66
  simplified objectives, 139
  SIOP® Model aligned with, 51
  skill requirements, 73
communicative demands, in second-language acquisition, 36–37, 37f
community, classroom involvement of, 97–99
comparative case study, 61–69
  activity worksheet, 63–64, 63f
  advertisement activity, 65–66, 66f
  chronology of four-day unit, 62f
  content objectives, 62
  discussion of, 67–69
  label-reading activity, 64–65, 65f
  language objectives, 62
complexity of assignments, modifying, 140–141
comprehensibility, paraphrasing for increasing, 78

comprehensible input
    in authentic communicative contexts, 35
    in service sessions, 147
    in sheltered instruction, 21
    in SIOP® Model, 51, 52f
    visual images used to teach, 110
Comprehensible Input component, in SIOP®
    Model, 52f
comprehensible lessons, SIOP techniques for,
    58–60
    bulletin boards, 60
    demonstration, 60
    graphic depiction, 60
    maps, 60
    modeling, 58
    pictures, 59
    realia, 58
    technology, 59–60, 59f
    timelines, 60
comprehension level, in SOLOM assessment,
    15f, 16
concepts
    in cognitive learning theory, 45
    instructional conversations for developing,
        80–86
connected talk, in instructional
    conversations, 84
content area instruction
    language demands, 12–13
    learning strategies in
        examples of, 107–113
        focusing on important learning
            strategies, 119
        grade-level reading words found
            in, 121
        native-language speakers and, 107
        for optimal strategy instruction, 116
        reading strategies, 108–110
        writing strategies, 110–113,
            111f, 113f
    native-language speakers and, 97
    sheltered instruction in (see SIOP® Model)
content knowledge, for building academic
    proficiency, 127–128
content objectives
    in sheltered instruction compared to
        effective instruction, 50f, 62
    in SIOP® Model, 51, 52f, 53f, 54f, 56, 58
conversational language, 12, 14f, 36
cooperative grouping, 94, 140
COPS (capitalization, overall appearance,
    punctuation, spelling) strategy, 115,
    115f, 116, 117, 118, 118f
Cornell note taking system, 141–142
correction. see error correction
cross-cultural understanding promoted by
    teacher, 100–101
CSR (Collaborative Strategic Reading), 140
CTEL (California Teachers of English
    Learners), 11–12, 11f, 123, 124
cultural connections, focusing on, 92–93
cultural diversity, 97
Cummins, J.
    conceptualization of language proficiency,
        12–13
    theory of second-language acquisition,
        36–38, 37f

D

DBE (developmental bilingual education), 7t, 8
demonstration
    for modifying lesson plans and text, 138
    in SIOP® model, 60
developing (level 3) in ELD, 17f, 18
developmental bilingual education (DBE), 7t, 8
developmental learning theory, 44
differentiated instruction
    academic proficiency and, building,
        127–128
        academic proficiency skills, 128
        content knowledge, 127–128
    background knowledge and, providing,
        126–127, 126f
        phases for, 126f
    language development opportunities,
        providing, 129–132
        academic language, 130–131
        discipline-specific vocabulary
            development, 131–132
        language proficiency, 129–130
    lesson plans and texts in, modifying,
        132–144
    sensitivity to cultural and linguistic
        diversity, 124–126
disabilities. see learning disabilities
disability culture, 97
discipline-specific vocabulary development,
    131–132
discourse
    in adjusting language with sheltered
        instruction, 78–80
    in instructional conversations, 84–86
discovery learning, 45, 46, 47
discussion, in instructional conversations
    (ICs), 84
due process procedures, 33

E

educational reform movement, 35
education of ELs, history of
    educational reform movement, 35
    gap in achievement/performance, 33–34
    history of, 32–35
    immigration, 32
    programs for ELs, 33–35
    rights of ELs, 32–33
    students with disabilities, 33
effective instruction
    adjusting language with sheltered
        instruction compared to, 78–80
    sheltered instruction compared to, 50–51,
        50f (see also comparative case study;
        SIOP® Model)
    SIOP® Model compared to, 50–51, 50f
        academic engaged time and
            lesson preparation, 58
        consistency and repetition, 57
        contextualized instruction, 58
        linguistic interactions, 58
        linguistic load of teachers' speech,
            reducing, 57
        more pauses between phrases, 57
        real-life activity assignments, 56

    student interaction with one another and
        with teacher, 57–58
    text adapted to meet students' needs, 56
    vocabulary instruction, 57
    well-planned lessons, 56
effective teachers, SIOP® Model and, 51
ELD. see English language development (ELD)
elicitation techniques, in instructional
    conversation, 81–83
ELLs (English language learners). see ELs
    (English learners)
ELs (English learners)
    academic background, 21
    affective issues and
        actively involving learners, 93–94
        expectations for learners, 99–100
    assessment
        academic background and school
            experience, 21
        home language survey and, 6, 14
        native-language knowledge, 6
    with disabilities, 33 (see also learning
        disabilities; special education)
    diverse backgrounds among, 1–2
    evaluation, 4–5
    factors affecting, 3–4, 4f
    history of education of (see education of
        ELs, history of)
    instructional approaches to (see instruction
        of ELs; learning theories)
    native-language, 5–10
        instructional models, 6–10, 7t
        skills-assessment, 5f, 6
    profiles, 2–3, 28–29
    school experience, 19–21
    school programs for (see school programs
        for ELs)
    SIOP® Model for (see SIOP® Model)
emotions. see affective issues
English language development (ELD), 7t, 9–10.
        see also ESL (English as a second
        language)
    important considerations in, 9–10, 10f
    instructional conversations for, 80–86
    instructional programs for, 16–19, 17f, 20f
    language objectives and, 74–75
    learning contexts in, 16
    opportunities, providing, 129–132
        academic language, 130–131
        discipline-specific vocabulary
            development, 131–132
        language proficiency, 129–130
    stages of, 17–18, 17f
    time dedicated to, 17
English language learners (ELLs). see ELs
    (English learners)
English proficiency
    assessment, 14–16, 15f
    attaining, 10–19
    instruction, 16–19, 20f
    levels
        SOLOM, 14–16, 15f, 20f
        WIDA, 17–18, 17f
entering (level 1) in ELD, 17, 17f
environment for learning. see learning
    environment
Erikson's stages of psychosocial development, 44

error correction
  modeling for, 118
  providing, affective issues and, 91–92
  to teach learning strategies, 120–121
ESL (English as a second language). *see also* English language development (ELD)
  programs for ELs and, 7t, 34
  rights of ELs and, 32
  specialists, 9, 34
essay strategy, 112–113, 113f
evaluation
  nondiscriminatory, 33
  self-evaluation, in reflective practice, 151–156, 152–153f
expanding (level 3) in ELD, 17f, 18
explicit teaching, 36, 37
extroverts, second-language acquisition and, 40

F

facts, in cognitive learning theory, 45
family, in second-language acquisition, 41–42
  classroom involvement of, 97–99
  "Family Literacy Nights," 98
  home-use literacy strategies and, 98–99
"Family Literacy Nights," 98
feelings. *see* affective issues
first-language development, 38, 40, 88. *see also* native-language knowledge
fluency level, in SOLOM assessment, 15f, 16
"folk theory" (or implicit theory), 43
four-square strategy, 105
four-stage note-taking strategy, 141–142
framed outline, 136, 136f
"A Framework for K–12 Science Education" (NCES), 126

G

gap in achievement/performance, 33–34
goal-setting
  for learner, 27–28
  in reflective practice, 151–156, 152–153f
  for teacher, 27–28
good-listening strategy, 117, 117f
grade-appropriate practice, 121
grammar level, in SOLOM assessment, 15f, 16
graphic depictions
  for modifying lesson plans and text, 132, 134–135
  in SIOP® model, 60
graphic organizers, 45, 134–136, 136f
grouping of students
  alternate strategies, 94–95
  cooperative, 94, 140
  for linguistic interactions in SIOP® Model, 58
  oral discussions in, 140

H

hands-on materials/manipulatives, in SIOP® Model, 50f, 53f
high-interest–low-vocabulary books, 138
home language survey, 6, 14
home-use literacy strategies, 98–99

homework, 142
humanistic learning theory, 43–44

I

IAs (instructional aides), 8
iceberg analogy, language proficiency and, 13, 14f
ICs. *see* instructional conversations (ICs)
IDEA (Individuals with Disabilities Education Act), 33
Idea Proficiency Test (IPT), 14
IDEIA (Individuals with Disabilities Education Improvement Act), 26
immigration, EL education and, 32
implicit theory (or "folk theory"), 43
Individualized Education Plan (IEP), 21, 33
  elements of, 27
Individuals with Disabilities Education Act (IDEA), 33
Individuals with Disabilities Education Improvement Act (IDEIA), 26
Initiation/Response/Evaluation (IRE), 85
Initiation/Response/Feedback (IRF), 85
inservice sessions, for professional development, 147
instructional conversations (ICs)
  atmosphere of, 84
  for concept development, 80–86
  connected talk in, 84
  discourse used during, 85–86
  discussion following opportunities by students' contributions, 83–84
  elements that characterize, 81–84
  goal of, 80
  interaction in, 85
  for language development, 80–86
  learning disabilities and, 81
  model for conducting, 81
  participation by all students encouraged in, 84
  quality interaction and, 85
  questions in, 82–83
  rich discussion involving connected talk, 84
  student characteristics and, 81
  teacher in, role of, 81
  themes in lesson planning and, 81
instruction models for teaching ELs, 6–10, 7t
instruction of ELs. *see also* school programs for ELs
  academic background and, 19, 21
  approaches to (*see* learning theories)
  differentiating (*see* differentiated instruction)
  ELD/ESL, 16–19, 20f
  learning contexts for, 16
  models/approaches to, 6–10, 7t
  quality of, access to, 42
  reflecting on approach to, 43
  three-tiered intervention model applied to, 23–27, 23f
instrumental motivation, 38–39
integrative motivation, 38–39
interaction, in instructional conversations, 85
Interaction component, in SIOP® Model, 53f, 57–58
  linguistic interactions, 58
  student interaction with one another and with teacher, 57–58

intermediate level, language acquisition, 17f, 18
interventions. *see also* Response-to-Intervention (RTI)
  tier 1, 23f, 24–25
  tier 2, 23f, 25–26
  tier 3, 23f, 27
IPT (Idea Proficiency Test), 14
IRE (Initiation/Response/Evaluation), 85
IRF (Initiation/Response/Feedback), 85

K

knowledge
  background (*see* background knowledge)
  content area (*see* academic proficiency)
  content knowledge of language (*see* language knowledge)
"known-answer" questions, in instructional conversation, 83
Kohlberg's stages of moral reasoning, 44
Krashen's theory of second-language acquisition, 35–36

L

label-reading activity, in comparative case study, 64–65, 65f
language, academic. *see* academic language
Language Assessment Scales (LAS), 14
language development. *see* English language development (ELD)
language knowledge
  domains of, 11–12, 11f
  levels of
    SOLOM, 14–16, 15f, 20f
    WIDA, 17–18, 17f
  native language
    instructional models and, 6–10, 7t
    skills assessment in, 5f, 6
language objectives
  in sheltered instruction compared to effective instruction, 50f, 62
  in SIOP® Model, 51, 52f, 53f, 54f, 56, 58
language proficiency. *see also* English proficiency
  academic, 9, 12, 13, 14f, 36
  benefits of, 76
  case example, 13
  Cummins's conceptualization of, 12–13
  developing, 76
  iceberg analogy, 13, 14f
  opportunities for developing, providing, 129–130
LAS (Language Assessment Scales), 14
Lau Remedies, 32, 33
Lau v. Nichols, 6, 33
learners. *see* ELs (English learners)
learning disabilities, 22–25. *see also* special education
  characteristics of students with, 23, 24
  ELs with, 33
  instructional conversations and, 81
  interventions for, 23f, 24–25
  minority students and, 22
  Ole program and, 89, 96
  SIOP® Model and, 69–70, 70f
  strategy instruction for, 104–105

learning environment
    adjusting to meet students' needs, 151
    cultural and personal diversity in, 101
    least restrictive, 27, 33
    Ole program, 89, 96
learning strategies. *see also* strategy instruction
    adapting to language proficiency levels, 105
    benefits of, 104–105
    cognitive behavioral psychological
        principles in, 104
    in cognitive learning theory, 45
    in content areas, 106
        examples of, 107–113
        focusing on important learning
            strategies, 119
        grade-level reading words found in, 121
        native-language speakers and, 107
        for optimal strategy instruction, 116
        reading strategies, 108–110
        writing strategies, 110–113, 111f, 113f
    defined, 104
    to enhance academic and English
        proficiency, 105
    to enhance language acquisition, 106
    to enhance second-language skills, 106
    essay strategy, 112–113, 113f
    four-square strategy, 105
    good-listening strategy, 117, 117f
    history of using, 104
    interpersonal strategies, 106–107
    main ideas, finding
        mini-lessons for, 105f, 106
        modeling for, 108–109, 108f
    science strategy, 105f, 106
    selecting, guidelines for, 113–115
        decide order of instruction, 115
        determine levels of knowledge and
            language proficiency, 114
        determine most useful strategies, 114–115
        use simple wording and fewest number
            of steps, 115
    social skills strategies, 106–107, 107f
    teaching, 116–121 (*see also* mini-lessons)
        body, 117
        closing, 118
        opening, 117–118
        presentation methods in (*see*
            presentation methods to teach
            learning strategies)
        preskills, determining and preteaching,
            116–117
        reading strategies in content-area classes,
            108–110
        requirements of, 116
        writing strategies in content-area classes,
            110–113, 111f, 113f
    types of, 104–107
    use-of-cognates strategy, 106, 106f
    writing-as-a-process, 110–111, 111f, 120
learning theories, 43–47
    behavioral, 46–47
    cognitive, 45–46
    of Cummins, 36–38, 37f
    developmental, 44
    "folk theory" (or implicit theory), 43
    humanistic, 43–44
    of Krashen, 35–36

    of Piaget, 44
    social interactionist, 45
    of Vygotsky, 44
least restrictive environment (LRE), 27, 33
length of assignments, modifying, 140–141
Lesson Delivery component, in SIOP®
    Model, 53f
lesson planning. *see also* SIOP® lesson plan
    effective sheltered lessons, 61, 66–67
    language objectives in, 75
    modifying plans (*see* lesson plans,
        modifying)
    in sheltered instruction compared to
        effective instruction, 56
    student engagement and, 58
    themes, in instructional conversations, 81
lesson plans, modifying, 132–144
    advanced academic engagement, preparing
        for, 141–144
        assessment and instruction cycle,
            142–143
        cooperative efforts among teachers,
            encouraging, 143–144
        main points, highlighting, 143
        note taking, 141–142
        rewriting by students, 143
        study resource guides, 143
        study sheets and homework, 142
    assignments, modifying, 138–141
        length and complexity of assignments,
            140–141
        maps or pictorial representations, 139
        objectives, 139
        oral discussions in pairs or small
            groups, 140
    methods of, 132–138
        by adding graphic depictions, 132,
            134–135
        by audio taping text versions, 138
        graphic organizers, 134–136, 136f
        by outlining text, 136, 136f
        by providing live demonstrations, 138
        by rewriting text, 137–138, 137f
        sources and adaptations, 133–134f
        by using alternate books, 138
        visualization strategies, 134–135, 135f
Lesson Preparation component, in SIOP®
    Model, 52f, 58
linguistic interdependence model, 36–37
LRE (least restrictive environment), 27, 33

M

main ideas, finding
    mini-lessons for, 105f, 106
    modeling for, 108–109, 108f
main points, highlighting, 143
manipulatives, for promoting physical
    learning, 94
maps
    for modifying assignments, 139
    in SIOP® model, 60
Marsh and Shavelson's structure of self-
    concept, 44
Maslow's hierarchy of needs, 44
memory, in cognitive learning theory, 45
metacognition, in cognitive learning theory, 45

mini-lessons, 106
    for finding main ideas, 105f, 106
    revision format presented in, 112
    strategy instruction, 117–118
    time management in, 118, 119f
minority students, in special education, 22
mnemonic strategies, 46
modeling. *see also* three-tiered model
    for error correction, 118
    for finding main ideas, 108–109, 108f
    instruction models, for teaching ELs, 6–10, 7t
    for optimal strategy instruction, 116
    pacing, 120
    in SIOP® model, 58
    think-aloud, to teach report writing,
        108–109, 108f
    two-stage, 117–118, 117f
        physical model, 118
        verbal rehearsal, 117–118, 117f
    visual, 108–109, 109f
moral reasoning, Kohlberg's stages of, 44
motivation, in second-language acquisition,
    38–39
multimedia, 59–60

N

National Assessment for Educational
    Progress, 33
National Center for Educational Statistics, 126
National Literacy Panel, 98
"The Nation's Report Card," 33
native-language knowledge, 5–10
    affective issues, 95–96
    assessment in, 5f, 6
    instruction in, models for, 6–10, 7t
    second language acquisition and, 40–41
needs, Maslow's hierarchy of, 44
newcomer programs, 7t, 10
Next Generation Science Standards, 126
next generation standards, 9
No Child Left Behind, 33
nondiscriminatory evaluation, 33
note taking, 141–142

O

objectives
    language, 74–75
    short-term, 27–28
    simplified, 139
Ole (optimal learning environment), 89, 96
open-ended questions, in instructional
    conversation, 83
opening, in strategy instruction, 117–118
optimal learning environment (Ole), 89, 96
oral discussions in pairs or small groups, 140
oral language proficiency. *see* language
    proficiency
outcome-based accountability, 142
outlining text, 136, 136f
overall appearance, in COPS strategy, 115, 115f

P

pacing, to teach learning strategies, 120
paraphrasing for increasing comprehensibility, 78

parental participation, right of, 33
partner sharing, 25, 94, 97
peer pairs, 112
peer tutoring, 94, 112, 133f
perception, in cognitive learning theory, 45
personality, in second-language acquisition, 40
physical learning, manipulatives for
    promoting, 94
physical model, 118
Piaget's developmental theory, 44
pictures
    for modifying assignments, 139
    in SIOP® model, 59
planning, lessons. *see* lesson planning
PLCs (professional learning communities),
    148–149
practice
    providing, 91–92
    to teach learning strategies, 121
Practice & Application component, in SIOP®
    Model, 53f
presentation methods to teach learning
    strategies, 119–121
    error correction, 120–121
    pacing, 120
    practice, 121
    student involvement, 119–120
preservice teachers, 34
preskills, determining and preteaching,
    116–117
problem solving, in cognitive learning theory, 45
professional development, 146–149
    action research for, 147–148
    conditions recommended for optimal,
      146–147
    inservice sessions for, 147
    professional learning communities for,
      148–149
professional learning communities (PLCs),
    148–149
pronunciation level, in SOLOM assessment,
    15f, 16
psychosocial development, Erikson's stages
    of, 44
punctuation, in COPS strategy, 115, 115f,
    116, 117

Q

quality of instruction, in second-language
    acquisition, 42
questions, in instructional conversation, 82–83

R

reaching (level 3) in ELD, 17f, 18
reading strategies in content-area classes,
    108–110
realia, in SIOP® model, 58
reasoning
    in cognitive learning theory, 45
    moral, Kohlberg's stages of, 44
reflective practice
    importance of, 145–146
    professional development and, 146–149
    self-evaluation and goal-setting in, 151–156,
      152–153f

student vignettes and, revisiting, 153–156
    video reflection and analysis in, 150–151
repetition
    in SIOP® model, 57
    in social interactionist learning theory, 45
report writing, think-aloud modeling to teach,
    108–109, 108f
Response-to-Intervention (RTI), 26–27
responsiveness, second-language acquisition
    and, 40
Review & Assessment component, in SIOP®
    Model, 53f
rewriting
    by students, for advanced academic
      engagement, 143
    by teachers, for modifying lesson plans
      and text, 137–138, 137f
rights of ELs, 6, 32–33
risk taking, second-language acquisition
    and, 40
RTI. *see* Response-to-Intervention (RTI)

S

scaffolding
    defined, 68–69
    in sheltered instruction compared to
      effective instruction, 50f, 69
    in SIOP® model, 53f
    verbal, 69
*Scaffolding Reading Experiences for English
    Language Learners* (Fitzgerald and
    Graves), 89
school experience, assessment of, 21
school programs for ELs, 33–35. *see also*
    instruction of ELs
    characteristics of, 34
    educational reform movement, 35
    historical perspective on, 33–34
    implementation of effective, 34
    teachers of, 34
school supports, three-tiered model, 23–28, 23f
    instruction, 26–28
    tier 1, 24–25
    tier 2, 25–26
    tier 3, 26
science strategy, 105f, 106
SDAIE (Specially Designed Academic
    Instruction in English), 50, 51. *see
    also* sheltered instruction (SI)
second-language acquisition, 10–19
    content area instruction and, 17–19, 17f
    factors affecting, 38–42
      language learner factors, 38–41
      socio-contextual factors, 41–42
    levels of
      impact on development, 40
      SOLOM, 14–16, 15f, 20f
      WIDA, 17–18, 17f
    sheltered instruction for, 35
    theories of, 35–38
      Cummins, 36–38, 37f
      Krashen, 35–36
self-concept, Marsh and Shavelson's structure
    of, 44
self-evaluation, in reflective practice, 151–156,
    152–153f

sheltered instruction (SI), 7–8, 7t
    adjusting language with, 76–80
      compared to effective instruction,
        78–80
      integrating into lessons, 77–78
      modifications, 76–77
      paraphrasing for increasing
        comprehensibility, 78
    defined, 50–51
    effective instruction compared to, 50–51,
      50f (*see also* comparative case study;
      SIOP® Model)
    goals of, 38, 43
    model for (*see* SIOP® Model)
    for second-language acquisition, 35
    theories of second-language development
      (*see* learning theories)
Sheltered Instruction Observation protocol
    (SIOP) Model. *see* SIOP® Model;
    SIOP® Model
short-term objectives, 27–28
SI. *see* sheltered instruction (SI)
SIOP® lesson plan. *see also* comprehensible
    lessons, SIOP techniques for
key academic terms in, 57
preparation time, 56
sample, 54–55f
SIOP® Model
    components of, 51, 52–53f
      Building Background, 52f
      Comprehensible Input, 52f
      Interaction, 53f, 57–58
      Lesson Delivery, 53f
      Lesson Preparation, 52f, 58
      Practice & Application, 53f
      Review & Assessment, 53f
      Strategies, 53f
    effective instruction compared to,
      50–51, 50f
      academic engaged time and lesson
        preparation, 58
      consistency and repetition, 57
      contextualized instruction, 58
      linguistic interactions, 58
      linguistic load of teachers' speech,
        reducing, 57
      more pauses between phrases, 57
      real-life activity assignments, 56
      student interaction with one another and
        with teacher, 57–58
      text adapted to meet students' needs, 56
      vocabulary instruction, 57
      well-planned lessons, 56
    features of, 51, 55–56
      effectiveness of, 55, 60
      overview of, 52–53f
      text adapted to meet students' needs, 56
    learning disabilities and, 69–70, 70f
    lessons (*see* SIOP® lesson plan)
    sample lesson plan, 54–55f
social identity, in second-language
    acquisition, 39
social interactionist learning theory, 45
social studies, in sheltered instruction compared
    to effective instruction, 61–69. *see
    also* comparative case study
sociocultural theory, of Vygotsky, 9

SOLOM (Student Oral Language Observation Matrix), 14–16, 15f, 20f
special education
    characteristics of students with learning disabilities, 23, 24
    interventions for, 23f, 24–25
    minority students and, 22
Specially Designed Academic Instruction in English (SDAIE), 50, 51. see also sheltered instruction (SI)
speech of teacher, reducing linguistic load of, 57
spelling, in COPS strategy, 115, 115f, 116
story mapping, 134, 135, 136f, 139
Strategies component, in SIOP® Model, 53f
strategy instruction. see also learning strategies; mini-lessons
    body in, 117
    closing in, 118
    COPS strategy in, 115, 115f, 116, 117, 118, 118f
    for learning disabilities, 104–105
    modeling in
        for error correction, 118
        for finding main ideas, 108–109, 108f
        for optimal strategy instruction, 116
        pacing, 120
        think-aloud, to teach report writing, 108–109, 108f
        two-stage, 117–118, 117f
        visual, 108–109, 109f
    opening in, 117–118
    student involvement, to teach learning strategies, 119–120
Student Oral Language Observation Matrix (SOLOM), 14–16, 15f, 20f
student pairs, 112
students. see ELs (English learners)
study resource guides, 143
study sheets, 142
supplementary materials, 143

T

talkativeness, second-language acquisition and, 40
TBE (transitional bilingual education), 7t, 8, 32
teachers. see also reflective practice
    of bilingual education, 34
    cooperative efforts among, encouraging, 143–144
    cross-cultural understanding promoted by, 100–101
    effective, SIOP® Model and, 51
    elicitation techniques used by, 81–83
    in instructional conversations, 81
    language learning in the classroom, promoting, 129–130
    as language teachers, 73–74
    preparation programs for, 34
    preservice, 34
    speech of, reducing linguistic load of, 57

teaching
    English language development, 129–132
        academic language, 130–131
        discipline-specific vocabulary development, 131–132
        language proficiency, 129–130
    explicit, 36, 37
    learning strategies, 116–121 (see also mini-lessons)
        body, 117
        closing, 118
        opening, 117–118
        presentation methods in (see presentation methods to teach learning strategies)
        preskills, determining and preteaching, 116–117
        reading strategies in content-area classes, 108–110
        requirements of, 116
        writing strategies in content-area classes, 110–113, 111f, 113f
    social interactionist approach, 45
    theory to practice, 43–47 (see also learning theories)
Teaching English to Speakers of Other Languages (TESOL) standards, 75, 134, 147
Teaching Strategies GOLD®, 14
technology, in SIOP® model, 59–60, 59f
TESOL (Teaching English to Speakers of Other Languages) standards, 75, 134, 147
text, modifying, 132–144
    advanced academic engagement, preparing for, 141–144
        assessment and instruction cycle, 142–143
        cooperative efforts among teachers, encouraging, 143–144
        main points, highlighting, 143
        note taking, 141–142
        rewriting by students, 143
        study resource guides, 143
        study sheets and homework, 142
    assignments, modifying, 138–141
        length and complexity of assignments, changing, 140–141
        maps or pictorial representations, drawing, 139
        objectives, 139
        oral discussions in pairs or small groups, 140
    methods of, 132–138
        by adding graphic depictions, 132, 134–135
        by audio taping text versions, 138
        graphic organizers, 134–136, 136f
        original text, 134f
        by outlining text, 136, 136f
        by providing live demonstrations, 138
        by rewriting text, 137–138, 137f
        sources and adaptations, 133–134f
        by using alternate books, 138
        visualization strategies, 134–135, 135f

text adaptation, in SIOP® Model, 56
text "chunking," in instructional conversations, 83
theories of second-language development. see learning theories
think-aloud modeling to teach report writing, 108–109, 108f
thinking, Piaget's theory of development of, 44
three-tiered model
    to increase academic proficiency skills, 128
    instruction, 26–28
    tier 1, 24–25, 128
    tier 2, 25–26, 128
    tier 3, 26, 128
timelines, in SIOP® model, 60
transitional bilingual education (TBE), 7t, 8, 32
two-stage modeling, 117–118, 117f
    physical model, 118
    verbal rehearsal, 117–118, 117f
two-way immersion (TWI), 7t, 8–9

U

use-of-cognates strategy, 106, 106f

V

Venn diagram, 135–136
verbal rehearsal, 117–118, 117f
verbal scaffolding, 69
video reflection, in reflective practice, 150–151
visualization strategies, for modifying lesson plans and text, 134–135, 135f
visual modeling, 108–109, 109f
vocabulary
    in academic language, 74, 130
    brainstorming for words, 57
    cognitive learning theory and, 46
    complexity of, in first-language development, 40
    discipline-specific, development of, 131–132
    everyday vs. subject-specific, 12
    explicit teaching and, 36
    introducing, 62
    key academic terms in SIOP® lesson plan, 57
    personality and, 40
    repetition to reinforce, 57
    in SIOP® Model compared to effective instruction, 57
    social interactionist learning theory and, 45
vocabulary level, in SOLOM assessment, 15f, 16
Vygotsky, L. S.
    developmental theories, 44
    sociocultural theory, 9

W

Writer's Workshop, 89, 110–111, 120, 142
writing-as-a-process, 110–111, 111f, 120
writing strategies in content-area classes, 110–113, 111f, 113f